SO-AQL-687

Promoting Adult Growth in Schools

The Promise of Professional Development

Sarah L. Levine

Association of Independent Schools in New England, Inc.
Braintree, Massachusetts

Promoting Adult
Growth in Schools

The Promise of
Professional Development

Revised Edition

Published by
Association of Independent Schools in New England, Inc.
Suite 301, 100 Grossman Drive
Braintree, Massachusetts 02184
(617)849-3080

Copyright © 1995 by Sarah L. Levine. All rights reserved. No part of this book may be reproduced in any form without permission in writing from the publisher, except for the inclusion of brief quotations by reviewers. Printed in USA. ISBN 0-9636513-2-3.

Promoting Adult Growth in Schools

The Promise of Professional Development

For Jim —
Best wishes
Sarah L. Levine

To my very special family
Randy, Seth, and Johanna

Table of Contents

Illustrations

Tables

Foreword

This morning I left the harbor, taking my small boat to a nearby island where I hoped to pick mussels for dinner. I had also just finished rereading *Promoting Adult Growth in Schools* which is now being reissued in paperback.

I had a passenger on board who had never been in these waters. As we approached the island's north side, we saw high dunes and grass, gulls and terns. "There can't be any mussels *there*," said my passenger.

Our destination was on the western end. To reach it we would have to stay in the channel, making a full circumnavigation. So we swung east. From that vantage point, the shore offered a thicket of rosa rugosa and beach plum, a few old foundations and a wall. "No mussels *here*," said my companion again.

We turned to run along the south shore of the island which sloped out gently in a wide arc of beach. "No mussels *here*," my companion repeated.

Then we approached the western end with its rocky ledges, tidal pools, and swirling seaweed. "But plenty of mussels *here*," I said.

One island, but many faces. One permanent location recorded on maps, but shifting aspects whose contours, edges, and channels constantly widen or narrow as the waters move the sand. This morning's voyage evoked Sarah Levine's book which is like a chart, a compass, a depth finder, and yes, an anchor as we explore adult human development.

While many educators have learned to see children from different per-spectives, noting and accommodating their learning styles, their levels, their areas of vulnerability and resilience, most of us have not thought to extend that vision to other adults. It is as though once people are old enough to be teachers, they are fully formed or "finished." This book shows us a different reality.

The author points out how adults' fears, hopes, and priorities change as they move through their stages of personal development. Unmarried teachers who develop longings for intimacy and family may feel marooned in the islands of their classrooms. Teachers new to the profession, eager and idealistic, want to harness their untarnished energies to climb the dune and see the far horizon. Experienced teachers, those who are content with sameness and repetition, may see professional life as a gentle swim in protected waters.

I think back over some of the faculty meetings I've attended which went awry but no one seemed to know why. Now I see how often the various players were approaching the island from different points of the compass. Antagonisms between people who seemed like-minded were often expressions of different vantage points rather than true animosity.

By coincidence, Sarah Levine's father, Bert James Loewenberg, was my professor many years ago at Sarah Lawrence College. He taught his students the unspoken truth that, just as each person has a finite supply of physical energy, each has finite supplies of psychological and intellectual energies. The physically weary person is restored by rest or sleep; the psychologically and/or intellectually depleted person is just as deeply in need of replenishment, which can come from finding new challenges, shifting focus from vocation to avocation, or just plain restoring oneself in enjoyable aesthetic domains. Psychological and intellectual energies are just as susceptible to drain-down as physical buoyancy but the indicators aren't as easy to see. To be at odds with one's fellow workers, to be misunderstood, to be pointed toward ill-fitting goals dictated by other people steals power from those psychological and intellectual energies needed for teaching.

If we are to tap into the strength, benevolence, and creativity which brought most people into teaching in the first place, Sarah Levine points out that we must see adults in schools as individuals on different levels of development, setting our expectations accordingly, and helping them find safe and exciting courses to their various destinations. How? That is for the reader to discover. Practical suggestions stand up like buoys, beacons, and lighthouses throughout the text.

This book is a compass rose.

Priscilla L. Vail

Preface

Promoting Adult Growth in Schools: The Promise of Professional Development is a book for and about the adults who work in schools. It is about professional development; it is also about adult development. In fact, this book's novelty derives from bringing professional and adult development together, from applying what we know about adult growth to what we do as teachers, administrators, and staff developers.

This book offers an in-depth look at the professional lives of four teachers. It extends the role of principal to include educational leader, manager, and adult developer. And it describes an array of practices that can foster adult development.

In *Promoting Adult Growth in Schools* you will have the opportunity to learn a great deal about how adults grow. You will have a chance to consider possible differences between the ways men and women develop. You will see how ideas about adult growth can broaden strategies for staff development; and you will discover a great deal about yourself.

Individuals are at the heart of development and central to this book. It is for this reason that the voices of practitioners are prevalent throughout. In addition to the teacher portraits, there are frequent comments and reactions by teachers and administrators. In Chapter 6, four school practitioners write about the impact of an adult development perspective on their lives. In Chapter 9, the case stories of two school principals bring developmental theories to life.

I am convinced that most teachers and administrators have deeply felt, positive experiences of their work. They also have an enormous wealth of wisdom about teaching and learning. Most of what is written about schools captures neither. This book is meant to celebrate both.

Sarah L. Levine

Acknowledgments

Many people contributed to the development of this book. I am particularly grateful to the teachers and principal of the Archer School for their willingness to share and to learn, as well as to the other practitioners who contributed through their writings or interviews and wish to remain anonymous.

I am grateful to Hiram Howard, my original editor at Allyn and Bacon, who sought me out and encouraged me to begin the project, and to Sean Wakely, my current editor, who guided the project to completion. Ken Haskins, colleague and friend, helped me create time for writing in the midst of an already busy work schedule. My husband and children – Randy, Seth, and Johanna – lived with me and cheered me in many ways as I started, continued, continued, continued, and finished the book.

Jean Nicholas and Mark Kaufman read and reread early drafts. Dick Drew took over where they left off. Other colleagues and friends contributed by reading or writing: Pat Ashby, Roberta Bernstein, Marilyn Blight, Kathleen Buckley, Gil Cass, Carolyn Caveny, Ryan Champeau, Chuck Christensen, Helene Cohen, Dale Devine, Laura Dickey, Ed Fraktman, John Halfacre, Rusty Hlavacek, Bill Howe, Vicki Jacobs, Jo Ann Jasin, Angela Javora, Spike Jorgensen, Jerry Katz, Matt King, Margaret Loeffler, Broadus Mayfield, Jeff Nelson, Steve Piltch, Bruno Ponterio, Lou Rodrick, Adelaide Sanford, Susan Sellers, Len Sirotzki, Stan Thompson, Dick Voso, Bruce Wellman, Ruby Whalley, Bill Wibel, Kay Woelfel, Tim Woodward, and Alex Wyeth. Anne Wierum was an ace typist and proofreader. Gopa Khandwala searched and re-searched every reference. Jean Pendleton and Theresa Pease accomplished the technical and design apects of republication with skill and care.

Finally, these colleagues reviewed and critiqued part or all of the completed manuscript with care and insight: Roland Barth, Arthur Blumberg, Nancy Broude, Dick Drew, Ginger Hovenic, Robert Kegan, Randy Levine, Jane Loevinger, Susan Loucks-Horsely, Carolee Matsumoto, Norma Sprinthall, and Lois Thies-Sprinthall. The book and the author have been enriched by their influence.

Introduction

This is a book about the adults who work in schools. It reviews stages and phases of adult growth and draws from them implications for teaching and learning. In this book you will discover how adults change throughout their adult years and what these changes might mean for professional development and school leadership. But most of all, if you are an adult who works or might work in schools, this book is for and about *you*.

Traditionally, staff development focuses on getting *other* people to change. Teachers work at helping children to learn and grow, principals try to create supportive contexts for teachers, central office personnel look out for the well-being of principals, and so on. Since we know that growth starts from within, the most effective forms of staff development begin with the *self*. The more you know about yourself, the better able you are to model effective learning, support the growth of others, and create a climate conducive to individual and group growth. My hope for you as you read this book is that the way you understand yourself – and thereby others – expands and deepens.

Like development, this book begins and ends with *individuals*. Its organization reflects my interest in and concern for specific adults and their particular growing needs. The book focuses on individual development to draw attention to and capitalize on knowledge of adult development. Such knowledge has yet to be exploited as a professional development and school leadership resource.

The book also parallels development by stressing *context*. Teachers and administrators function in schools, systems, and communities. While it is essential to provide individual supports and incentives for growth, it is equally important to offer structural supports and a school culture that values and creates opportunities for personal and professional development. Without supporting structures and a fertile school culture, growth will be isolated and idiosyncratic, its impact minimal and unsustained. As important as it is for the adults who work in schools to understand themselves and their colleagues, integrating internal and external needs and goals is imperative.

Many schools do not provide a work environment conducive to adult development. Teachers cannot leave their classrooms without finding someone to take their places. During the school day, adults have little or no time to work or to socialize in groups. As a result, adults who work in schools can feel isolated and powerless. Not only are individuals impoverished by such circumstances, but schools become less effective and less exciting working and learning environments. A great deal more needs to be said and learned about the adults who work in schools and the schools, systems, and communities in which they develop.

ORGANIZATION AND DEVELOPMENT

The book is divided into five parts. Part One focuses on teachers and schools. In Chapter 1, four teachers introduce themselves and their school. Chapter 2 looks at schools in general and Archer Elementary School in particular. Not only are individuals and contexts basic elements of development, but the experiences of teachers and the nature of schools serve as examples of how adults change and grow and illustrate the ways in which schools can facilitate or impede their development.

Part Two of the book introduces adult development theories and suggests their implications for staff development. Chapter 3 introduces phase theories of development, which focus on the major life tasks or conflicts that stimulate growth at relatively specific times in the life cycle. Here I explore the theories of Erik Erikson, Daniel Levinson, and Roger Gould. In Chapter 4, on stage theories, I review the work of Lawrence Kohlberg and Jane Loevinger and discuss in detail the work of Robert Kegan, whose conception of development is central to the book. Stages of development, modeled on the work of Jean Piaget, are not age specific. They unfold in sequence over the life span and account for the ways individuals understand themselves and their worlds.

Chapter 5 focuses on the topic of male/female developmental differences. Recognizing differences can help us become more aware of ourselves as well as the men and women with whom we work. Knowledge of differences among and between *all* adults further complicates our understanding of human development and suggests a view of adulthood that may transcend gender-related differences – a point taken up and expanded in the chapter that follows.

Chapter 6, the final chapter in Part Two, includes reactions by school practitioners to the developmental framework. Throughout the book the voices of practitioners bring to life the theories and their implications. They also demonstrate the thoughtfulness and expertise of the adults who work in schools. In Chapter 6, there are reactions to the idea of male/ female differences as well as more general reflections upon theories of adult development.

Part Three of the book is a bridge between theory and practice and the beginning of an extended examination of the potential applications of adult development theories to schools. In Chapter 7, I return to the four teachers who initially introduced themselves and their school and examine their personal and professional lives in light of the developmental framework. What can be learned from listening closely to teachers talking about their schools, about their experiences of teaching, and about themselves? Can adult development theories suggest specific professional development strategies?

The role and the person of the principal emerged spontaneously as the initial topic in interviews with Archer's teachers. Because of the principal's importance to this school and in the literature on school improvement, I explore the principal's role in Chapter 8. Chapter 9 concludes Part Three with two case studies illustrative of the influence of the developmental perspective on school leaders and their schools.

Part Four of the book focuses on practice. In three chapters, I identify and describe a range of activities and programs that have the potential to influence adult development. Chapter 10 deals with writing. I begin with an extended discussion and illustrations of writing because of its enormous and largely untapped potential as a professional development resource. Chapter 11 explores individual and group supports, including independent learning, peer-assisted leadership, mentor programs, coaching, role taking, and support groups. Chapter 12 presents organizational supports: a visiting practitioner program, principals' centers and leadership academies, a teachers' network, and a staff development center. The promising practices in Part Four are designed or adaptable for use by teachers and administrators. Consistent with my beliefs and experiences about effective practice, all the practices I describe require a commitment of training and time.

Part Five of the book is both an ending and a beginning. In Chapter 13, I review the major conclusions, underscore the importance of the adult development perspective, and suggest several future steps.

Six years after the initial study, I returned to Archer Elementary to catch up with the principal and the teachers. Chapter 14 captures these adults' changes and similarities since the first study. You will recognize the power of the developmental perspective as a guide to understanding the personal and professional growth of these and other adults in schools, as well as your own.

The reader should especially note that the name and location of the school and the names of the teachers and the principal portrayed in this book are disguised. If the names of persons or schools in this book bear any similarity to those of actual persons or schools, the similarity is purely fortuitous. The names of other practitioner-contributors are real or disguised as indicated, at the discretion of each contributor.

WAYS OF PROCEEDING: THERE ARE MORE THAN ONE

If you are like me, you start a book on page one and read until you reach the end, trusting that the author wrote with a logic you would be wise to follow. Having friends who read the final chapter of a mystery before the beginning and colleagues who first review a study's findings, I recognize there are alternative ways of proceeding. Even if my life experiences did not confirm this, my understanding of individual differences would. Bearing this in mind, I want to suggest several fruitful ways of profiting from this book.

If you are someone who likes to learn about people's lives as they describe them and to find out about a story's setting, you will want to begin at the beginning, where four teachers talk about themselves and their work environment. You will then want to move directly on to Chapter 2 to learn more about teachers and schools and the specific school, Archer Elementary.

If it is important for you to begin with a framework within which to understand your own and others' experiences, I have a different suggestion: Begin with the chapters in Part Two, which introduce conceptions of adult development and explore differences between and among men and women. You can then return to Chapters 1 and 2 with the theory as background.

In either case you will want to read Parts One and Two before Part Three, which builds upon and integrates the chapters in the first two sections. Chapters 7 and 8 put the lives of the four teachers into developmental perspective and examine the role of the principal, and Chapter 9 presents two cases in which the lives of adults and children have been affected by a knowledge of adult development.

On one level, Part Four can be read in or out of sequence. In it, I describe a range of practices – from writing to a teachers' network and a staff development center – that holds promise for supporting and sustaining adult growth. Although the value of these practices grows out of the adult development perspective and can thus be understood more completely with this perspective as background, each practice also stands on its own.

You will notice that the tone of the book shifts in Part Four, which is essentially pragmatic in nature. If you find your attention riveted to the four teachers whose development you have been following, you may want to move ahead to the final chapter, which describes their lives six years after they were introduced. If you are eager to put ideas into direct use, you will want to forge ahead to learn about practices that build on an adult development perspective.

I recommend reading Chapters 13 and 14 in that order. Again, I tend to read books from beginning to end; to me it makes sense to find out what happens to people and ideas after I know about them. Still I recognize that others may want to decide beforehand if the people and ideas are worth knowing!

TWO FINAL SUGGESTIONS AND ONE REQUEST

First, I want to point to the margins as a place to respond in writing to the text. Here you can keep a running account of your thoughts and feelings as well as initiate a dialogue with the people and ideas as you first meet and then get to know them. In addition, some readers may want to keep a separate journal to record in greater detail their experiences and reflections. The value of such writing will become clearer in Chapter 10, where I and others present writing as a tool for professional development.

To write Part Four of the book, on promising practices, I called on staff developers, principals, and teachers all over the country to ask for suggestions. I was surprised that so many adults who work in schools believe practices that support adult growth are lacking. I am certain that many such practices and programs with unrecognized potential or influence are in existence. Readers who are involved in such practices or know about them are invited to write to me so that the repertoire of promising practices for adult growth and development can be shared and expanded. If you adopt or adapt something from the book, I would also be pleased to learn about it.

You are about to embark on a journey that will demand your attention, provoke your thinking, and stir your feelings. It is my hope that you, like the adults in the book, will not remain unchanged.

Part One

Teachers and Schools

Teacher Portraits

How we gain understanding of another person's experience of work should be no easy matter....The experience of work...is so extraordinarily complicated and so private, so determined by culture and tradition, so much the organizing center of our lives, and so much a developmental process that it is small wonder we as individuals have difficulty taking distance from "our work," i.e., from ourselves.[1]

In this opening chapter, four teachers, all in their early to mid-thirties, introduce themselves and their shared work environment. They speak of the changes that have taken place within the school and within their lives. In their own terms, they frame the issues that are important to them. They sketch a picture of the school, but, more fundamentally, they paint portraits of themselves.

I begin with the voices of teachers quite intentionally. The usefulness of understanding human development hinges upon paying attention to the complexities of individual lives. Because all people make their own meanings, it is essential that we perceive what they say, how they think, how they feel, and how they understand.

As you listen to these teachers, you will begin to hear both similarities and differences. The similarities, such as the importance of the principal, point to some of the most powerful influences in the school; the differences underscore the ways in which these teachers experience themselves and their environment uniquely. Differences in their experiences provide important clues for working with and supporting adults in schools. They describe how a teacher grows and changes and his or her primary preoccupations, hopes, and values. In turn, this knowledge forms a basis for creating appropriate plans and goals for individual, group, and school improvement.

While reading the portraits, you may want to envision yourself having a conversation with each teacher, listening to how he or she makes sense of the school, of the principal, of teaching, and of his or her relationships to children. How might these teachers respond to you? How do you respond to them? Can you identify particular strengths and weaknesses in the teachers as well as in yourself? What do these teachers say that you or they could use to design strategies to support or enhance their personal satisfaction and professional effectiveness? Whether you are a teacher or an administrator, consider yourself a colleague with interests in and responsibilities for your own and others' personal and professional development.

The portraits that follow are based upon in-depth interviews with teachers at the Archer School. Throughout the book, I will be referring to these teachers, using their experiences to illustrate the power of a developmental perspective for understanding and working with the adults in schools.

JUDY CUBBINS: A THIRD-GRADE TEACHER

I am much more of a total person than I was when I started teaching. I have my parts put together so that I'm complete. I don't mean to say there aren't fine points that need polishing, things to be added and things to be taken away. But I'm not a compartmentalized person now. Now I wear all my hats at the same time. Whereas before I was always taking a hat off and putting a hat on, now I'm just me and me is what I do here at school; and when I leave, I don't live, eat, breathe, sleep, and drink school anymore…I happen to think I'm a very good teacher. I'm happier with myself too.

I began my career as a third-grade teacher at Archer Elementary, where I have remained for the past ten years. Over the years, there have been changes in my approach to teaching, as well as in my understanding and acceptance of myself. I would describe myself as happy and growing, with no immediate plans of making a change.

When I think about what stands out for me since I've been at Archer, I think first about the change in principals. The first principal we had was Sam Ellis. I liked Sam a lot. As a matter of fact, I've liked all three principals – as people. But as a new teacher, not having experience with other principals, I thought Sam was the end-all and the be-all. Sam supported the staff in an open-ended way. You felt he would let you do whatever you wanted; he trusted your ability as a professional. But he was afraid of parents – something I didn't realize at the time.

At that point in Archer's development, teachers were terrified of parents. The school was not moving smoothly. There were behavior problems. The staff were all friends, but there was no cohesiveness about how we handled kids. That made everything uncertain. A parent might come in and literally back you into a corner, and Sam couldn't come to your defense. So during my first three years here, one of the major problems was communication with parents.

Then Bob Slater came. He was just the opposite of Sam Ellis. What he said, went. I felt supported by Bob because he liked me...and there were definitely people he didn't like. There were certain personal or professional qualities that a person might have that would make him automatically not like you. I was one of the lucky ones; I had no strikes against me, so he liked me. As a matter of fact, we were pretty good friends, though you can probably imagine that it was difficult for me, being liked by a principal some people hated.

Bob was a stern authoritarian, but I think he came at a good time for the school. He established some kind of order here, which was something Sam was incapable of doing. Bob made us firmer and better able to cope with the kids. I think parents were a little afraid of him. And a combination of teachers a little afraid, and parents a little afraid, and kids a little afraid pulled us together – almost as a means of protection.

When Peter Samson arrived, we were really ready for him. Peter was someone we had taught with, that we knew and appreciated. By the time he came, we were together and headed down the right road, and Peter's the type of principal who pats you on the back – not constantly, but when you really deserve it. He says "thanks" in some way, and the school's an entirely different place from what it was.

The change in principals stands out for me because I believe the principal's role is so important. The principal affects the whole school. One thing about having a self-contained classroom is that if something you don't like is going on down the hall or in another classroom, you can shut the door and pretend it doesn't exist. But you can't do that with something that cuts across the school. If you're anxious because Parents' Night is coming up and you know that parents will be critical about things that aren't your fault, you feel out of control. The whole school felt that way. It was just like a cloud hanging over everyone. When Peter came, the cloud was gone. He's just made the school entirely different.

The principal's role is important, but it's also the person. I think Peter is a very special person. You need a position like principal, a role that cuts across the school, and you need the person in the position to be a good, consistent, intelligent, fair-minded person.

Having a principal like Peter makes it easier to be a teacher. But I like teaching for a lot of reasons. One of the most important is my interest in putting together curriculum materials. I love to create. I like to color. I love bulletin boards. That's me, and teaching gives me these opportunities. Teaching also fulfills me on another level. Besides doing something that I like, I think I'm doing something important.

When I started, teaching was my life. Just trying to keep my head above water during the first two or three years was a struggle. I ate, slept, and dreamed school. I was married then, and my marriage was faltering.

In some ways, that made it even easier to immerse myself in my career. My husband was having problems, and as a result, I had them too. Now that I'm married again, I'm glad that I've been teaching for ten years. I can be a person as well as a teacher. My marriage is very different, too, because I see myself as more separate from my husband – in a positive sense.

Before, I think my identity was always dovetailed to whatever environment I found myself in. The most comfortable environment then was the school environment, so I carried it around with me all the time. Now I shed my environments like skins. I do think of leaving someday. I think of having a family, and I wonder if I'll want to go back to teaching. I think of getting more involved with teaching people to teach or creating materials for teaching. But in a way, it's scary, because I'm very happy here; change is scary.

If I wanted to leave, I would. It's a question of deciding if I really want to. Even now, I'm thinking about what I'll do when we have a family. If I don't work, what will I do? I really wonder because I know that when I'm not teaching during the summer I'm going crazy. By the middle of August, I want to feel productive again. And teaching makes me feel productive, whereas keeping a house clean is just a vicious circle. You cook a nice dinner, you've got dirty dishes. Whatever you've done gets undone by something else. Teaching feels productive because what you do lasts and you see results. You have to be patient, but you do see results.

Staying in the same grade helps too. I can see the expectations that parents have. Even if they haven't had an experience with me, they know about me and some of them have high hopes that their children will have me. And it's nice to feel needed and wanted, as well as knowing that you can do something important and useful.

Seeing the results of my work is what makes me happy. I know I would be far less satisfied if I were just creating materials and they were ending up in a catalog and I was getting money. It's much more satisfying to see the children in my room sit down on the rug and use what I've made and then to see on their achievement tests that their language scores have gone up. I feel a sense of satisfaction because I know I had something to do with it. I planned for it; I made it work.

This year I am teaching alone, but for the past several years I was working in a partnership. There were a lot of things about that arrangement that were great. I got to know the children very well, seeing them through my eyes as well as my partner's. Depending on the group, I either had a lot of release time to plan dynamic things or far less. Either way, I was involved with greater numbers of children with a wider range of needs and abilities.

This year I'm lonelier teaching by myself. I miss my partner; I miss a lot of things. But I'd choose a self-contained classroom again if you asked me to make a decision right now – not because I like the isolation at school, but because I have more time at home. If I weren't married, I'd probably feel different about it. But right now I'd say I want a self-contained classroom because of the way I use my time outside of school. Having a self-contained classroom means having more of a life of my own.

When I was team teaching, I also missed the feeling of autonomy. I missed being able to go home and spend all evening rewriting a curriculum unit and then being able to implement it the next day. Instead, I would have to tell my partner and we'd need to go over it together. By then some of the enthusiasm would be gone. I do feel lonely teaching by myself – much more so than I ever did before – but I also have more freedom, more control, and more time.

Within my classroom, I make my own decisions. If I want to teach reading in the afternoon instead of in the morning, I just do it. I simply say to the kids, "We're going to try something new. We're going to have reading in the afternoon." It's my decision when I'm going to do it. We all decide as a faculty *what* programs we're going to use; *how* and *when* we use them is at each teacher's individual discretion.

When I don't agree with a school-wide decision, modifying it to meet my needs takes a little more initiative, but it's still possible. Let me give you an example. I'm of a dissenting opinion about how much science and how much social studies have to be taught. The curriculum guides tell me that I'm supposed to teach at least three units in each. I don't have time to teach three units well. So I made the decision to do only two units in science this year. I talked with the science specialist, and we sat down to find out what would be most appropriate. So you can make changes, but you have to take the initiative or you get locked into something and someone else makes the decision for you.

Your first couple of years' teaching, you think you have to teach so many hours of science, so many hours of social studies; you take everything as gospel, no deviations. Well, you realize with experience that there are a lot of deviations. What you do after you really learn how to teach is what is best for the kids, not necessarily what it says in the curriculum. I guess it's also important to say that I don't feel I always need to go to Peter to get things changed. I know from experience that whenever I make a thoughtful decision he will back me up.

Things can even be changed at the system level if you're willing to work with the central office. I took a supervision course two years ago and designed a report card that I'd love the system to adopt. I hate the report card we use now, and I know parents and students don't like it. I could talk with the superintendent or join the report card committee, but I think the red tape of the school administration is far too complex.

Working with the central administration would demand a great deal of energy and time. Right now, I don't want to take anything away from my teaching. But again, that's my decision.

Looking back over my ten years of teaching, I think the biggest change has been in my personal sense of confidence. When everyone else is telling you that you're good, you have to keep going to prove to yourself they're right. But it's a nice day when you realize that you're competent. That was a lot longer in coming, you know, really believing it...*really* believing it!

In the beginning all the pieces of myself were going in different directions. Now I am much more of a total person. I have my parts put together so that I'm complete. I don't mean to say there aren't fine points that need polishing, things to be added and things to be taken away. But I'm not a compartmentalized person now. Now I wear all my hats at the same time. Whereas before I was always taking a hat off and putting a hat on, now I'm just me and me is what I do here at school; and when I leave, I don't live, eat, breathe, sleep, drink school anymore. I still wake up in the middle of the night with ideas. I still keep a pad of paper by my bed. But it's not the same. I'm still very organized, still a very forceful person. I still have to watch out for my tendency to be bossy. I mean, things may change in the way you interpret them, but they don't change in reality.

I hope I think of kids differently now too. I hope that I've become more aware of them as individuals than I was in the beginning of my teaching. In the beginning I had to put much more of my focus on what I was doing than on what they were doing. Now what I'm doing is secondary. In general, I think that I'm far more outgoing than I used to be, toward everyone – less toward kids, maybe, because kids are far less threatening than peers. I think I've always felt very comfortable with kids. But you feel much more comfortable with anybody when you feel comfortable with yourself.

I've also changed as a woman, but I don't really feel that it had that much to do with my profession. My profession offered me something stable to hold onto while I went through some pretty big changes in my own identity. But my identity within the profession, I think, has remained basically stable. Except for my level of confidence, I think it has stayed the same. The fact that I am a teacher at Archer and that I teach the third grade has been my stability. Especially when I've gone through hard times in the other parts of my life, teaching here has been a guarantee that tomorrow was going to come and that I would be able to do something organized and productive so that I would feel like a worthwhile human being.

Working in a woman's environment has never been a problem. It is an issue for some of my unmarried friends because they're not meeting men. My bone of contention there is: "Of course you're not. You're working with women. Go out and meet men." When I was unmarried, I went out and I met men.

Right now I feel very good about my teaching, but I don't want to lose my touch. Having taught third grade for a number of years, I don't want it to become mundane: "Well, I've done this unit before, so I can just take out the lesson plans and do it again." I don't want to get so involved with the rest of my life that I become stale. I can see doing that very easily, especially now that I'm thinking of starting a family. I don't want to get so involved with things outside the classroom that I don't consider the needs of individual children. If that happened, I wouldn't be doing what was best for the kids. Teaching this group of children is not at all like teaching last year's group. Students' needs are always very different

The other day my husband asked me about burnout. "Why are you still teaching third grade? Don't you want to teach another grade? Don't you feel like you're doing the same thing year after year?" I said no, because I'd never enjoy the same thing year after year. The curriculum changes; the needs of the kids change. This year's group of children is entirely different from the class before them. I can be a different authority figure to them. I can be a different person. I can be a different friend. I can be a different source of information. That, to me, is why I've never gotten tired of teaching third grade. Each year is entirely different.

There's a nice balance for me here. I can institute my own changes. I think there are some individuals who are fearful of change because the change might not be something they could handle or they might not get the change they want. So it's safer to hold on to what you've got. Part of that might be my reason too. In all honesty, I don't really know. For now, I happen to think I'm a very good teacher. I'm happier with myself too.

JANET KRAMER: A SIXTH-GRADE TEACHER

At the beginning of teaching, you're very, very enthusiastic. You know, the sun, the moon, and the stars are your class, and you kind of wear out, or burn out, after a number of years. I don't have the same enthusiasm that I did eleven years ago. I definitely don't. I still care about kids and I want them to learn...but I just don't have the same excitement. I'm tired of my job.

I have taught sixth grade for the past twelve years – four years at a public school in Maryland and eight years at Archer Elementary. I went to graduate school directly after completing undergraduate work at the University of Maryland, then went right into teaching and have continued to teach both during the year and in the summers. I am now in my mid-thirties and unmarried. In looking back upon my years at Archer, I confess that I feel dissatisfied with my job and with my life.

As I look back, Archer has gone through a lot of changes. When I first came to this school, there was another principal, and I found him difficult to work with. I don't think he had a great understanding of children, teachers, or parents. It was difficult working with him and under him, but he only lasted here a few years because other people felt the same way – especially the parents. Often, I think, the attitude of teachers is a reflection of how they're treated and how their principal looks at them, and I didn't have a good feeling from this principal. That changed dramatically after Peter came. There was a marked change in the attitude of everyone, and even though he stepped into a difficult position, he was always very supportive of the teachers and that made a gigantic difference in your own caring about what kind of job you did.

I've always found Peter to be very supportive, intelligent, and under- standing. I think that it's rare to find a principal with that combination.

When he comes to observe in your classroom, he doesn't just sit there and take notes; he participates in the activity, whatever it is. And the things he writes up are always on a positive note. It's not that we're all super-duper teachers, but he writes up his comments in a way that makes you feel good, and positive reinforcement works with adults just like it works with children. You make them feel like they're doing a good job, and they try even harder. I think that's the biggest plus.

Even though Peter's not physically here in my room or at our team meetings, he knows what's going on in my classroom. He may know through the kids, through the parents, or through the grapevine, but he always seems to know. If you have a problem, you can go to him. He knows the kids and the school very well. All these things help. I don't know exactly why he's so nice, but you want to do a good job because you know it's a reflection on him.

This is a school that has a lot of parental pressures. That's the next thing that stands out for me when I think about Archer. If you didn't have a principal who supported you with this type of parent, it would be impossible to survive here. It's certainly nice to have the support of other teachers; it's nice that our team gets along fairly well, and team members are supportive if there's a problem with a parent or even something personal. But the principal's support is crucial. The parents are really a driving force. I mean, they drove the first principal out!

Parents can be very difficult. They don't always have an accurate picture of their children's abilities, but they always want them to succeed. Sometimes I think the pressure is too great. Parents want to help, but it's too much. I don't know how you can control it. Oftentimes I feel if you don't give parents the answers they want to hear, they're very unsupportive. You want to live a happy life, and sometimes I give in just to make life easier. Now this has changed in my eight years here. It used to be that if I really believed in something strongly, I wouldn't give in to parents. Now, just to make my life easier, I might try to convince a child's parents that the way they saw something wasn't the way I saw it. But I'd probably give in just because I'd like my year to be a pleasant one. I don't want parents making my life miserable. It's unfortunate.

Last year I had one parent who blamed her son's lack of success on my inability to get through to him in reading. Two years before, I had her older son and I was Superteacher for him. So here I was, the same me a couple of years later, doing basically the same kinds of things, and this time I had destroyed the child, according to his mother. Well, I happened to run into her last week, and when she saw me in the hall, she was very cold to me. It made me feel terrible, and I mentioned it to Peter. Now this is an example of Peter's support. He told me she thinks that of all of us, and that is, unfortunately, her problem. He just tried to make me feel better about it, which is all you can do, because the fact remains that you feel bad. You can't please all the people all the time, but you try, and it's nice when you can.

Of course, some parents are very helpful. They write nice notes at the end of the year, and you get little positive reinforcements here and there. When the negative things happen, though, they seem to overshadow the nice things. Still, this school has positive aspects that my other school didn't. There, parents didn't really care. It's from one extreme to the other.

Things have really changed since I first started teaching. In the beginning I was structured, and I've returned to that. I'm not a very strict disciplinarian, but I certainly like to have an orderly classroom. During the '60s, I'd say, I was much more open. The open-space concept was "in," and kids were freer – I don't even know if that's the right word. But we experimented with curricula and did a lot of projects and activities. Now I've returned to the basics. I never really left the basics, but my approach to them has changed.

I guess I'd have to say at this point that the most important thing to me in my work here is personal satisfaction – and hoping that at the end of the year I can look at the kids individually and say: "I reached this child; I made a difference." My ultimate goal is to let kids see that learning can be fun – an important and serious experience, but also an enjoyable one. That's my number-one goal. Another goal I have is to teach the children to show some respect. I'd like to have that from the parents and the principal too. I don't know. As longtime teachers, we've had a lot of training and experience. It would just be nice if it were recognized – kind of a thanks and an appreciation for the effort that you're putting forward. Teaching is a funny profession. You don't get a lot of positive feedback. You really have to rely on your own feelings about how things are going. And if the kids or parents show some appreciation and respect for what's going on, that, I guess, is the kind of feedback that keeps you going. You hear if you do something great or if you do something terrible, but you don't hear much of anything about all that goes on in between.

There are a lot of pressures here. At the moment, my mind is on the new reading program we're supposed to administer, conquering that. We have a curriculum that we're supposed to follow. It's a loose curriculum, but in some areas it's not so loose. In math, we have to follow eighteen levels; in science, we're supposed to do certain units; in social studies, we're supposed to do certain things. And now we are just shoved in the face with a reading program. There's just not enough hours in the day; it seems impossible.

First of all, we don't know this program. The sixth-grade teachers got together last Thursday and just found out how it worked. Now you could turn it around and say we could have looked into it four years ago when it was first mentioned, but it wasn't facing us until this year, so it seems like we're being hit with it all of a sudden. I think it's asking too much, because we have so much that we *have* to do. I don't know how we're going to do it. I mean, I'm sure I'll find a way, but it's a little overwhelming.

When I think about my day, I think about time with children. I think that's what it has to be if you're teaching. It's nice to have time with adults, but basically you're here to be with and guide the children. For me, I have enough time with adults, breaks, and lunchtime. No, I can't really complain. Now if you asked me this question at the end of the year, I might then be losing my mind and say, "One more minute with these children and I'll scream!" But at the beginning of the year it's okay.

It would probably be different if I were teaching with somebody else. I haven't had a lot of that kind of experience because I've always had a self-contained classroom. This past summer I worked in the summer school with another teacher. That was a nice experience. If I had it here, I'd probably like it, but I don't. It was also nice working with a man.

It bothers me that there are so many women teaching. I don't think it makes that much difference for the kids, but it sure bothers me. I'd like to work in an environment where there were more men around – for my own sense of female identity or something. Men and women are different, I think. It's hard for me to pinpoint why. There aren't many men around here, and you just feel like you're missing something. You know, society is male-female, and here it's so female oriented. I don't know, I think I tend to view women as not as objective, sometimes more emotional. I know these are generalizations, but I do think women tend to be moody, that they tend to show preferences, things like that. You can certainly have an incompetent male principal, but there's something about the female personality that's different.

Personally, I'd much prefer having a male principal. I've never had a female principal, but I know in other schools in Scribner there are some female principals and teachers aren't always happy with them. Now it can happen with a male principal too. It happened here with the first principal. I think working with a male principal, an authority figure – it's been good for me, so that's why I talk in personal terms.

As I look back over all my years of teaching, I guess that I've changed. At the beginning of teaching, you're very, very enthusiastic. You know, the sun, the moon, and the stars are your class, and you kind of wear out, or burn out, after a number of years. I don't have the same enthusiasm that I did eleven years ago. I definitely don't. I still care about kids, I want them to learn, and I happen to like this class, but I just don't have the excitement. I'm tired of my job.

If there were an alternative job that I felt would give me some meaning, I'd probably turn to it, but I haven't come up with anything. I've volunteered in hospitals, and I thought that might be an interesting environment, a mixed environment – men, women – stimulating. My mother's a nurse, and I've always thought in the back of my mind that I should have been a nurse. My father was a teacher, and I became a teacher. He directed me, and I'm not sorry, because it's been a good profession. But I miss stimulation.

I don't find that it's intellectually stimulating here. There are certainly some bright people, but it's a very stagnating, closed kind of society in this school. I'm not blaming anyone. A lot of it is my own laziness. It's a circular thing. You just keep going around in circles. You're bored with what you're doing, and you know you could make it better if you went and took some courses, but you just don't want to, and it just keeps going on and on.

I think a lot of the way I feel about teaching has to do with what's going on in the rest of my life. If I were married and had a family, I don't think I'd be so overwhelmed by this feeling [of incompleteness] in teaching. Marriage is something I need for fulfillment, and I haven't had it, so there's a black cloud over me that affects the way I see everything. It's too bad, but that's the way I am. It probably didn't bother me this much ten years ago, but it bothers me more now, so that must have something to do with the way I view myself. I feel cheated. I think that it has some effect on my teaching. Somehow, at some point, I think of having my own family. I hadn't really thought of it before because it really didn't bother me. I just wanted to have a relationship, and then, you know, it would be nice if it led to something else, but I didn't really think of children. Now, as I'm getting older, I'm thinking that time is running out and I'd better think about it. I'm getting tired of taking care of other people's children; it would be nice to have my own kids too. I guess if I stopped teaching for a while and came back to it and that part of my life were somewhat settled, I'd have a better attitude about teaching. If that other aspect of your life isn't fulfilled, then you really feel like your life isn't full; somehow it's just not complete.

It always sounds like you're blaming somebody else for the circumstance you're in, but when you're not dealing with the public and you're in kind of a closed society, you're limited to the number of people you meet and it has an effect. I think that teaching for a lot of teachers here is all-encompassing; it's their family, an important part of their life. But, at this stage in my life, it's not. I'm not saying it should or shouldn't be; it just isn't. It's a place where I come to do a job. I try to do a good job while I'm here, and I hope that I have some positive effects. It's an important job; education is very important. I still believe that, even after all this time, or I don't think I could do it. I don't hate teaching. I'm just tired and frustrated knowing that it's the same and that it will be the same if I let it be.

DON BOLTER: A FOURTH-GRADE TEACHER

For me to be successful, I want to observe positive changes in kids.... It's important to me because that's part of my definition of what a teacher is; and if I'm a teacher, that's what I should be looking for in my performance.

Changing myself is also important to me. Most of the changes I see in myself have been changes for the better. I don't know whether I see change as part of my role as a teacher or part of my role as a person. My own growth is important to me because I see myself as not being what I used to be, but still not being what I want to be. So I'm going to get better! There are areas in my life that I think need to be improved, and part of my job is to expose those to myself, or have somebody expose them to me, and to work on them.

I began teaching in the 1960s. After teaching for eleven years, I am confident about my abilities and comfortable in my current position. Except for summer jobs, teaching has been my only occupation. I intend to remain a classroom teacher.

What stands out in my mind is that when I first came to Archer, I didn't like it. I had been teaching in an inner-city school in Milwaukee where the kids were very needy, and I felt the students here were privileged and spoiled. I had a difficult time making the transition, but I think that's typical of me. Every time I make a change, I feel unsettled at the beginning.

I left Wisconsin because I wanted to return to where I'm from originally. I came looking for a job – that was my basic objective. I needed to work and that was it. I was more interested in being in this area of the country than in anything else. Where I worked was secondary.

I was attracted to the inner city because I had had a good experience there and I was satisfied with what I was doing. I didn't want too many changes at once; moving from one system to another was enough. And I suppose I didn't want to tamper with success. When I discovered the red tape involved in breaking into urban education back here, I started to look in the suburbs.

By the time I got here, I had little patience for students from the suburbs. I thought they didn't realize how good they had it. After a few months I discovered that they had a lot of needs, some even more severe than the needs of the kids I had been teaching in the city. They didn't necessarily have economic or material needs, but they certainly had educational and emotional needs. They were kids, and they had needs.

One thing that always makes it easier to like people is if they like you, and I guess that definitely happened to me by Christmas of the first year. Christmastime basically makes everything look better, but it was also a time when I began to sense that I was being appreciated.

When I first came to Archer, most of the staff were unhappy with the way things were being run. There was a lot of criticism of the principal who was here then. Actually, he and I got along very well. You probably haven't heard that from a lot of other people. We came the same year. The feeling in the system was that things were a little out of control, that things were a little too wild. Bob Slater was hired to straighten things out, and he took a tough approach. People felt threatened by him, but I think his approach worked because things weren't so wild after he came.

I'd probably feel even more comfortable with Slater now than I did then because I've changed, but one of the things that made me very uncomfortable then was his insistence on giving teachers permission if they wanted to do anything even a little out of the ordinary. Not only was it annoying to have to ask permission, but Slater's first response was always no. This was his technique. I talked to him about it. He understood that it was a technique, and he thought it was appropriate. I'm not sure that it's not appropriate. As a matter of fact, I find myself doing it a lot of times.

When you think about the situation Slater was coming into, you can understand why his immediate response was negative. He was probably thinking that it didn't make sense to change things when we needed to set a stable course. So his first response was to turn his back on any new idea, which meant you were supposed to try to convince him to change his mind. A lot of people just decided it wasn't worth the effort. They thought he should have seen the merit in their ideas from the beginning. But I kept pushing. I think I was young enough and new enough to the system so that

I didn't get discouraged. Sure, I wish I could have walked in and had him say yes right away to the things I wanted to do, but I didn't stop. I didn't like it, but I didn't let it get in my way. I can't think of anything that I didn't do as a result of it.

Several years later, Peter Samson was appointed principal, and that's what has really turned the school around, in my opinion. Peter's a rare and unusual person. He's free, informal, easy to talk to, and easy to get to know. Communications with him are open. He doesn't set up barriers because of his position.

Peter has a way of making you feel you're important and that you're doing a good job. I think he looks for opportunities to tell you that something you've done is good. He seems to spend more time looking for the positive than picking things apart. That doesn't mean he won't offer suggestions or voice his opinion. But he's genuine, and he's constructive.

I can't think of anything I've ever done that Peter hasn't approved. There are times when kids are running in the halls or to the bus, but then he puts out a bulletin to all the teachers, and even when he does that, it's in a humorous fashion. When he's reprimanding you, he makes it easy to take because he's not overbearing. If a child in your class has been making trouble in the cafeteria – usually it's things outside the classroom – he might put a note in your mailbox describing the incident. It's a way of informing you. Then he assumes the next time you see that person you'll talk to her or him about it. Maybe it's his way of saying, "Your kids were acting up in the lunchroom, and you need to talk to them about it." But he doesn't say that. What he says is, "I found so-and-so acting up in the lunchroom." He leaves it at that, so you can evaluate the situation and decide what to do about it.

For me to be successful, I want to observe positive changes in kids. There have been plenty of times when I haven't observed those things, but there have been enough times that I have that I still think what I'm doing is important. It's important to me because that's part of my definition of what a teacher is; and if I'm a teacher, that's what I should be looking for in my performance.

Changing myself is also important to me. Most of the changes I see in myself have been changes for the better. I don't know whether I see change as part of my role as a teacher or part of my role as a person. My own growth is important to me because I see myself as not being what I used to be, but still not being what I want to be. So I'm going to get better! There are areas in my life that I think need to be improved, and part of my job is to expose those to myself, or have somebody expose them to me, and to work on them.

Some of the impetus for my growth comes from within the school and in the system, where there are a large number of professional-development activities. A lot of the stimulus and encouragement for my growth also comes from my family.

My teaching has changed over the years – and gotten better. I used to spend less time thinking about kids, less time teaching and more time on techniques, catchy little things to be doing with kids. Having a good time was first, and learning was second. It seemed like education was supposed to be like that. I remember when I first started teaching, I found two old couches and an old rug from somewhere. I had a comfortable room, and we all used to have a good time in there. When I think about it now, I think about the messages I was conveying. You know, when you put trash in your room and expect kids to use it, maybe you're telling the kids that that's what they're worth. I wanted to be unique back then. Now I'm less concerned about me; I spend my time worrying and thinking about whether kids are learning.

In every way, I'm more conservative than I used to be. I would have cringed at this thought a few years ago. But I like myself and I recognize that's happened, so I think it's okay. Things have changed in the system, become better defined. I've made the changes that have been needed, and some, I suppose, have been changes that have been imposed on me, but I haven't felt that. I've felt that I've changed as the trends have changed – back to basics.

To me, the curriculum here is not confining. There's a lot of latitude. As time goes on, I think there will be fewer options; that seems to be the trend, and I'm comfortable with it. Some people are crying out in opposition, but I'm not. In general, I don't find it comfortable to do something very different from whatever is going on at the time. I certainly don't see myself as being radical or revolutionary.

Right now I'd have to say friends and colleagues are not as important to me as they were. They've become less important as I've gotten older. In college, if everybody else was doing it, I was going to do it too. Fortunately, the kinds of things that everyone was doing weren't so bad. Getting married, having kids – suddenly outside influences have become less important. I spend more time with my family, and I like it.

I wouldn't say my relationships here aren't important, but I'm satisfied with the casual way things are. I guess if I were teaching in a high school, where there might be more male faculty members and a broader spectrum of activities, I might want to establish closer ties. I don't see a tremendous amount of potential for that here. There are a lot of single, female teachers at

Archer, and I get along with all of them, but I don't see myself wanting to establish any close friendships. When you're married and have a family, I think your interests shift.

Rarely do I think about working in an all-female environment. Except for summer jobs, I've always worked in environments like this, so I really don't think about it. Other people think about it more than I do. People ask me about it, and that's the only time it ever comes up. It's not an issue for me at all.

The most negative thing that could happen to me here would be to get fired, but I don't think it could happen. I don't fear being laid off. I know some people do, but I don't know why they're so upset about it. I think we've had enough years of layoffs. If I thought I was doing a poor job, then I might worry. But I have a complete sense of confidence that as long as I want the job, I've got it.

As far as classroom matters go, I work with my teaching partner, whom I've been teaming with for several years. Teaming has a number of advantages. Aside from providing a ready source of help for classroom issues, teaming offers a chance to have someone observe and critique your teaching. I see that as being an advantage, though I can see where some people might not like it. I think it's good to have someone in continuous observation of you. You can help each other by pointing out your successes as well as failures, and you can try to improve yourself that way. I think we've done less of that than we could, and I don't know why, but I see that as a potential advantage that we haven't really exploited.

Most of my "adult time" is spent with my partner, then with other members of the team. The team structure demands that you be together for certain portions of the day, so those are the people you get to know and those are the people you gravitate toward. I know there's a feeling of separation between the two school teams as a result of the way the school's organized, but it doesn't bother me.

Not being involved in a lot of decision-making doesn't bother me either. I don't worry about having to do something that I wasn't involved in determining. I think there should be things that I'm told to do. I'm not at the top. It's okay to ask people for their opinions and to get input, but I think those people in the positions to make decisions are the ones who should make them. I can disagree, and I can expect to have my disagreements heard, but I think it's their responsibility to make the decisions and, if they're wrong, to accept the responsibility. I'm perfectly comfortable with that. In fact, at the moment, I'm comfortable at the school and in the system.

NAN JOHNSON: A FIFTH-GRADE TEACHER

I'm an outward-seeking person – with a great need for time to myself. I'm very happy with my life....I love to do adventurous new things, but when it comes to changing my life-style, I'm really conservative....

As a teacher, I've come into my own. I feel comfortable enough in my routines and in what I do in the classroom. I'm always willing to change. There are things I'm never doing well enough. I always like to try new ways of dealing with kids and of presenting materials. I've really gotten to be much more conscious of curriculum in the last couple of years, I guess partly because that's the push here in Scribner. But what I'm teaching and how I'm teaching are becoming much more important to me. So maybe after all these years I'm really coming around full circle to what teaching is all about.

From the time I was seven, I really knew that I wanted to teach. I was one of those classic types who never even thought about anything else. For several years I worked at an inner-city elementary school, where I loved the children but grew weary of constant pressures and battles with the administration. In the suburbs I regained my enthusiasm. For the past eight years I have taught fifth grade at Archer Elementary. While I would describe the present as an even period, I am uncertain and ambivalent about some aspects of my life.

The arrival of Peter is what stands out in my mind. It was a very nerve-racking, tense school with a poor reputation when I came. The principal who was here right before Peter had a very hard time dealing with people and dealing with problems that later became crises. Everything was in a constant state of turmoil one hundred percent of the time.

It was hard to know how one stood with the former principal. I think he had a hard time defining his role and deciding what principals were supposed to be like. He was actually a very nice person, but when he came into your classroom, he would scare the children. He never smiled; he never commented about the kinds of things they were doing. And he was a very large man, tall and heavyset, so even physically he was intimidating. It was just very hard, and things were tense the whole time. You sort of prayed that he would leave you alone – and for the most part, he did. I guess it was not until the end of the last year that I finally learned to stand up to him a little bit. And when I realized that I wouldn't lose my job, it was wonderful!

Needless to say, I was very glad when those days ended and Peter came.

It was like a breath of spring air had come into this whole building, and everybody just sighed in relief, that all of the hassles that used to go on were being taken care of by someone.

Another thing that was super was that whenever Peter came into your room – even for just a few minutes – he wrote you a note. I began to know that he really sensed the kinds of things I was doing; he knew what it was like to be in a classroom. It was very obvious after the first year that he was principal, that he never truly forgot what it was like to be a teacher. I think that's one of the things that makes him stand out from any principal I've ever known.

Peter doesn't actually have direct impact on my teaching. The most important thing he does is to give me his complete support. He lets me know that I'm doing a good job through things that he says, the notes that he writes, the way...the day, I guess, that he looked at me and said, "Nan, I'd like my kids to have you as a fifth-grade teacher." Those are the kinds of things that let me know that what I'm doing must be okay.

The other thing I know – and I think he knows it about me – is that I'm probably much tougher on myself than any supervisor would ever need to be. I have very high goals for myself. I think Peter knows that about me. I don't know quite how he knows. Probably it's because I talk to him a lot and because he's such a good listener. Maybe he picks up on these things that I try to tell him.

I do know that I have Peter's complete support, that whatever I decide to do in this classroom with these twenty-two kids that I feel has some educational value, chances are ninety-nine and ninety-nine one hundredths percent that he would say: "Terrific. Go right ahead." In most cases, I wouldn't even need to ask him.

I enjoy the people here, but I don't really feel that I have any close, close friends. With the team structure, there's always a certain amount of competition and comparing of the ways each part of the school works with children. But I don't feel bad. I guess it's because I get so many good feelings from my children. It's nice having other adults around, and I certainly enjoy spending time talking to the adults that are here, but I'm so busy during the day, I guess I just don't miss adult interactions. If I had to describe myself, I'd say I'm an outward-seeking person – with a great need for time to myself. I'm very happy with my life and I guess that's the only thing that's kind of scary in a way. I love to do adventurous new things, but when it comes to changing my lifestyle, I'm really conservative. Any time I've made a change in my life, it's felt hard.

As a teacher, I've come into my own. I feel comfortable enough in my routines and in what I do in the classroom. I'm always willing to change. There are things I'm never doing well enough. I always like to try new ways of dealing with kids and of presenting materials. I've really gotten to be much more conscious of curriculum in the last couple of years, I guess partly because that's the push here in Scribner. But what I'm teaching and how I'm teaching is becoming much more important to me. So maybe after all these years I'm really coming around full circle to what teaching is all about.

I certainly see myself in the last three years as moving outward into the system, as really being a leader, I suppose. I was recognized for my leadership ability two years ago when I put together a new computer program. I'm a fairly competitive person, always keeping an eye on other people and comparing myself all along with what other people are doing or thinking. I like to know that I'm doing a good job.

Sometimes I think my mind-set is somewhere between about age ten and age twelve. I think I'm one of those classic good little kids. I guess there's still this child inside of me that I like and that is a part of me. In fact, I think that's one of the things that helps me relate to kids some of the time and enjoy being with them. Then, in terms of the staff, I see myself still as a little sister. I guess that partly comes from the school's having a rather stable faculty and the fact that there aren't any people younger than I am here. I was one of the younger people to begin with, and I have remained so because nobody much younger has arrived since I came. I do see myself as an adult too, I guess. I must, because I certainly perform in an adult world and I do all those adult kinds of things that need to be done. I certainly don't need taking care of, although there are times when I suppose it would be nice. But I know it would drive me crazy after about ten minutes because I'm too independent. I know my own mind.

And you know, it's very interesting. The time when I was becoming more comfortable with myself as a teacher – more savvy in terms of hunting up an interesting curriculum and being involved in planning and writing – was a real turning point in my life. It was the year we bought a house and moved out of the city. If I hadn't had school, I would have gone directly to a mental ward without passing "Go." I was miserable for three months, and school was the one place where I knew I could find a pair of scissors and colored paper.

I'm really torn, because I am very adventurous and I love doing new things; but I also get myself established in routines, and I love my life so much that I don't want to change it. I don't know where the adventurous side comes in – I mean, in terms of doing new things, in terms of saying, "Okay, kids, we're going to do something that's never been done before." That's just another part of me. It comes out in small chunks, when I know that I can come back to something safe, where I don't have to be adventurous in everything. A large risk, like quitting my job and doing something completely different, is probably a little bit too great at this point.

Now I look at my life, and I'm not sure I want to have a child. That biological clock is ticking very quickly, and we really have to decide. Anyway, the change is not going to be easy, and I'm almost saying: Maybe if I'm not going to be able to have a child, I will accept that; it will get decided. If someone were to offer me some guarantee that if it didn't work out, that if I weren't happy, I could come back – that would be different. But the problem in this day and age, with this kind of job market, is that there are no guarantees.

In general, I'm pretty pleased with the kinds of things I'm doing. I think I may have proved to myself that I can do it, that I am a good teacher, that I can do things that other people – say, my family or my husband's family – think are good. I'm probably ready to move on. Right now is an even period, and I don't know if something will come along and jolt me. Probably having a child will, taking at least *some* time off. Then what I'm really hoping for is something new and different. I'd like to come back to Scribner, but I'd probably be interested in forging ahead into some new territory and trying out something like partnership teaching or a shared classroom. To be perfectly honest, I see myself not being able to stay away.

I'm not dissatisfied at this point. I think it would be easier to become dissatisfied in other systems. I know for a fact that burnout would probably have occurred around year three if I had stayed in the city – just because the kinds of tensions there were and the rewards that I was getting were so minimal in comparison to the kinds of efforts that I was having to put forth. I think that's where burnout comes from. And I guess here I just get the feeling that I'm worthwhile as a person, that I'm doing my share and maybe more, that I'm an important link, that if I weren't here I would be missed.

2   *Understanding the Context for Development*

WORKING IN SCHOOLS: PERSONAL AND PROFESSIONAL REFLECTIONS

Why look at the school setting, the profession, and the recent educational climate? How will this view add to an understanding of adult development? Developmental psychologists agree that growth is a complicated and interactive process influenced by many forces both inside and outside the individual. The environment is not only a context within which growth takes place. More fundamentally, it is a major component of a dynamic interaction. To understand the potentials for adult growth in schools, adults *and* schools must be examined.

In this chapter I draw upon practice and research. I weave together my own two decades of experience as a teacher and administrator, the reported experiences of other practitioners, and the results of past and current analyses. I explore how the structure of schools and the roles of teacher and administrator facilitate or interfere with adult growth. I raise these questions: What past or present conditions might influence the way Archer Elementary and its adult workers are functioning? To what extent do the conditions shape the individuals; to what extent are the conditions shaped by the individuals? Is the educational climate supportive, undermining, or neutral? How do persistent attitudes toward education affect the day-to-day experiences of children and adults in schools?

The Nature of Teaching and Schools

When I first started teaching in the late 1960s, there was an air of excitement about professional service. Even though the pay was dismal, it was a vocation that had purpose and meaning. As I look back on that time with an understanding of adult development, I suspect the optimistic view of teaching as a profession was tinged with the idealism of young adulthood. A generation spawned by the baby boom after World War II was coming of age, and there were enough of us to influence public outlook and opinion.

The late 1960s and early 1970s were times particularly well suited to my needs as a fledgling adult. It was a time of exploration and innovation. Large sums of federal money were available for curriculum development and program planning. The school I taught at was one of the first in the country to adopt the English model of open education for the primary grades. At the upper level of the school where I worked, English, history, science, and art teachers collaborated to test a similar model for early adolescents. While administrators, veteran teachers, and parents often frustrated our efforts with wisdom and logic, we struggled for four years to transform our dreams into practice. Many exciting things happened in those years, not all of which were productive for all children. Typical of young adults, we were persistent, tenacious, unyielding, and perhaps somewhat myopic.

The school where I worked provided an unusually supportive work environment. I had a relatively small class of twenty-five students, interesting colleagues, a work space, and a great deal of freedom. Even so, I soon began to feel something was missing. My needs as a developing adult were not being satisfied by work in a school or by my constant exposure to children.

This first school was likely more conducive to my young-adult needs for career exploration and experimentation than many. Nevertheless, I was soon frustrated by my needs for recognition and advancement. Once I had progressed from an English and history teacher to the head of an interdisciplinary team, I had completed the existing road of career advancement. Except for administrative positions, which were unlikely to become vacant, my occupational climb within the school was finished.

Work in schools is not structured like the many professions where there are clear paths to promotion through the hierarchy of the organization. Teachers cannot generally advance without leaving the classroom. Even outside the classroom, opportunities for advancement are limited. Teachers may become discouraged as they look toward the future and may gradually begin to seek their rewards in the present. This limited outlook contributes to an emphasis on the demands of the moment, reinforcing teachers' dependence on their relationships with students. More fundamentally, it encourages educators to focus on the way schools are, rather than the ways they might be – an orientation more conducive to maintaining the status quo than to encouraging innovation.

At some time and for some adults, education's static structure served a purpose. This was so when women would teach until they married and started a family, leave to raise their children, and return after some years to a school that had essentially remained the same. Although women were just beginning to combine the roles of mother and worker when I decided to have my first child, the fact that I would lose little professional ground by taking time off certainly influenced my decision. For those who choose to move in and out of teaching, taking time to develop themselves, their families, or alternative career options, this aspect of school work is encouraging. For others who prefer a prolonged and uninterrupted career in education, lack of change can be stagnating. Even after teaching for twenty or thirty years, a veteran educator can have hardly any greater responsibility than a novice. One experienced teacher explains:

> Forty years…is a long time to stay at the same job, a job that permits no significant changes. Not many teachers today can enter the classroom in their twenties and still be happy and fulfilled in their work when they retire at sixty-five.[2]

The organizational structure of schools directly influences teacher and administrator satisfaction. Teachers are often frustrated by the lack of opportunities to advance and gain recognition. In contrast, some administrators find they have lost the essence of being an educator when they move out of the classroom. Most young teachers do not consider classroom teaching a permanent occupation. Men seem to want to move on to other work or into administration. Women often have marriage and family on their minds. If neither promotion nor marriage is realized, there can be a general feeling of loss or incompleteness. Some of Janet Kramer's unhappiness with teaching may be associated with unfulfilled expectations for this type of career pattern.

Though women tend to expand their work commitments when they believe they will remain unmarried, their level of satisfaction can vary. Married women, on the other hand, both devote less of their "life space" to teaching and derive more satisfaction from it.[3] This has certainly been the way Judy Cubbins has adjusted her life. Her decision to shift from a partnership to self-contained teaching was directly related to her desire to devote more time to her life outside of school and to her husband. Is there an inverse relationship between involvement in teaching and level of satisfaction? Might it be predicted that reducing the amount of time adults spend in schools or encouraging adults to focus their energies on nonwork activities could provide an antidote to negative working conditions? When researchers replicated Lortie's 1975 study of school teachers, they learned that a very important aspect of teaching identified by teachers in the 1980s was the amount of vacation time it afforded. Satisfaction was linked to time *away* from the job.[4]

The rewards of working in schools have historically favored adults who make less than a full commitment to their work and who plan to be involved in teaching for short or intermittent periods. Lortie concluded that "the career system in teaching continues to favor recruitment rather than retention and low rather than high involvement."[5] Most schools in the 1980s were staffed by veteran teachers and administrators. At the same time, a sharp reduction in the pool of young adults entering the profession seriously hindered recruitment. Could it be that dissatisfaction with working in schools reflects a mismatch between persistent features of the occupation and the characteristics of the teacher and administrator population?

School people changed during the 1970s and 1980s. They were older, more experienced, racially and culturally more diverse, and better educated. Yet schools have remained basically unchanged. A result of these mismatched realities may be a significant cause of dissatisfaction.

In my case, lacking the opportunity for promotion, I riveted my attention and energies on teaching. I could never do enough, and there was never sufficient time. I arrived at school at the crack of dawn and left after dark. Every night, I corrected papers and prepared lessons. My job became all-encompassing. Before long, I felt tired and I was beginning to experience the conflicts inherent in the teaching role and the limitations of a teacher's status.

By its nature, teaching immerses the adult in the lives of children. One consequence of this immersion may be a need to hold one's adult status in abeyance. Balancing demands to become involved in the values, attitudes, and thought processes of children, while still remaining an adult, can be a source of conflict. I remember a conversation I had with one of my supervisors: Was it appropriate for me to wear jeans to class so I could freely take part in the activities of my students? Or did I need to don a skirt or dress so teacher and child would be clearly distinguished? It has been suggested that the happiest and most effective teachers may never have completely transcended aspects of their own childhood and adolescence.[6] While this developmental reality may make it easier to teach, it may also impede satisfactory peer relationships and arrest personal and professional development.

In addition to the liabilities of immersion in the world of children, dependence on students for feedback and a sense of achievement can be limiting. Teachers persistently say that the primary rewards of teaching come from their interactions with students. As classes become larger and more heterogeneous, does this source of rewards for the adults in schools become diffused? When teachers are not sufficiently gratified by their work with students, where else can they turn for support?

Although I was greatly rewarded by my relationships with students, the repetitive nature of teaching gradually became stressful and tiring. Modifying the curriculum requires time and autonomy. Adhering to the same curriculum year after year can gradually engender diminished enthusiasm and a feeling of arrested growth. Routine thinking and behavior can come from the constant demands of teaching. Required to *give* of themselves continually in a role where getting is elusive and infrequent, teachers may adopt routines for protection. "One of the consequences of a marked disparity between giving and getting is development of a routine that can reduce the demand for giving."[7] This insight helped me to understand both my own diminished enthusiasm for teaching over time and the low levels of energy and interest I have observed in veteran educators who lack opportunities to renew their skills and refocus their professional energies.

Feelings of isolation, exhaustion, and frustration can overtake idealism and enthusiasm for adults who work continually with children. One teacher who started her teaching career in the 1960s explains:

> I worked tirelessly, tried all kinds of experiments, came in on Saturdays. It was exhilarating – for the first few years. But as the years wore on and on, I began to notice that the drive was being replaced by myriad frustrations. Many teachers who had arrived with me on the crest of the '60s waves felt tethered in place. We became less experimental, angrier, found it harder to give, more isolated.[8]

Once, when I was talking with a group of teachers, the issue of isolation kept surfacing. Teachers want and need contact with other adults. As a teacher, I often felt alone: as the only adult in a classroom filled with children; in the solitude of correcting papers and preparing lesson plans; and during times when I was free, but when other adults were usually teaching. The organizational structures of most schools separate adults within self-contained classrooms. Physical separation can also mean social, psychological, and professional isolation. Yet peer interaction is a key component of school improvement; likewise, it is an essential aspect of adult development.

Recognition is an important – and often missing – ingredient of teacher satisfaction. Describing the potential stresses of teaching, several teachers commented that even the most difficult days are brightened by the acknowledgments of colleagues, supervisors, and parents. Janet Kramer explains:

> Teaching is a funny profession. You don't get a lot of positive feedback. You really have to rely on your own feelings about how things are going....You hear if you do something great or if you do something terrible, but you don't hear much of anything about all that goes on in between.

In this country, teaching has historically held an anomalous status: On the one hand, education is revered and teachers are expected to be faultless; on the other hand, education is demeaned as a profession and those who cannot develop skills in other, more notable pursuits teach. This double-edged sword gives educators ambiguous messages about the importance of their work. It also raises unattainable expectations for their performances. Writing about teaching, Myron Brenton explains:

> The successful teacher is buoyant, considerate, cooperative, emotionally stable, ethical, expressive, forceful, intelligent, objective, resourceful, reliable, mature, vital, punctual, magnetic, enthusiastic, energetic, uses judgment, possesses a sense of humor and has scholastic proficiency.[9]

Teachers who internalize such expectations are destined for frustration and disappointment.

The norms of teaching can often be more conducive to discontent than satisfaction. Norms – unwritten rules for behavior – are numerous and slow to change in schools. Adults in most schools do not share their expertise. They do not customarily visit each other's classrooms. They do not typically create and evaluate materials together. They do not frequently talk about the practice of teaching. Yet these behaviors are critical to the establishment of newer norms of experimentation and collegiality linked to enhanced professionalism and continued school improvement.[10]

The nature of teaching and the organizational structure of schools influence the lives of teachers, the operation of schools, and the public perception of schooling. Attitudes toward the profession are likely to be an outgrowth of these conditions.

Attitudes Toward Schooling

I left teaching and administering in schools because I found it confining. I wanted to break out, to develop myself and my skills, and to expand my influence. Though I continue to work with schools and consider myself a practitioner first and a researcher second, I have not yet found a way to stay in the schools *and* promote my own growth, as well as the growth of other adults and children. My disposition toward schools remains hopeful and positive. I love to teach, and I think teaching offers very special rewards that few other professions can claim. I am interested in the persistence of my own positive attitudes and curious about the attitudes of others who remain committed to schooling. Has the teaching force changed over the past decades? Have the attitudes and perceptions of teachers and administrators shifted or remained stable during this time?

We were told that school people in the 1980s were tired and demoralized. Many did not plan to continue working in schools. Most would not choose working in schools again if given a second chance to make a career decision. While the need for teachers was escalating, the number of students choosing to major in education was low, and those who did decide to pursue a teaching career were not generally among the most capable. Talented women and minorities who once chose to become educators, because other options were not open to them, were turning away from teaching. Of those who did become teachers and administrators, it was the most capable who tended to leave soonest.[11]

In 1986, three researchers published the results of a follow-up study to Dan Lortie's work on the nature of teaching.[12] The sample of teachers surveyed and interviewed came from a diverse community with a variety of school types. Lortie and these researchers contended that the sample was thus representative of many sections of the nation and that the results could be broadly generalized.

Overall, the researchers found teachers slightly less satisfied with the job of teaching and conditions in the workplace than they were twenty years earlier. In 1964, 81 percent expressed some level of satisfaction with teaching as a job; in 1984, only 76 percent did. In 1964, 80 percent of the teachers sampled expressed some level of satisfaction with their schools; in 1984, only 68 percent did.[13]

Though teachers in 1964 and 1984 relied most often on their perceptions of student learning to judge their effectiveness, the weight given to this factor had eroded. In 1984, teachers appeared to rely more often than their 1964 counterparts on external indicators of effectiveness, such as test scores and evaluations. Since teachers' sense of efficacy is a significant factor in school improvement, and since teachers spend most of their day isolated from other adults, understanding where they derive their sense of effectiveness is important. Over the twenty-year period between the studies, the proportion of the teaching sample who cited external indicators of effectiveness in contrast to self-assessment more than doubled. The percentage of teachers indicating that they received no satisfaction at all from outside sources, however, also doubled. Again, the most frequently cited reward related to the objective characteristics of teaching was the teaching schedule, particularly the time it allowed teachers to be away from work.[14]

A critical element of professionalism is displaced when educators devalue their own knowledge and skills as the standards of excellence. School people also ally themselves with others who limit the measure of school improvement to outside input and, most commonly, to scores on standardized tests. Goodlad comments:

> Perhaps the most serious bar to understanding or improving our schools is the inadequate measures we use in seeking to determine their health. We use test scores, such as those on the SAT, as though they tell us something about the condition of school.[15]

Dependence on external rather than internal measures of success makes school people even more vulnerable to public criticism.

Diminished satisfaction with working in schools, retirements of large numbers of experienced teachers and administrators, and waning interest in teaching as a viable career option all suggest the need to make schools more attractive work environments and the job of teaching more valued, more highly rewarded, and more satisfying. As these needs have been recognized, an array of possible solutions to enhance the teaching profession has been generated, including career ladders, increased salaries, merit pay, relevant professional training, and more rigorous certification requirements. My understanding of the ways schools change and my experience as a teacher and administrator lead me to believe that solutions that influence the school directly, that enhance the quality of relationships among adults and between adults and children, and that give teachers and administrators increased control over their work lives will be those most likely to make a sustained difference.

Adults in schools need to work with each other in mutually supporting, collegial relationships focused on important facets of teaching and learning. School people must have expanded roles in decision-making about issues that affect their work lives. To professionalize education, control must revert to those in the business of teaching and administering. Giving teachers and administrators discretion over their work is an essential form of empowerment. Teachers will also want opportunities to work outside of the classroom *without* leaving teaching. Teachers can combine teaching and research, teaching and curriculum development, teaching and teacher training, or teaching and administration. In turn, administrators can reacquaint themselves with curriculum and instruction by working on curriculum projects and participating in classroom teaching. If principals are to be instructional leaders, periodic involvement of this kind is imperative. The principal of Archer Elementary recognizes the importance of this involvement:

> Being outside the classroom diminishes my potential for educational leadership. The longer I'm not in the classroom, the less current I become with curriculum materials and methods of instruction. If you're teaching, you have a different – and, I think, richer – perspective.

Other avenues of growth, renewal, and enhanced professionalism might include the reinstatement of sabbaticals or leaves to give educators time and resources to follow their teaching and nonteaching interests. The establishment of support groups within the school can provide a context for sharing and discussion. Creating opportunities for practitioners to continue and combine teaching and administrative responsibilities will increase alternatives for experimentation, variety, recognition, and advancement without severing the important relationships between adults and children.

The professionalization of teaching and administration will require that learning be an expectation and goal not only for students but also for adults. A profession is continually expanding and modifying its knowledge base; likewise, learning and growing are continuous. Not only is the ongoing learning and development of adults necessary for the growth and well-being of children, but growing and changing are part of a lifelong process to which both adults and children are entitled.

[T]he professional development of individual teachers is more than a means toward the end of delivering services. It should also be an end in itself....Until teachers are seen as being worthy of receiving services, especially the service of adult education, they will see themselves neither as learners nor as professionals.[16]

Conditions that support teacher and administrator professionalism promise to buttress flagging enthusiasm and increase overall satisfaction. As positively oriented educators have a positive influence on the school and in the classroom, it is critical to foster conditions that enhance rather than inhibit professional satisfaction. To the extent that present conditions impede the sense of efficacy and well-being of the adults in schools, it is in a largely negative context that schools and school people will be working.

Ample but Often Undisclosed Optimism
As I review the literature on teaching and teacher attitudes, I am continually struck by its negative cast. It is more often the limitations than the opportunities of working in schools that make their way into print. Clearly, there are serious professional and organizational constraints on educators. It is also true that the long-term effects of being a school teacher or administrator can be debilitating. Yet, I know from my own experiences as a teacher and administrator that working in and with schools is also an exhilarating experience – not only in the first few years, but over decades. Where do the positive aspects of the work lives of adults in schools find expression?

At the start of a recent meeting, an assistant principal turned to me and whispered:

> You know, I was walking around the building today, and I said to myself, "I really love this job. I love working with the teachers, and the kids are terrific! Am I crazy?"

Somewhere, permission for expressing the incomparable joys of working in schools has been lost. Not only is the sense of the joy and challenge of working in schools largely undisclosed, but the general educational climate seems to inhibit its unfettered expression. "Am I crazy?" the school administrator questions.

Talking with teachers and administrators about their work and asking them to share its wonders rather than its difficulties might yield a very different literature. When I was teaching, I discovered the unbounded energy and creativity of young adolescents. I remember the unparalleled pain and struggle of moving from a child to a young adult. I empathized with the naivete and idealism of youth. I capitalized on these qualities by encouraging seventh, eighth, and ninth graders to write poetry, to study utopian visions, and to read the words of philosophers. One aspect of teaching early adolescents I especially liked was the thoughtfulness of their questioning and reasoning about the real and the possible. Adolescents can also be brutally honest.

As my own children were tripping through adolescence, I had another opportunity to experience the pains and magic of this time of life. I sometimes think with regret about all the adults I know who go through each day and each year without the rejuvenating and challenging influences that accompany the presence of children in one's life. As a parent, I have a fleeting opportunity to reexperience these feelings. As an educator, this opportunity is an ongoing privilege.

I am convinced that most teachers and administrators have deeply felt positive experiences of their work. While they express similar concerns about the structures of schools and the limitations of the profession, they are buoyed by the excitement of working with children and by the possibilities of making a difference. A special needs teacher comments:

> I really love seeing children change and grow and feeling that I can be of assistance. Seeing children want to learn, especially children for whom school has been such a struggle, is very special. Teaching is exciting; teaching is fun.

A former second-grade teacher shares his experience:

> I was excited about exploring with young children. They're sponta-neous, they let you know they care, they don't hold back and posture. I loved the challenge of making learning happen. The prospect of reading a good book with second graders or teaching math, which I love doing, was a very high point.

Now as an elementary school principal, he continues:

> Just as I loved interactions with young children, I now love adult interactions. I love working with a group of adults and helping them to move to a different place – a better place. As a principal, you

can facilitate, you can move systems, you can move organizations, you can help people, you can produce change.

The School Reform Movement of the 1980s

The 1980s was not an easy time for people in education. The wave of reports on the status of schools that began with the release of *A Nation at Risk* in 1983 resulted in a wide range of national reports as well as state-initiated legislation.[17] Starting with an emphasis on the U.S. high school, attention grew to encompass primary and elementary school children as well as the special educational needs of young adolescents.

Many studies painted a bleak picture of schools – then, and for the future. Teachers and schools were described as inadequate, and everything from teacher and administrative certification requirements to academic standards and test scores for students was evaluated and found lacking. This is certainly not the first time schools have undergone such intense scrutiny. Reports of dissatisfaction with education have been common throughout the history of the United States, and many of the same issues and questions have been reiterated. Schools have become accustomed to receiving low grades from outside critics. What impact do these critiques have on those within the schools? Have they finally built firm walls of resistance to outside criticism? Are they immune after years of attacks?

During this period, I had opportunities to visit schools and talk with school people from all over the country and abroad. What struck me most from these observations and conversations was the incredible strength and resiliency that school teachers and administrators continued to exhibit. While controversy and criticism are swirling around the school building, the business of teaching and learning goes on. Sometimes, it is even positively affected.

One curious and hopeful pattern that has been observed after the inevitable swings of school reform is the sense of optimism that typically accompanies each period of criticism.[18] The school reform movement of the 1980s appeared to leave the same enthusiasm in its wake. Not only did schools benefit from the renewed focus of public attention and interest, but conversations among school people and between school people and researchers began to take place. National interest in education has also led to state-level legislation and local school improvement efforts.

A principal writes about the impact of national and state reform efforts and the attitudes toward reform they have influenced:

In all candor, the publication *A Nation at Risk* and other recent reports have had little direct impact on my school practices or my educational philosophy. The current school reform movement, however, has helped to provide an impetus for new legislation in my state. The resulting local public school improvement act has had a direct impact on schools, providing funds for teacher salaries, the establishment of school improvement councils, and the initiation of teacher grants.

The furor and publicity over the reports have also fostered discussion among many school constituents: parents, teachers, administrators, and students. The ripple effects from these discussions are just beginning to surface in tangible activities by the school committee and other influential legislative bodies.

However, I want to clearly state that it is often the less visible currents that prove to be the most effective movers in education; it is the subtle shift in the current of public school opinion that impacts most vigorously on schools.

I believe the tides have begun to shift, momentum is picking up, and exciting times lie ahead. Some credit for this has to be given to the reform movement.

Whatever influence school reform movements have, they do seem to stimulate teachers and administrators to think and reflect upon practice. This effect alone makes them valuable. A high school math teacher writes:

I have spent a great deal of time considering *A Nation at Risk* and am willing to acknowledge the lack of achievement of our students in many areas. The places most often singled out are reading and math. While low scores do suggest a problem, it's not my sense that improving them would mean the problem would be overcome. In my mind, the problems at hand revolve around motivation and interest, not just performance.

The more I think about things, the more I believe that enthusiasm and interest are the two qualities necessary to be an effective teacher. People learn much more easily when they know someone genuinely cares.

An elementary principal from rural New Hampshire states:

We constantly change the focus of what we want our schools to do and be. The climate is fast approaching one of expected levels of performance by the public: "Teach us to read, but also mainstream us, individualize us, reach for our gifts and talents, feed us, discipline us for school and home, transport us, and then provide us with after-school care." In addition, you should be able to interpret all types of texts, meet all forms of administrative procedures, and satisfy expectations to raise test scores. Remember, you have to be nice to the public, too.

We want effective schools with effective leaders, staff, and support groups, but what do we do to preserve the integrity and worth of those who live the profession? We criticize, malign, insult, belittle, underpay, intimidate, and wrap in red tape those adult professionals responsible for trying to educate the youth of today.

Then there are the school reform reports, almost every one written without the input and insights of teachers and administrators.

A veteran teacher and administrator from a poor, minority community in New York City offers:

The school reform reports have not had significant influence on my practice. Practice seems to be influenced by pressure groups on the state and national level. The pressures they impose may or may not be related to public interest. In a large system, changes are imposed in a crisis-like atmosphere without the kinds of structural changes and training necessary to ground them in solid practice based on understanding and acceptance. On-the-job training and instant teachers and staff proliferate.

Teachers are feeling overwhelmed and frustrated. Many to whom I speak feel they have a vision of what they would like to do, but they feel they can't because of external regulations. Teachers have been treated poorly by administrators. They have not been encouraged to experiment, initiate, and grow. I've thought about these conditions as I've been reading the reports.

School people are thinking and talking about educational reform. They are also arriving at schools each day to work with children and adults. They are functioning within difficult roles and complex organizations with constant internal and external pressures and mixed support. Many are tired and defeated. Many more are committed and engaged. As we turn the corner on our way to Archer Elementary, it is natural to wonder just how the broad context of education affects the lives of the children and adults who are variously wending their way toward school.

You have already discovered that Judy Cubbins, Janet Kramer, Don Bolter, and Nan Johnson each experiences Archer somewhat differently, depending, in part, on how they perceive themselves and the people and things around them. As another adult and as an outsider, my view of the school will be different, as will yours. In the next section, I describe what I saw when I visited Archer. I ask you to look through my eyes and beyond to your own perceptions. How does your school compare to Archer? What makes Archer a positive work environment for many adults? What do you see as potential problems? What do you recognize as areas for expanded opportunities?

When Archer's faculty and the principal talk about the school in the third section, they reveal still different shades of understanding. It will be interesting to notice, for example, that contrary to Mae West's protestations, too much of a good thing may *not* always be wonderful. Some teachers feel overwhelmed by the professional-development opportunities at the school and in the district. Their reactions are an important reminder that educators cannot construct the "perfect" school environment. Focusing, instead, on the needs of individual adults may be a more fruitful path to effective and satisfying personal and professional growth and staff development.

ARCHER ELEMENTARY: OUTSIDE LOOKING IN

Driving south on the main highway out of the city, I notice that traffic is relatively light. In contrast, a stream of slow-moving vehicles is heading in the opposite direction toward the city. After only a few miles, trees and fields replace the brick and wood structures and the sidewalks, bus stops, and rows of parked cars that line the streets of the city. A winding exit leads me into the western section of Scribner, where, for a moment, it feels like country. Here the roads do not have sidewalks, and an abundance of trees frame or even hide the homes. Off to one side, a horse grazes in a field not far beyond a large wood and stone house. At the next turn, a sign directs me to the Archer School.

Turning right, I find myself in a residential area. Sidewalks reappear and, along one, a small child is dawdling, lunch box banging against one knee. The houses here are two-story buildings, each with a two-car garage. In many of the driveways, several cars are parked. Neatly trimmed lawns separate one house from another.   A yellow school bus passes by, negotiating a final curve before stopping at the school's front door.

Archer School is a long, low, brick building. A road runs along the front side, and behind the school, playgrounds and fields are flanked by park land. While children climb from the buses or chain their bikes to the rack near the front door, teachers are parking their cars in a far lot and entering at the side of the building. It is just before eight-thirty. The school is still quiet. As I walk down the corridor toward the front office, I see that most classrooms are dark and their doors are closed.   Midway down the hall I see three teachers in a room chatting about the events of the weekend. In another room, a teacher sits at her desk reviewing the day's plans.

At eight-thirty I hear the sounds of children beginning to filter through the halls. Two girls bound into the room where their teacher is working and immediately command her attention with stories about the weekend and questions about the day ahead. Another child enters, proudly displaying a drawing he has completed at home. The teacher admires his efforts and asks if he would like to share his work with the class sometime during the morning. Out in the hall an adult voice can be heard cautioning a group of children: "Walk. Don't run!" Another day at the Archer Elementary School is about to begin.

I spent several months at Archer. I sat in classrooms and in meetings. I listened to students, parents, teachers, and the principal. I collected past and current documents: memos, reports, notices. And I formed a number of impressions.

The town of Scribner appears to be a middle- to upper-class, professional, suburban community. Families live in large homes with substantial grounds. Parents come to the school well dressed, often driving expensive new cars. The parents of many children are doctors, lawyers, university professors, or business people. The high value they place on schooling is demonstrated by the phone calls and visits they make to the school, by high attendance at school functions, by the number of enrichment activities in which they enroll their children, and by the frequent communication to children of the importance of school and high achievement. In some cases, parental interest and investment in education translate into pressures on teachers from parents and into competition among children; at the same time, parental involvement is a source of caring, support, and stimulation.

While most children at Archer are white Americans, there are fifty-four black or foreign students. Twenty-one black children come to Archer on buses each day through an outreach program. A plan for voluntary, one-way, urban-suburban integration, the program offers children from the city an opportunity to attend suburban schools. Most of these students remain at the school for the duration of their elementary education. Foreign students are often at the school for only six months or a year while one of their parents works at a local university or business. During the time I spent at Archer, there were students from China, France, Greece, Italy, Israel, South Korea, the Netherlands, Sweden, Armenia, and the Philippines.

From the Early Years to the Present

Archer School is a relatively new addition to the town of Scribner. Built as an "overflow school" in the 1960s, when the population was expanding, the school opened its doors in the fall of 1967. While it was designed to accommodate six hundred, the enrollment was almost seven hundred in the first year. Slides taken at that time picture an art lesson taught in a hallway – the bottoms of cubbies serving as seats, the walls functioning as partitions. What is now the teachers' lunch area was then a classroom. At the time of construction, Archer was designated a "team-teaching school." Folding doors form flexible walls between a number of rooms. This year, only the doors in the sixth-grade rooms are intermittently opened. Sometimes two teachers work together, dividing specific teaching responsibilities, but the most common structure for teaching is self-contained.

Archer was originally organized into three teams. Kindergarten and first and second grades were grouped together; grades three and four were a unit; and fifth and sixth grades formed the upper division. In the early days, when enrollment was at its peak, these units operated almost as three separate schools. Current records show enrollment at less than 350 children. There were four kindergarten sessions. Now the program runs one session in the afternoon. Where students once squeezed into the cubby area to have an art lesson, extra chairs and cabinets are stored. One room stands empty, and most classes have fewer than twenty-five children. Enrollment patterns at Archer are reflected throughout the town. Several schools have already been closed, and it is likely that Archer will receive additional teachers and children when a nearby elementary school closes.

As the school has grown smaller, there have been corresponding organizational changes. Instead of three teams, there are now two. The Lower Team is made up of the kindergarten and grades one, two, and three; the fourth, fifth and sixth grades compose the Upper Team. Now there are two lunch shifts instead of three. Archer used to have both a principal and a vice principal; now the position of vice principal has been eliminated. The principal, Peter Samson, currently coordinates a staff of nineteen classroom teachers (including two teaching assistants), eleven specialists, a secretary, five aides, three cafeteria workers, and three custodians. Of the classroom teachers, two are males and seventeen are women; of the eleven specialists, eight are women and three are men. A walk through the halls at mid-morning reveals twenty-one separate classrooms. In each room, one or sometimes two adults and a group of children are busily engaged in activities. At first glance, these appear to be different from the activities of a similarly composed group in a neighboring room.

Archer Elementary has a large, centrally located library, a learning dis-abilities center (which serves the district), a cafeteria, and a gym. Along one of the gym walls, there is a stage. On occasion, this space is converted into an auditorium. Flanking one side of the library is a large area subdivided into several sections. I rarely saw children in this part of the building, where work areas for teachers, teacher aides, and specialists were arranged. Next to this area is a teachers' lunchroom. Two vinyl couches, with a low table in between, face each other along one wall. Along another wall are two refrigerators. And at the opposite end of the room, there is a bulletin board with notices pinned to it about teacher workshops and with other adult communications. Teachers come and go from this room all during the day, finding a place at the central table for fifteen or twenty minutes at lunchtime.

Inside Archer's Classrooms

I can hear the soft sounds of music as I enter a third-grade room. Children sit quietly at their desks writing. Close to the door, there is a much larger desk where the teacher works. After several minutes, she looks over her shoulder at the clock on the wall and asks the children to put their papers away in preparation for the Pledge of Allegiance. After turning the record player off, she asks the boy whose job is "pledge leader" to take his position at the front of the class. Everyone stands and recites together. This is followed by sharing time. One by one, children who raise their hands are called upon by the teacher to stand in front of the class and make a contribution. Then, looking up at the clock again, the teacher announces that it is time for math. As some children leave, others take out their books, soon to be joined by students from a neighboring classroom.

"One, two, three," the teacher counts slowly and deliberately, and the noise of transition lessens. "There are people who should have math papers for me," the teacher continues, reading off individual names. While some children crowd around the teacher's desk to turn in papers and ask questions, others take out their folders and talk with friends. After handing everyone a piece of paper, the teacher says, "On your mark, get set, go." The room is instantly quiet. The scratching noises of pencils and pens are the only audible sounds. A timed math exercise has begun.

While the children work, I look around the room. Along the walls are numerous colorful bulletin boards. Different portions of the room seem to be set up for distinct functions. There is a rug in one corner on which the children will later have a group discussion. Not far away, a mobile hangs from the ceiling, displaying the message: "Key Word: Whisper." Along the back wall, a desk and a globe are positioned together with a sign that reads: "Get familiar with your world." Between this area and another, where the focus is cursive writing, there is a small partition. Near the teacher's desk, a series of shelves holds a variety of games. And in the center of the room, twenty desks are arranged in a square.

"Stop! Please exchange your papers," directs the teacher. The timed exercise is finished. After reviewing the answers and recording each child's score, a lesson on decimals begins.

At the far end of the building, fifth graders are returning to their room after recess. Individual desks are grouped here to form tables. Not far from the door is a much larger desk, where the teacher sits. A clock, a flag, and a phone occupy the wall behind. They are joined by several posters and framed paintings. On the other side of the door, a round table and chairs are positioned. A square rug occupies one corner, and there is a small book cart not far behind.

As children find their seats, the teacher begins the lesson with a question: "What two things do you have to have for a complete sentence?" Several children raise their hands, and each is called on in turn. Once a definition has been established, the teacher asks everyone to take out his or her language workbook and turn to a specific section. The teacher guides the class through two of the questions before passing out paper and asking the students to complete the exercise on their own. This is to be individual work, she stresses, and there should be no talking.

Almost as soon as work begins, hands pop into the air, and the teacher circulates around the room responding to individual questions. When all are momentarily answered, she goes over to the round table and sits down. Once there, several children approach her with additional questions. One boy comes over to work at the table and continues from this position to ask a flurry of questions. After responding several times, the teacher tells him he needs to work them out on his own. Some time passes before the teacher looks up at the clock and announces that it is time for them to put their books away. Anyone who has not finished, she explains, should complete the exercise for homework. It is time to work on creative writing.

As I leave this end of the building and walk toward the kindergarten, I am struck by the changes in size. Between the ages of six and eleven there is a great deal of physical growth. Everything here is on a smaller scale, and coming in to visit, I am surprised to find how near to the ground I come before sitting on a chair appropriately proportioned for the room's occupants.

As in other classes, this room has several defined areas. An easel is located not far from a sink where paintbrushes are soaking before being cleaned. A long table is set up beyond with papers and Magic Markers laid out on it and shelves full of books behind them. A door leads out from the back wall to the playground. On one side is a worktable holding saws and hammers. Next to it, a miniature kitchen is set up, complete with table and chairs, stove and cabinet. A piano is nearby, its back serving as a partition between this area and a block corner at the other end. Here a rug on the floor makes the area appear like a comfortable place for building. Shelves with games on them form another divider. The teacher tells the children they can take the games out whenever they want to play with them. In front of the shelves are several tables. One has a number scale set up on it and large cards with holes and yarn for practice sewing. Finally, there is a small table near the front door with large sheets of white paper, Magic Markers, and boxes of crayons. In the middle of the class, there is a ladder-like structure upon which several children are climbing. Nearby, a small mat is the place the children jockey for position as they begin to talk about the activities for the afternoon.

During the activity time that follows, children circulate freely around the room. Some settle at the long table, where a student teacher begins to engage them in drawing. The principal comes in to visit and begins to play catch with three children at one end of the room. Boys and girls work together. One little girl sets out several dishes on the kitchen table. Soon she is joined by another child, and the preparation of supper begins. The teacher asks several wandering children if they would like to color. One agrees; another goes off to find a game. Many activities are going on simultaneously. The children make choices about what will occupy them. After some time, the teacher glances up at the clock and says that it is time to clean up. She asks everyone to gather on the mat for an exercise game.

With forty-five minutes left before dismissal, there is time to see one last classroom. The self-contained class for third- and fourth-grade students with learning disabilities is set up in a now familiar fashion. A teacher's desk is near the door. The room is divided into several sections. There is an area with a rug forming a "quiet corner." Blackboards and bulletins occupy the walls. In the center of the room, seven student desks are arranged in rows. Another large desk is positioned at the front of the room. In most other classes, there is only one adult consistently present. Here there are two adults: a head teacher and an assistant.

A reading period is in progress. At a round table in the back of the room, the teacher is working with two students. As one reads aloud, keeping his place with a marker, the teacher monitors his progress and provides assistance in forming some sounds. "Good work; nice job; good reading," she tells him intermittently after several sentences. Another child is reading silently by her side. A third child, not at the moment under the vigilance of an adult, wanders around the room, making noises. Each of the two teachers speaks with him in turn, asking him to take his seat and suggesting ways he might make use of the next few minutes. He returns to his seat. Before long, he is up and wandering again, and the cycle repeats itself.

At the front of the room, the teaching assistant is sitting at a table with a child who has just completed a book. After answering questions about the story, the child counts up the number of pages she has read successfully. With help, she discovers that she has finished 102 pages since the last counting. Jumping up and down, she proclaims that she is eligible for a star. The assistant congratulates her and tells her she may take one from the desk. Grinning from ear to ear, she makes just the right selection and returns to her seat. A card on her desk has her name printed on it in bold letters. Each child can find his or her name similarly positioned.

"It's two-thirty," one of the students reminds the teacher. "Isn't reading period over?" "Oh, thank you, Tommy," the assistant replies. "Can you all put your books away and get ready for science?" Several children respond immediately, putting their reading books inside their desks and sitting up straight in their seats. The assistant says, "I'm very proud of Tommy and Jasmine. They're ready for science." Then she asks them to hand her the cards they have on their desks; she puts a check mark on each of them. As others show that they are also ready, they are also given check marks by the assistant.

A general discussion begins about snakes. When a child raises her hand, she is praised and her card checked. Several children give long accounts of their experiences with snakes. After fifteen minutes, the assistant begins the science topic for the day: the care and cleaning of teeth. In ten minutes, it will be time to go home.

Meetings

Most meetings among staff take place after children have gone home. In addition, school is dismissed early on Wednesdays, and an extended series of staff development courses coordinated by the central office is offered for in-service credit. During a typical semester, as many as fifty individual workshops and courses are available, almost half of which are organized and taught by classroom teachers and counselors from within the system. Outside curriculum specialists, coordinators, and consultants are responsible for the rest. Classes range in content from seminars on models of teaching and large-group management to sessions on phonics and social studies curricula. At Archer, the principal estimates that as many as 80 percent of Archer's teachers are currently enrolled in some form of professional development.

Three other types of meetings periodically involve some or all staff. Every other Tuesday afternoon, there is a meeting of the Senate. The Senate is a small group of staff, generally eight to ten members, chaired by the principal. The group meets to discuss school issues and to make recommendations or decisions on matters pertaining to school life. The leader from each team and representatives of various groups – such as aides, resource teachers, and specialists – attend.

At Senate sessions, decision-making is orchestrated by the principal in a very deliberate manner. Everyone's opinion is solicited before there is an evaluation of the sense of the group. Where there is still dissatisfaction, the principal acknowledges it and attempts to generate alternative solutions. During one meeting I observed, each representative took notes on Ditto masters, which were then copied and distributed. Some information, such as a scheduled faculty meeting with the superintendent, was merely to be communicated; some decisions, such as a rule that hats could not be worn in the building, were to be discussed among the groups and decided by consensus. Finally, a suggestion from the Lower Team to institute an honor roll was referred back to teachers from both teams for more discussion.

Every couple of weeks, the teams meet. The Upper Team generally gathers for lunch in one of the classrooms on Wednesday afternoon. Frequently, these meetings are short because of the press of other professional commitments. The Lower Team comes together before school at eight a.m., currently the only time everyone is free. Once a month, Lower Team members meet for a longer period on a Wednesday afternoon.

Full-faculty meetings are not common. After one such meeting, held the day before school opened, there were no others until mid-October. Faculty meetings take place in the library, where teachers sit at a variety of tables facing in different directions. The principal or key speaker generally sits alone at a table near the front of the room, separated from the group by a noticeable distance.

Faculty meetings operate differently from Senate discussions. Teachers raise their hands to be recognized. Whereas the principal deliberately solicits individual opinions at the Senate, there are many teachers who come to faculty meetings and remain silent. Here, as at Senate sessions, a consensus is sought. In setting the instructional goals for the school year, the principal asked for suggestions and then called for a vote.

For the most part, meetings are scheduled for the afternoons and end before five p.m. There are, however, special evening gatherings. Parents' Night is one such event. The Parents' Night I attended went like clockwork. Parents arrived and headed straight for their children's classrooms. Teachers arrived uncharacteristically dressed up and visibly nervous. After brief presentations, questions focused on class content and homework requirements. Though parents were asked to refrain from asking about the progress of individual children, most did corner teachers as the formal part of the meeting ended. The night was scheduled to end at eight p.m. At five after eight, I pulled out of the faculty parking lot. Most cars were gone, and the building was dark.

A VIEW FROM INSIDE

Overall, Archer faculty describes the school as a warm, friendly, and happy environment, a setting in which the needs of children are carefully and caringly addressed. Teachers describe the atmosphere in the school as cheerful and industrious. Though the school sits in the middle of a suburb, its proximity to park land gives it an almost rural feeling.

The adults who describe the school say it is a bright, cheery place. All but one of the teachers describe Archer in positive terms. Significantly, it is Janet Kramer, the only teacher describing herself as burned out, who sees the school somewhat differently. "I think the first thing that I would be impressed with is the physical layout of the school, because I don't think it's very attractive. The walls are gray cinder block; it's just a very cold, factory-looking building."

Beyond disliking the school's physical appearance, Janet agrees with others that the school provides children with a good education. "Objectively, I would have to say if you were thinking of sending your children to the school, they would have opportunities that aren't given to children in a lot of school systems. Archer has many facilities, including a learning disabilities center which serves the district. The center has a lot of teaching materials, and system specialists are often available there to answer questions or help with planning. We also often use the library."

As they describe Archer, several teachers note that the school has changed – in particular, the principalship and the attitudes and activities of parents. While parents are variously viewed as threatening or cooperative, the general attitude of parents and the community toward the school is now perceived as positive. This was not always the case. Veteran teachers explain that the community used to be highly critical of the school. When it first opened, Archer had the reputation of being "inconsistent, undisciplined, and chaotic." Many attribute the change in atmosphere and the subsequent shift of community sentiment to the present principal. Teachers note that there has been very little staff turnover. At the same time, they say there has been a large increase in the number of working mothers and in the number of single-parent families, a situation that often brings mothers back into the work force. Many parents simply lack the time and energy to become involved in the school.

Still, the influence of parents continues to be felt. For the most part, parents are thought of as interested and supportive. However, many staff members feel parents put excessive pressures on teachers and students. Parents are anxious about how well their children are doing and have specific opinions about the content of the curriculum and the ways it is taught. One teacher believes it is the parents who have the greatest amount of power in the system. She explains, "Even though they're not here visibly, I would say they have the strongest influence."

In addition to parents, Archer teachers talk about the principal when they describe what life is like for them in the school. Teachers say that Peter Samson protects and supports them. Even though he may not directly intervene in their everyday affairs, the attitude of respect and trust that teachers feel he communicates seems to give them a sense of personal efficacy and confidence. Explaining what life might be like for a new staff member, a teacher states: "You'll have a very supportive principal who will not sit you down and say, 'Do this, this, and that,' but who will care about what you are doing. The principal here trusts you, and because he trusts you, you work even harder."

On the whole, Peter Samson is seen as a principal who gives teachers a lot of freedom to make the decisions that affect their lives. To feel comfortable in the school, many teachers believe they must have both initiative and a desire to be independent. "You have to want to be independent, not be told what to do all the time. Because with Peter as principal, you're not going to be told what to do. You're going to be given a very free hand."

While teachers are encouraged to be independent, sharing is also valued. While the principal does not place many restrictions and pressures on teachers, the system is seen to be constraining and demanding as well as stimulating. Describing the life of a teacher at Archer and in the town, Peter Samson says:

> [Life is], in a word, busy – also productive and challenging. I think you would have to be a teacher who liked to share with other teachers and could give and receive from other teachers. You would not be living a life of isolation by any means. In this school, the job requires that teachers interact with others on their team and with specialists in the building. A classroom teacher is also required to put a great deal of him- or herself into developing the curriculum – not writing curriculum, but designing ways in which to implement it. The math program, in particular, requires a lot of teacher time and preparation.
>
> Your life outside the building in relation to the rest of the system would also be a demanding as well as an enriching one. You can become as involved as you wish in in-service workshops and committee work. There are many opportunities for people to grow in their profession, to become involved in the educational life of the school system.

Referring to his own early years as a teacher, Samson remembers, "It was fun, but it was also very demanding."

For some teachers, system-wide opportunities seem less like a choice and more like an expectation. A sense of stimulation is mixed with feelings of pressure and exhaustion:

> As a teacher in Scribner, you would be expected to go to a great many meetings, and that can be very, very tiring. Many of the programs say that they are voluntary, but that is not the feeling I have when I get notices from the administration saying only so-and-so signed up for this course. All voluntary – attendance is taken. People know when you don't show up. The opportunities are fantastic, the in-service training is wonderful. But, especially when you're an elementary teacher, there's very little time left for yourself. If your

last bus leaves at three-thirty and you have to be at a meeting from four to six, it's too hard. I think sometimes they forget that. If you wanted to, you could be doing something enriching, something fantastic every single day, twenty days a month while you're in school. You'd either be dead or you'd be very, very stimulated.

Within the school, teachers generally see the staff as friendly and cohesive. Some speak of closer personal relationships with both teachers and parents; others feel there is a professional cohesiveness that masks personal differences. In a school where so many of the teachers have been together for so long, both strong ties and clear differences have had time to develop. On one level or another, the staff has evolved ways of being and working together as a group. For some, the environment "feels close, comfortable, and safe;" for others, the arrival of a new adult is an exciting prospect. There is a sense of community; there are "limitations in terms of the contacts you can make." On balance, staff members speak positively about working at Archer. They have varied reactions to pressures and opportunities within the system.

Teachers often wonder about the effects of extended working relation-ships on Archer's staff. As student enrollments have declined and teaching positions diminished, teachers have remained in their jobs, and the arrival of a new teacher is an increasingly rare occurrence. One teacher reports that there has not been a new classroom teacher at Archer in more than five years. Perhaps teachers can be independent here, they speculated, because they are so familiar with their work. A long-term relationship with the principal may also lay the groundwork for mutual trust and respect.

Many teachers believe that the initiative they say they must take in the school is also related to the particular nature of a veteran staff. One staff member reflected that new teachers would find initial support from col-leagues but would soon be on their own because everyone is so absorbed in his or her own projects. "I think if you're new anywhere, you have to have a lot of initiative, but you have to have a lot more now than in the past because there are very few new people on the staff here and the rest of us can forget what it's like." Similarly, the principal states that after so many years, most people have their programs well in hand. He assumes that each teacher knows the resources that are available and will not hesitate to ask for help. In his view, teachers who have worked together over some time may feel more comfortable taking the initiative. Predicted increases in elementary school enrollments, impending retirements, and teacher shortages are likely to change all of these dynamics.

Consistent with the emphasis on individuality at Archer are some teachers' feelings about the presence of educational leadership. As one teacher defines it: "I think an educational leader is somebody who stretches your imagination and your belief that there are more possibilities in education than what you're doing or there may be different ways to do something than the way you're doing it. I think there are a lot of people here who do some of that at some times, but I don't see it coming from a single source."

Teachers see the principal as accessible and supportive, and Peter Samson uses similar words to describe himself. But neither he nor the staff typically describes him as an educational leader. Samson reflects:

> Am I an educational leader? Not entirely. I think there are people in the school who know a lot more than I do. In one respect, I'm not in as close touch with some aspects of teaching or with the classroom situation as I once was. I do keep an eye out for things that might be helpful to people and might represent a change or a new direction. I also try to make myself accessible to people, to help them in their classrooms or their lives. I guess I see myself more as a clearinghouse and a clinician than as a real leader: an original thinker with an original philosophy that I want to bring to a school, saying, "Follow this; follow me."

The sentiments of many teachers are captured by one teacher's comments:

> I wouldn't say Peter is an educational leader. You will find him to be a supportive principal, one who will answer anything you'd like to know and will be very open. But it's the type of thing where you would have to know what the question is in order to get the answer; he might not anticipate the question for you.

In fact, this teacher and others have a broad view of leadership, believing it can be shared by a number of adults in the school, particularly by teachers: "If you mean, by educational leadership, people who are outstanding teachers and in that way are educational leaders – yes, you would find a lot of that here."

Just as it is perceived that leadership is shared at Archer, so, too, is power available to anyone who wants to assume it, including children. One teacher relates:

I think everyone here has some power. The children, for example, wanted to change the lunchroom, and this year we've done it. Starting from the bottom, or maybe it's the top, the children have some power in making changes and decisions, and so can everyone else.

Teachers at Archer see power as the capacity to perform effectively, rather than the might to impose one's will on another: "I think everyone has power here, but it doesn't seem that one has power *over* others." Almost all of the staff say they feel a sense of personal efficacy, at least in deciding what happens in their own classrooms. Those teachers who do not feel influential in the school or in the system say they do not choose to be. If there were something they wanted to get done, however, each feels it would be possible to accomplish it, either alone or with help through the channels that exist.

If leadership, power, and independence at Archer result in feelings of efficacy, they also lead to diverse educational values and teaching methods. While staff agree on the broad goals of education, there is no clear consensus on the means. Providing children with excellent academic training in a caring manner is a shared objective; the ways in which this goal is achieved are various. Several staff members point out that some teachers emphasize social skills while others stress academics; some are strict disciplinarians, others are not. For the most part, this diversity is accepted. One teacher explains:

I might not do what somebody else might do in a classroom, but they have a right to do what they do if it's not educationally totally unsound and is not hurting kids. I just might think that's a very different way to react to kids and that I would not be very good doing things their way any more than they might be good at doing things my way. It doesn't suit them, but it might suit kids, so that's okay.

Some staff members would like more consistency in policies and procedures throughout the school. Stricter discipline is an issue that several mention. More broadly, one staff member suggests:

I would like to see a more consistent system of values. I think that kids get mixed messages about what's right and what's wrong, what's acceptable and what's not acceptable. I think the school is a reflection of society in that respect, but I don't like it.

Finally, the principal concludes that diversity is a given:

> There's going to be diversity whether you like it or not, and most
> people are close enough to the way I feel, I suppose. I don't have *the*
> answer to the way children should be taught. There are some basic
> things like being nice to kids and allowing them to move at their own
> rate, but if some people are more autocratic, while others are so-called
> more democratic, I think there are many ways to get to the same
> point. There are some instances where I would not do it that way,
> but if the kids are happy and they're learning and if the teacher is
> doing it in a humane way, it's all right with me. I accept variation and
> diversity. I also think it's healthy for a school because we can offer
> different classes to different kids. Our student population is not
> homogeneous, nor is our parent population.

Although one teacher acknowledges differences in styles and values, she
does not believe that teachers could remain in the school for extended
periods if there were significant differences. In her view, teachers have
become more alike as they have worked together over the years. System-wide
implementation of a uniform town curriculum in the last several years, she
believes, has also helped to make class content more consistent.

One way to learn about what life is like in a school is to ask people to
identify the unwritten rules for behavior: the dos and don'ts that are not
necessarily talked about but that everyone seems to follow. At Archer, the
most frequently identified unwritten rules are:

- Don't intrude upon another teacher's classroom. "Each person's
  classroom is his or her castle." "Everybody has a certain amount of
  power or control of the classroom that no one else should touch."
- Don't undermine the professionalism of a colleague by suggesting
  a method of your own.
- Don't criticize a colleague's teaching.
- Don't speak negatively about a teacher in front of the principal.
- Don't confront. Be diplomatic if you have a disagreement. "Don't
  rock the boat."
- Do get along professionally, even if you have personal differences.
- Do consider the children first and your own ego second.

For a school that places a high value on sharing, some teachers point out that the caveats about open communication are striking. Both principal and teachers shy away from direct criticism, and efforts at confrontation are often so careful that the critical message is lost. As a result, communications are often indirect or clandestine and adults learn to be selective or keep quiet.

While there is no unwritten rule barring teachers from observing one another's classrooms, and there has been at least one instance of two teachers exchanging observations in the past, increasing pressures for accountability in the system seem to have made teachers more cautious: "After people became obsessed with accountability, there was less visiting in one another's classroom." The range of styles and methods within the school also lends itself to a certain amount of separation, even defensiveness: "I think people are often afraid to air their views because they don't know whether other people perceive them as right or wrong. And sometimes, they don't know how to perceive them themselves." Another teacher shares:

> I think we shy away from mutual evaluation and confrontation because there aren't really avenues for dealing in a comfortable way with the things you might like to deal with. People tend to get defensive about their particular styles, and it's often difficult to address an issue without involving style differences. That seems like a hard thing to separate out.

Given the school and the system, what changes might they like to see to make their work more rewarding? In general, the adults are content with the way things work at Archer and in the Scribner system. Everyone agrees that the professional-development opportunities for staff and the individualized instruction for students are important. Teachers consistently point to the principal as one critical reason for the school's positive environment. Only a few teachers have suggestions for change. One wants more schoolwide rules; another wishes for less input from parents. A teacher expresses a desire to have more contact with other adults during the day. Another would like to see partnership teaching resurface. A teacher has this plan:

> I'd like to mix everybody around from all the different schools: "Sorry guys, it's time to revitalize. Who would like to go where? You still have job security. I give you my support, but try to see what it feels like to teach sixth grade. Then maybe when you're in another school teaching first grade you'll have greater understanding of what it's like to be a sixth-grade teacher." It would also facilitate communica-

tion. I mean after I was in the sixth-grade room for just fifteen minutes, I wanted to say, "My word! How do you get them to listen? I know how to get first graders to listen, but how do you get sixth graders to listen?" I guess it would just help since we all work in schools with a number of grade levels....We would have a more coordinated feel for it.

I would also juggle rooms so that you might have a fifth-grade class next to the kindergarten. This would increase the options in terms of having kids work with my kids, being able to drop in, just getting to talk to them.

Making a lot of the equipment and materials that we use in the lower grades available and seen as part of the supplies and curriculum for the upper grades, I think, would also be a positive change. I mean, why can't older kids play with finger paint and watercolors? It might expand the possibilities for their learning.

The ideas, issues, and perceptions of the Archer staff describe a school with relatively high teacher satisfaction. Archer Elementary appears to be a positive environment for children; it also seems to satisfy many adults.

CONCLUDING COMMENTS

As researchers traveled across the United States to gather evidence for the most recent reports on schooling, they rediscovered much that was familiar from their own school days. They saw large numbers of children and adolescents, most often separated by age and ability into individual classrooms. In most of these rooms, they saw students sitting and adults standing, students following and adults directing, students disordered and adults ordering, students relatively quiet and teachers persistently talking. Schooling everywhere is very much the same, and much of what goes on at Archer Elementary sounds and feels familiar. Yet Archer, like all individual schools, is different.

Schools differ; *schooling* is everywhere very much the same. Schools differ in the way they conduct their business and in the way the people in them relate to one another in conducting that business. But the business is everywhere very much the same.[19]

Looking back at the various levels on which we have observed the context of schooling and Archer Elementary, several things are initially striking.

Despite the rather bleak context in which schools in the 1980s were operating, adults and children were going about the business of teaching and learning. Perhaps they had read some of the current publications or, more likely – because of their busy schedules – had skimmed excerpts in professional journals, newspapers, or magazines. Perhaps there was fleeting conversation in the staff room or a new professional-development course dealing with research and possible school reactions. Perhaps a few children had heard the high school described as a shopping mall and others, through reports in the news or discussions with parents, had some sense of the problems facing education. A thirteen-year-old announced to me at the time:

> I hope you won't take this personally, but I would never be an educator. Teachers work too hard and get paid too little. It's not easy working with kids. And besides, no one seems to think that being a teacher is such a good thing.

Maybe adults at Archer were less affected by suggestions for educational reforms because of their primary focus on high schools. For whatever reasons, it is striking to see the contrast between what was being said on the outside about schools and how insiders continued facing everyday issues and solving problems.

The highly positive view that we get of Archer Elementary from many of the adults who work there is also striking. I deliberately chose a school that teachers, principal, and community members believed was functioning well, with the idea that the existence of differences among the adults in perception and experience, particularly negative ones, would clearly underscore the importance of addressing adult needs in schools more generally. In such a positive setting, it is especially hard for those with less favorable views since their feelings and perceptions seem so discordant. Janet Kramer suggests that there are other adults at Archer who are reluctant to express their negative views for that very reason. She says she would never share her feelings publicly. The resulting strain makes her work life and perhaps the work lives of some of her colleagues extremely difficult.

Janet's and others' dissatisfaction in a largely supportive working environment raises an important question: To what degree are the school and the system responsible for promoting adult growth? At some point, responsibility for personal and professional development may fall squarely, or at least more evenly, on the shoulders of individual teachers and administrators.

Given the overall positive assessment of Archer and the fact that teachers and the principal are pleased with the way children are cared for and how much they are learning, it is also interesting to note that the principal is not the charismatic, visionary leader that the literature on school effectiveness and reform would have us believe is requisite for such success. According to Peter Samson, the main roles he plays are those of "clearinghouse and clinician." Rather than leading teachers forward, Samson gives them information and provides support.

Perhaps creating the conditions for leadership is just as important as providing leadership directly. In fact, if the school principal effectively carries out this function, he or she expands the opportunities for leadership in the school, making it possible for leadership to be shared. At a time when education is becoming an increasingly complex enterprise, such expanded leadership may be imperative. Not only will shared leadership of this kind be a more reasonable way of accomplishing the multiple tasks of schooling, but the results of such sharing will empower the adults in the school, establishing an important precondition for personal and professional development. The way in which adults at Archer talk about power is a direct consequence of this more general pattern of shared leadership. Particularly within their classrooms, and more generally within the school, teachers believe adults and children can make a difference.

Some aspects of life for adults at Archer Elementary are more problematic. It is interesting to think about the implications of a veteran staff. When mobility in the profession was more common, teachers and administrators came and went, changing the configuration of adults in the school. As they came, they often brought fresh ideas and energy. As they went, they may have disrupted ongoing projects and disbanded both good and poor working relationships. When teachers and administrators grow old together, there is more time for either planned change or stagnation. Motivating an aging staff has become a critical issue for staff development.

In some schools, when adults retire, another phenomenon emerges: veteran educators at one end of the spectrum, novices at the other – young professionals with "new" ideas and veteran professionals who have already tried and discarded them. A developmental perspective expands the alternatives for looking at and responding to this situation. Young adults want and need to create and experiment. That they create and experiment is far more important than *what* they create and attempt. Once experienced staff understand this and recognize its developmental importance, they have the opportunity to support new staff, benefiting indirectly from the energy they exude and quite directly in terms of their own developmental needs to guide the next generation. Jealousy or competitiveness may be accompanying feelings that veteran staff will have to face.

On the other hand, young staff often stereotype experienced teachers and administrators as unimaginative and set in their ways. When a fifty-year-old teacher found his flexibility and creativity validated by a developmental perspective, he shared at a staff meeting in the company of two hundred colleagues:

> I'm glad to hear you say this because flexible and creative is exactly how I feel; but no one will give me a chance to be that way because I'm supposed to be the old teacher, with very little left to contribute.

At Archer, sharing is explicitly valued. The principal speaks about the importance of sharing, and structures within the school – such as a common work area for teachers and the team configuration – support it. The level and depth of sharing, however, may fall short of the kind of honest, open communication and criticism of teaching and learning necessary for continuous school improvement. In this sense, the adults at Archer may be more *congenial* than collegial. On the whole, desires to get along and to be cohesive seem stronger than the willingness to tackle significant differences. Adults at Archer do not generally confront one another, there is little peer observation and evaluation, and there is a wide range of diversity in style and methods of teaching.

The issue of diversity is particularly interesting. Teachers can feel independent and empowered when they have the freedom to implement curricula as they deem appropriate. Clearly, adults have different styles and personalities as well as distinct philosophies of education. On the other hand, large differences in approach and philosophy may be confusing to children, and not all methods are equally effective. While a degree of flexibility is crucial to accommodate differences in teaching and learning styles, lack of continuity may pull a school in divergent directions. Some schools publicize their stated philosophy, and both teachers and children are expected to support it. Independent schools are well known for taking this approach. Can public schools be similarly directed and still serve the diverse needs of their multiple constituents? Is it enough to agree on the broad goals of schooling without reaching consensus on the means?

Ironically, the rich professional-development opportunities provided within the system may detract from a school-based approach to improvement. Instead of (or in addition to) leaving the school at three-thirty to attend a workshop on classroom management, it may be important for adults to focus their energies on particular issues in particular classrooms within the school. The school can also serve as a context for expanding, deepening, and sustaining system-wide professional-development efforts. But individual schools miss the opportunity to improve current practice and initiate change when they look only outside the school for the ideas and tools of professional growth and school improvement.

Adults at Archer have a number of interesting ideas for change that could easily be tried within the school. Changing room assignments is one good idea for altering relationships among both teachers and students. Sharing equipment and materials, normally used by one grade, in other grades or in different subjects is also an intriguingly simple way to expand teaching and learning options.

John Goodlad has argued for individual school assessment, rather than generalized prescriptions for reform. Looking at the school in the broad context of education, obtaining outside input, and, most importantly, gathering and sharing the perceptions, ideas, and experiences of present school participants as well as other vested constituents (e.g., parents, community, etc.) are steps toward that form of assessment. It is against this background that we will explore theories of adult development and expand our relationships with Judy Cubbins, Janet Kramer, Don Bolter, and Nan Johnson.

Part Two

The Developmental Framework and Its Implications

3 *Phases of Adult Development*

Phase theories of development focus on the major life tasks or conflicts that stimulate growth. These tasks or conflicts emerge at relatively specific times in the life cycle. The way we accomplish or resolve them continues to influence us for the rest of our lives.

Erik Erikson, Daniel Levinson, and Roger Gould have each described a theory of phase development. Common to all three perspectives is the basic idea that development is an ongoing process that takes place throughout the life cycle. All agree that growth unfolds through interactions between the self and the environment. They also believe there is a definable pattern and sequence to development. Erikson focuses on the conflicts that emerge from within the individual over the life cycle. Levinson identifies the major life tasks of men in early and middle adulthood. Gould pinpoints the assumptions that adults carry with them from childhood and the ways in which these assumptions influence how adults think, feel, and act.

In this chapter, I will outline the phase approaches of Erikson, Levinson, and Gould, pointing to similarities and differences in their perspectives. Following a summary of each theorist's views, I will explore the implications of their ideas for the adults who work in schools. Patterns of growth characteristic of men's and women's development will be addressed in Chapter 5.

TABLE 3.1
ERIK ERIKSON: THE LIFE PHASES

	1	2	3	4	5	6	7	8
A. Infancy	Trust vs. Mistrust: Hope							
B. Early Childhood		Autonomy vs. Shame & Doubt: Will						
C. Play Age			Initiative vs. Guilt: Purpose					
D. School Age				Industry vs. Inferiority: Competence				
E. Adolescence					Identity vs. Identity Confusion: Fidelity			
F. Young Adulthood						Intimacy vs. Isolation: Love		
G. Maturity							Generativity vs. Self-Absorption: Care	
H. Old Age								Integrity vs. Despair & Disgust: Wisdom

Source: Reproduced from "Adulthood," *Daedalus*, vol. 105, Spring 1976, by permission of the American Academy of Arts and Sciences.

THE PHASE THEORY OF ERIK ERIKSON

Life Cycle Phases

Erik Erikson's life phase theory is the earliest of the three theories. Erikson describes development as a series of crises or turning points evolving in a predictable sequence and at similar times. There are eight distinct phases between infancy and old age. At each phase, the dialectic surrounding a particular issue becomes most prominent. While specific issues or conflicts are salient at certain times, all of Erikson's developmental issues are continually re-resolved, never fully losing their importance. (See Table 3.1.)

Erikson gives trust a position of particular prominence, describing its establishment during infancy as "the cornerstone of a vital personality."[20] Though the balance between trust and mistrust depends on the consistency, continuity, and predictability of early parent-child interactions, trust remains a key factor throughout life.

Erikson believes past and future issues are continually mediated through the turning point of the moment. Table 3.2 illustrates the life phases elaborated around the issue of identity. The columns suggest the ways in which earlier and later issues will be interpreted through the dominant conflict. Understood in this way, all the issues Erikson identifies will be important factors in considering adult development.

Erikson's Phases of Adulthood

According to Erikson, adult development turns around three distinct conflicts: intimacy versus isolation, generativity versus self-absorption, and integrity versus despair. Balancing intimacy and isolation is the central concern of young adulthood, roughly spanning the ages of twenty to forty. During the middle adulthood years, from forty to sixty or sixty-five, generativity – or the interest in guiding the next generation – vies with self-absorption. The subsequent focus of old age, from sixty-five until death, is integrating past experiences and coming to terms with life as it has been lived.

At each of Erikson's life phases, successful resolution of the dominant conflict results in a specific capacity. Successful resolution of the conflicts between intimacy and isolation establishes the capacity to love. Caring is the ability that emerges as a consequence of balancing the conflicts between generativity and self-absorption. During late adulthood, wisdom develops from successfully balancing integrity and despair.

TABLE 3.2
ERIK ERIKSON: THE LIFE PHASES (ELABORATED AROUND THE ISSUE OF IDENTITY)

	1	2	3	4	5	6	7	8
VIII								INTEGRITY vs. DESPAIR
VII							GENERATIVITY vs. STAGNATION	
VI						INTIMACY vs. ISOLATION		
V	Temporal Perspective vs. Time Confusion	Self-Certainty vs. Self-Consciousness	Role Experimentation vs. Role Fixation	Apprenticeship vs. Work Paralysis	IDENTITY vs. IDENTITY CONFUSION	Sexual Polarization vs. Bisexual Confusion	Leader- & Followership vs. Authority Confusion	Ideological Commitment vs. Confusion of Values
IV				INDUSTRY vs. INFERIORITY	Task Identification vs. Sense of Futility			
III			INITIATIVE vs. GUILT	Anticipation of Roles vs. Role Inhibition	Will to Be Oneself vs. Self-Doubt			
II		AUTONOMY vs. SHAME & DOUBT			Mutual Recognition vs. Autistic Isolation			
I	TRUST vs. MISTRUST							

Source: Reproduced from *Identity, Youth, and Crisis*, by Erik H. Erikson, by permission of W. W. Norton & Co., Inc. Copyright © 1968 by W. W. Norton & Co., Inc.

Implications of Erikson's Phase Theory for the Adults Who Work in Schools
Any of Erikson's developmental variables can be a point of departure for thinking about schools and designing settings that support growth. Since trust is basic to development, schools will need to provide environments where both adults and children feel safe to share and to risk. They will have to be environments where there are feelings and *evidence* that individuals and groups can safely confide in one another, take chances, and succeed or fail without losing a sense of self-worth. Along with the particular importance of trust to development are the three dualities of adulthood. Adults need to interact with others, to guide the less experienced, and to consolidate their life experiences.

Schools are appropriately designed around the developmental needs of children and adolescents. Most schools are not organized to facilitate the developmental work of adulthood. The way schools are built, the way they operate, and the way they are structured more often deter than facilitate the development of the adults for whom the school is a workplace.

Intimacy Versus Isolation. Adults in schools often feel isolated. Although they may be constantly surrounded by students, they are frequently cut off from other adults. During the school day, teachers barely have time for themselves, let alone others. Though classes may be dismissed by mid-afternoon, teachers report that they are often exhausted from their concentrated exposure to children. Many extend their day into the late afternoon or into the evening with preparations and paperwork, and some have second jobs.

While administrators have different schedules and ostensibly more contact with adults, they, too, often feel isolated. Principals, assistant principals, and specialists are distanced from other adults by their administrative and evaluative responsibilities. As busy as they are, school administrators frequently complain about lack of time to reflect and share with colleagues.

Schools do not seem to be places where adults can easily develop collegial relationships. Interest in collegiality and shared leadership at the school level promises to translate gradually into practices that reduce the sense of isolation among adults in schools. Such efforts can enhance a school's climate and increase professional effectiveness.

The practice of specific behaviors among adults in schools increases collegiality and diminishes isolation. In successful and adaptable schools, teachers and administrators talk about the practice of teaching and learning frequently and in concrete, precise terms. They observe each other teaching and administering. They work together on planning, designing, researching, and evaluating instructional and administrative materials. They teach each other what they know about teaching, learning, and leading.[21]

Both modest and basic changes in schools can support the conditions necessary for the development of collegiality and successful resolution of conflicts between intimacy and isolation during adulthood. On the one hand, making use of available classroom space for a professional lounge or work area can provide a place for teachers and administrators to come together. Scheduling times when teachers share free blocks also creates opportunities for adults to meet and collaborate. More fundamentally, educators must espouse and practice collegial behaviors. In place of honoring traditional taboos against sharing and observing, principals and teachers can intentionally support and reward peer observations, discussion and analysis of teaching and administrative practices, and joint planning efforts. Activities that bring educators together to share and talk about their work reduce physical and psychological isolation, buttressing the processes of adult growth; they also encourage staff development and thereby increase school effectiveness.

In addition to broad changes that will affect teachers and administrators as a group, individually tailored modifications will also be important. Particular schools and individual adults will have idiosyncratic needs, demanding individualized responses. Diagnosing these needs and developing strategies to address them can also be guided by understanding the emerging conflicts of adulthood. Since needs will be satisfied beyond as well as within the workplace, knowledge of the specific life circumstances of individual teachers and administrators can help identify the unmet needs of adulthood and suggest developmentally appropriate responses. A teacher immersed in relationships outside of school may need time in school to work alone. Across the hall, a colleague with limited opportunities for social contacts may need and welcome peer interaction. Because job satisfaction and needs fulfillment are closely related and individual needs can be met in multiple ways, both general changes in the school setting and individually diagnosed and prescribed solutions are requisite. During early adulthood, successful resolution of the shared and idiosyncratic conflicts between intimacy and isolation is the primary developmental need that must be addressed.

Generativity Versus Self-Absorption. During the middle adulthood phase, generativity vies with self-absorption for prominence. Erikson defines generativity in a way that seems to make it particularly adaptive to teaching:

> Generativity is primarily the interest in establishing and guiding the next generation or whatever in a given case may become the absorbing object of a parental kind of responsibility.[22]

On the surface, this developmental issue and the demands of teaching seem well matched. The men and women who started teaching as young adults, however, have been nurturing children for fifteen years or more by the time they enter middle adulthood. It may be that educators need mid-life opportunities to develop *themselves* after years of nurturing others.

Although generativity frequently applies to nurturing others, it also signifies re-creation and revival that can be applied to oneself. This expanded definition of the term is especially important in a profession that demands constant caring for others. Schools can encourage midlife adults to take time during and after school to attend to their own needs. At one school, a teacher with a passion for nature leaves the school during a late morning period and takes a walk. When she returns, she is refreshed and ready for the afternoon's challenges. In many professions, adults have some freedom in structuring their time. Not only can they sometimes determine what they will accomplish and when, but they also have unstructured times for breaks and lunch. The demands and traditions of school work do not customarily offer similar freedoms. Leaving school for an appointment or even a work-related errand can engender feelings of guilt. While it may seem that these suggestions encourage self-absorption, the scale for educators has been so heavily weighted in the opposite direction that some time for oneself is needed to right this professionally induced imbalance.

The generative needs of adults imply both the support of children by adults and the nurturance of young adults by adults at midlife and during later adulthood. This latter developmental need is frequently unrecognized in schools. Increasing opportunities for adults to come together in schools expand the possibility that generative relationships will naturally develop. Novice and veteran educators can also be paired, and specific activities developed by experienced administrators and teachers for young adults can satisfy the developmental needs of both the midlife and older adults who are seeking ways to support the less experienced as well as the young adult who needs the contact and guidance.

While teachers often lack opportunities to work with adults, administrators may have only limited contact with children. On the one hand, emphasizing the aspects of their jobs that allow them to support and nurture adults is important. On the other hand, middle adulthood can be an ideal time to create opportunities for more nurturing tasks with children. Principals and specialists can take on classroom teaching assignments or supervise extracurricular activities. These arrangements have the added benefit of freeing teachers for administrative responsibilities or professional development.

Integrity Versus Despair. As school people have grown older, sustaining their interest and enthusiasm for education has become a major staff development objective. Erikson's theory suggests that a sense of integrity must prevail over feelings of despair and disgust. Older adults thrive when they are able to integrate their past experiences into the present. Advanced status, recognition from others, and chances to share the accumulated wisdom of growth are inherent in the resolution of the developmental conflict of old age.

Opportunities for obtaining and then displaying advanced status are limited for adults in schools. The horizontal nature of the profession minimizes chances to advance. The responsibilities and rewards for novice and veteran educators are not significantly different. An experienced educator comments, recognizing the missing link between this structural aspect of schools and adult development:

> The teaching profession, as it is traditionally construed, is flat. It deals inadequately with the developmental processes of adulthood, with aging, with the passage of time in a person's life. There is no sense of movement, no distinction between apprentice, journeyman, and master craftsman. A teacher is simply a teacher, whether it's his fourth year or his fortieth. His work profile, his responsibilities remain virtually unchanged over time.[23]

In part, the reality this teacher describes expresses a powerful norm among educators against special recognition or attention. Adults in schools, particularly teachers, are more often treated alike than distinguished. This norm is so powerful that efforts to grant recognition to teachers can create more ill will than enhanced status. Teachers frequently discourage efforts to acknowledge them, shying away from even informal recognition. Standing apart from the group can have serious consequences:

> Enthusiasm was suspect. It disturbed stability and raised questions....To complain too much or to boast too much were both

taboo....If you did not expect too much, you would not be disappointed. To boast was to blow your own horn at the expense of other teachers. To complain was to expose vulnerability and insecurity. Serious complaining became a demand for a kind of support and closeness that other teachers were unwilling to give. Or it revealed, just as boasting did, a higher level of expectation than was considered appropriate.[24]

Alternatively, the experiences, knowledge, and skills of all the adults in the school could be tapped as a resource for continuous school improvement. In particular, the expertise of veteran educators can enrich the school as well as support and capitalize upon the developmental needs of older adults during the final phase of their careers. Older adults can sustain a sense of past history and tradition within the school, they can serve as mentors to young colleagues, and they can be encouraged to organize and share their expertise in meetings and workshops. Though some societies esteem the members of the older generation, valuing youth has been the prevailing norm in Western cultures. As the cohort of older adults increases within the schools and in society, a gradual shift in attitudes may be a healthy result.

The need to change long-held norms and practices makes these suggestions formidable staff development objectives. Not all adults will respond positively even to the best intentions to foster growth. Teachers and administrators working to enrich the personal and professional development opportunities for adults in schools must allow for, and not be discouraged by, individual differences and sometimes a negative response. Overcoming taboos against sharing or granting and accepting advanced status and professional recognition will require commitment, tenacity, and risk. Most importantly, it will require strong leadership on the part of both teachers and administrators. These adults in schools must be willing to demonstrate by their expressed beliefs and practiced behaviors that newer norms of collegiality and experimentation can yield positive and satisfying results. The phase theory of Erik Erikson, in particular, and adult-development theory, more generally, support this premise. The ongoing development of the adults in schools, which should be a consequence of these practices, will provide further support and guidance.

Key Points in Erikson's Phase Theory

On the broadest level, Erikson's theory of phase development establishes the ongoing nature of growth. By identifying the specific turning points of adulthood, Erikson further highlights the changing nature of adult life. Adulthood is not a single or static phase following adolescence and maintaining its position until the end of life. Instead, the adult moves through three specific phases of growth: young adulthood, maturity, and old age. Each phase is characterized by specific conflicts.

Erikson's insistence on the continuing importance of life-phase issues serves as a guide to identifying the psychological variables in adult development. School environments can be designed with these variables in mind. For instance, professional-development experiences that allow adults to engage actively in the learning process can support the ongoing interest in industry. Activities focused on self-awareness and self-discovery can reinforce the continuing search for identity. Throughout adulthood, interactive and reflective experiences will complement the adult's focus on intimacy, generativity, and integrity.

Not only is Erikson's framework helpful in pointing the way toward conditions that support growth throughout the life cycle, but his dialectic approach reveals the conditions that threaten development. Lack of initiative can yield feelings of guilt; failure to develop a sense of purpose can create feelings of inferiority. Unresolved issues of adult development may result in feelings of isolation, self-absorption, and despair. By creating work environments that minimize these feelings, schools can foster rather than inhibit adult growth.

Identification of the general abilities that emerge from successful resolution of life's conflicts is another important contribution of Erikson's framework. From this we can pinpoint the abilities that adults evolve over time and intentionally focus on creating opportunities for these capacities to develop. During adulthood, schools can support adults in their development of the capacities to care and to integrate and then share their lifetime experiences.

Erikson's phase theory highlights the shifting conflicts and concerns of adults at different periods in their development. By making these conflicts and concerns explicit, Erikson offers school people insights into their lives and the lives of their colleagues. Although he does not detail the conditions that are most likely to ensure a favorable balance at each turning point, he opens the door for others to do so. In this way, conditions can be tailored to respond to the distant developmental needs of individuals and groups.

THE PHASE THEORY OF DANIEL LEVINSON

Seasons of a Man's Life

In his book *The Seasons of a Man's Life*, Daniel Levinson describes the results of an intensive study of forty men between the ages of thirty-five and forty-five. Levinson and his colleagues identify specific developmental tasks that appear to follow a pattern and gain prominence at very specific times in a man's life. The seasonal metaphor Levinson uses in his title captures the importance of time and sequence in his work:

> To speak of seasons is to say that the life course has a certain shape, that it evolves through a series of definable forms....Every season has its own time; it is important in its own right and needs to be understood in its own terms....It is an organic part of the total cycle, linking past and future and containing both within itself.[25]

Although Levinson writes about men's lives, he claims that the sequence of phases holds true for men *and* women of different cultures, classes, and historical times. Within this general framework of human development, however, there are many differences in how individuals work through or manifest their particular life patterns.

The Life Cycle

According to Levinson, the life cycle is broadly divided into four eras, each lasting approximately twenty-five years. Development proceeds through alternating periods of building and changing, stability and transition. Each phase is established for an average period of five to seven years and modified for approximately another five years. Transitional periods, which are generally times of turmoil and uncertainty, take up almost half of our adult lives.[26]

In contrast to other developmental theorists who postulate only a general relationship between phase or stage and time of life, Levinson finds that each period begins and ends at a well-defined average age. During adulthood, which begins around age seventeen, there are three basic, overlapping phases: Early Adulthood (ages seventeen to forty-five), Middle Adulthood (forty to sixty-five), and Late Adulthood (sixty and beyond). Within each phase, there are novice phases, culminating phases, and times of transition. Table 3.3 outlines the periods for men during early and middle adulthood.

In Erikson's phase theory, the ascendance of major psychological conflicts stimulates movement; in Levinson's paradigm, the prominence of key life tasks initiates growth:

> The developmental tasks are crucial to the evolution of the periods. The specific character of a period derives from the nature of its tasks. A period begins when its major tasks become prominent in a man's life. A period ends when its tasks lose their primacy and new tasks emerge to initiate a new period. The orderly progression of periods stems from the recurrent change in tasks.[27]

Table 3.4 describes the tasks for men aged seventeen to forty-five.

In the same way that Erikson establishes dualities at each successive growth phase, Levinson also pinpoints opposing tasks within each period. In the First Adult Life Structure, a young man must achieve a balance between exploring and making preliminary choices. During the Second Adult Life Structure, men are working to resolve tensions between settling down and progressing. During later adulthood, men look back on their lives and attempt to incorporate those elements that have been missing. Reflection, expansion, and resolution are characteristics of this time in men's lives.

TABLE 3.3
DANIEL LEVINSON:
DEVELOPMENTAL PERIODS IN EARLY AND MIDDLE ADULTHOOD

Early Adulthood (17-45)

Novice Phase	Early Adult Transition	(17-22)
	Entry Life Structure for Early Adulthood	(22-28)
	Age 30 Transition	(28-33)
Culminating Phase	Culminating Life Structure for Early Adulthood	(33-40)
	Midlife Transition	(40-45)

Middle Adulthood (40-65)

Novice Phase	Midlife Transition	(40-45)
	Entry Life Structure for Early Adulthood	(45-50)
	Age 50 Transition	(50-55)
Culminating Phase	Culminating Life Structure for Middle Adulthood	(55-60)
	Late Adult Transition	(60-65)

Late Adulthood (60-)

Source: Compiled from Daniel Levinson, "A Conception of Adult Development." *American Psychologist*, vol. 41, no. 1, Jan. 1986.

TABLE 3.4
DANIEL LEVINSON: TASKS OF MEN'S DEVELOPMENT, AGES SEVENTEEN TO FORTY-FIVE

PERIOD	AGE RANGE	TASKS	KEY VARIABLES
The Early Adult Transition	17-22	To start moving out of the pre-adult world To make a preliminary step into the adult world	1. Forming a dream and giving it a place in the life structure 2. Forming mentor relationships 3. Forming an occupation
The First Adult Life Structure	22-28	To fashion a provisional structure that provides a workable link between the valued self and the adult society (making and testing a variety of initial choices)	4. Forming love relationships: marriage and family
The Age-Thirty Transition	28-33	To change the first life structure: to make new choices or reaffirm old ones	
The Second Adult Life Structure	33-40	To establish a niche in society	
a. Early Settling Down	33-36	To progress and advance	
b. Becoming One's Own Man (BOOM)	36-40	To accomplish goals, advance on ladder, gain greater measure of authority	1. Breaking down of mentor relationship(s) 2. Establishing oneself as a mentor
Midlife Transition	40-45	To terminate Early Adulthood To initiate Middle Adulthood To deal with the polarities that are sources of deep division's in one's life	1. Modifying Dream 2. Accepting one's own mortality 3. Building a legacy
Entering Middle Adulthood: Building a new life structure	45-	To find a better balance between the needs of the self and the needs of society	

Source: Compiled from Daniel Levinson, et al., *The Seasons of a Man's Life* (New York: Knopf, 1978).

Life Cycle Tasks

Within each period, Levinson identifies specific work to be accomplished. The formation of a Dream and the support of a Mentor are examples of areas that influence male development in early adulthood. They have particular importance for thinking about development in the context of work. The Dream represents a visualization of the self in the world. Its formation in the early twenties facilitates the young man's entry into the world of adulthood. Throughout his life, the man continually modifies the Dream so that it becomes less a product of hopes and illusions and more congruent with the realities of the man's life.

According to Levinson, a man's work contributes significantly to his sense of self-worth. Images of the self in the workplace are therefore an important part of the Dream's content. To the extent that the Dream is clarified and the work environment can provide supports for both its expression and modification, resolution of this key component of development can be more easily accomplished.

One of the main functions of the Mentor is to facilitate the young man's work on the Dream. The mentor helps the young man shape and clarify his personal and professional objectives. Levinson believes the mentor relationship is one of the most complex and developmentally important relationships in early adulthood.

Between each phase, there is a period of transition lasting roughly five years. The age-thirty transition (ages twenty-eight to thirty-three) links the first and second structure of early adulthood. The midlife transition (ages forty to forty-five) bridges the eras of early and middle adulthood. The age-fifty transition (ages fifty to fifty-five) ties together the early and culminating structures of midlife. The late-adult transition (ages sixty to sixty-five) inaugurates the final phase of life. Levinson describes these intermittent periods as times of confusion and instability.

During the age-thirty transition, the young adult often feels anxious, confused, and depressed. Like all transitions, this is a time for reassessment and redirection. It is an opportunity to reappraise and modify the early structure of adulthood and to establish the foundation for the next phase of life.

The culminating life structure for early adulthood follows the age-thirty transition. The adult looks back at the provisional structures he has set up in his early-adult life phase and makes new choices or reaffirms old ones. During this period, men want to establish a place for themselves in society and advance in their careers. Early relationships with mentors gradually dissolve while the adult begins to establish himself as a mentor for younger colleagues. Accomplishment, recognition, and authority are the central concerns of this period.

Between ages forty and forty-five, adult men move through the midlife transition. This can be another tumultuous life shift. It serves both to terminate early adulthood and to initiate middle adulthood.

At midlife, men begin to review their lives, seeking to reclaim parts of themselves and their world that have been neglected. In particular, their efforts revolve around four polarities:

1. The young/old duality
2. The creative/destructive duality
3. The separate/attached duality
4. The male/female duality

Men struggle to balance the polarities in their lives and to restructure their work and relationships so that more of themselves can be expressed and experienced. Midlife adults recognize that they feel both young *and* old. As family and friends become ill or die, they begin to acknowledge their own mortality. In the first half of life, success meant getting *there*; now success depends on the quality of life *here*, as it is lived each day.

Adults begin to recognize the tragic nature of life during middle adulthood. They learn that no matter how hard they try, they cannot avoid hurting others or themselves. More than ever before, midlife adults need time with others and time alone. Finally, they need to balance the male and female parts of themselves.

Perhaps more important than the specific preoccupations in any individual's life during middle adulthood is the predictable tendency for concerns to shift. Educators who have been driven by career goals may begin to look away from work and toward family for more nurturing experiences; veteran teachers, who have worked contentedly in the classroom, may decide to push for promotion.

The age-fifty transition offers midlife adults the chance to modify the initial structures they have created in middle adulthood and sets the stage for movement into the final phase of midlife.

Although Levinson's focus is early adulthood and midlife, he does identify the era of late adulthood. Beginning at age sixty, this period lasts until death. Older adults are increasingly interested in and concerned about health and retirement. Further research is needed to learn more about this phase of development.

Implications of Levinson's Phase Theory for Adults Who Work in Schools
Because of its specificity, Levinson's phase theory can be an especially useful tool for understanding the lives of adults, particularly adult males, in schools. While Levinson's initial research has focused on the development of men's lives, many aspects of his phase theory are relevant to women too. In this section, I will generalize a number of Levinson's findings to suggest the potential applicability of the theory to both sexes.

Levinson identifies the times during which adults will be building and modifying the basic life structures and points to the specific life tasks that will be most important. This information can be used as a resource for responding to individual adults in the school, as well as for designing staff development activities. Knowing the life tasks of adulthood can help the principal or staff developer identify an adult's major preoccupations and suggest the kinds of supports most likely to be responsive to an adult's needs.

Early Adulthood. The First Adult Life Structure (ages seventeen to twenty-eight) is a time of exploration and discovery. Young adults want to try a variety of roles and relationships. They have energy, enthusiasm, and a sense of adventure. The optimism and idealism characteristic of this time of life is particularly well suited to the development and implementation of new skills and ideas. Profitable staff development activities can include opportunities to work on new teaching methods, to develop curricula, and to initiate projects. Career awareness and counseling are also appropriate staff development options for young adults.

Expecting young adults to make firm career commitments or even extended commitments to specific projects is likely to be unproductive. Young adulthood is an ideal time, however, to combine the roles of leader and learner. Not only does experience with this combination of roles offer good training for the young adult, but it provides a valuable model for adults and children in the school.

While foreclosing the option to learn is hazardous at any phase of life, it is particularly unfortunate during the era of early adulthood. Schools that appoint young adults to positions of leadership often miss the opportunity to capitalize on the young adult's need for trial and error, a need that can frequently lead to innovation. When young adults are asked to conform to a model of knowing rather than discovering, both schools and adults lose out. For example, not too long ago, a former school principal turned graduate student at age thirty-nine. Appointed to a principalship in his early twenties and expected more often to know than to question, he returned to graduate school during the second adult life structure to reclaim the piece of his development that had been attenuated earlier in his life.

Mentoring relationships are especially important facilitators of development for both the young adult, who is guided, and the older adult, who offers guidance. Establishing these kinds of relationships in schools, however, can be difficult. The formation of mentor bonds requires that adults have sustained contact. It is also essential that adults in the school community are at different periods in their development. As school populations have declined and fewer young people have entered teaching, school staffs have become increasingly homogeneous. Not only has the average age of school people advanced, but adults in the schools have aged together.

When mentoring relationships were first described by Levinson and others, it appeared that they evolved naturally, over time, when the chemistry between a young person and an older adult was right. The feasibility of designing such matches seemed contrived. Researchers have since suggested that *designing* such relationships can make a difference. In teaching, young adult teachers and administrators will have to be distinguished from mid-career practitioners to make these matches work. Making such distinctions is uncharacteristic of schools and may engender discomfort and distrust; on the other hand, all adults in the school might benefit. If older adults are working through the duality of integrity and despair in order to establish a sense of wisdom, making such distinctions will be in their best developmental interest. Adults in middle adulthood will also benefit from these relationships as their needs for generativity can be met by supporting young colleagues, as well as students.

During early adulthood, the importance of forming an individual Dream parallels the value of developing a vision for the school. Just as the personal Dream is a visualization of the self in the world, the school vision is a formulation of the school's values and practices. A Dream for the adult and a vision for the school can set the parameters for ongoing decisions and serve as sources of energy and motivation. School principals have been designated heralds of the school's vision; they might add to their educational leadership responsibilities the role of helping the adults in schools form, articulate, and gradually modify their developmental Dreams. When teachers share their Dreams, they provide access to the values and desires that can give their work meaning and direction. In turn, they suggest specific areas of personal and professional interest that can be translated into staff development practices.

Because young adults are experimenting with occupational choices, opportunities for career exploration within as well as outside the field can be important. Young adults can profitably assume a variety of roles in schools and school systems. Through committee work, job exchanges, or interim appointments, young adults can discover the range of options within the field as well as test their own strengths and limitations. Not only can principals help create these opportunities for young teachers, but they can establish the value and expectation that it is important for novice teachers to explore and expand their skills and knowledge of the profession.

By tapping the resources of veteran personnel to aid in this process, the principal can further support the needs of older adults for approval and recognition. Veteran educators can share their expertise by agreeing to be observed, by taking on apprentices, or by offering workshops.

Exploring career options outside of education is also essential for young adults if they are to make knowledgeable and responsible commitments to work that will sustain them through subsequent developmental periods. A good way to invigorate novice and veteran staff is to ask them to identify their hobbies or outside interests. One principal was formerly a house-builder. Not only did her expertise come into constant use in maintaining the school building, but the insights she shared with staff rekindled her enthusiasm and sparked others' interest. Adults in the school with second jobs or previous careers can describe their work; career materials and resources can be made available in faculty libraries and lounges. If adults choose to leave education in favor of work for which they are better suited, both adults and children ultimately benefit. If adults choose to work in schools with a clear knowledge of other options, chances are they and their students will gain from the clarity and strength of their commitment.

The Developmental Transition. From time to time, all adults manifest signs of restlessness and disillusionment. What seemed reasonable and logical several years before may now be in doubt. Adults in schools typically associate such feelings of professional malaise with burnout. The school no longer seems to provide for their needs, and they are tired and unexcited at work. By describing the turmoil of developmental transitions, Levinson suggests a new way of understanding these periodic and even predictable times of distress. Some of what may be experienced as professional burnout by adults in schools or other professions may be more accurately attributed to unresolved developmental tasks and to these periodic shifts in development.

Janet Kramer, a sixth-grade teacher working at Archer for the past eight years, introduced herself in the opening chapter. Now in her mid-thirties, she describes herself as burned out. As she reflects upon her feelings about teaching, she recognizes the influence of other unresolved issues in her life:

> I think a lot of the way I feel about teaching has to do with what's going on in the rest of my life. If I were married and had a family, I don't think I'd be so overwhelmed by this feeling [of incompleteness] in teaching. Marriage is something I need for fulfillment, and I haven't had it, so there's a black cloud over me that affects the way I see everything. It's too bad, but that's the way I am. I guess if I stopped teaching for a while and came back to it after that part of my life were somewhat settled, I'd have a better attitude about teaching. If that other aspect of your life isn't fulfilled, then you really feel like your life isn't full; somehow it's just not complete.

Janet was enormously relieved when she intuitively linked her sense of professional burnout to a developmental transition. Not only was it helpful for her to know that there was a potential explanation for her unrest, but it was comforting to realize that others experience similar feelings. Knowing something about adult development can help school people work effectively with other adults; it can also help adults understand and cope with their own development.

Levinson explains that developmental transitions make up almost half of our adult lives. Given this assertion, it is imperative that we expand our efforts to create supports for the adults who work in schools. Psychologist Robert Kegan makes this point:

> Developmentalists know something now about how to join the environment to stimulate development; but have we learned how to join or accompany the meaning-maker when he or she faces a world that is already heated up, already stimulating, even to the point of being meaning-threatening?[28]

Beyond traditional staff development efforts aimed at changing adult attitudes and behaviors, staff development activities can also be designed to *support* adults, who are already experiencing the uncertainties of development.

Early Adulthood. Tensions between settling down and becoming one's own person fill the culminating period of the Second Adult Life Structure (ages thirty-three to forty). During this period, establishing a place for oneself in society and advancing in the workplace are central objectives. Adults between the ages of thirty-three and forty want to be recognized for their accomplishments. They want to advance in their careers and assume some degree of authority. Often they want to share their experiences and serve as mentors to younger colleagues.

Adults in schools must be inventive in responding to these developmental needs. Education is an occupation with relatively few structures for mobility, authority, or recognition. Within schools, adults can sometimes become department heads, assistant principals, or principals. Within systems, adults can work in specialized areas – such as reading or counseling – that may put them in contact with more than one school, or they may aspire to a job in the central office. The majority of adults who begin their careers in teaching will remain in the classroom. Once they reach the top of the pay scale, they may receive only cost-of-living increments. After many years of service, the conditions and benefits of their jobs may vary little from those of a beginning teacher. How can adults working in schools satisfy their needs for advancement and recognition? How can excellence in the classroom be maintained and celebrated when it is often the most able teachers who get tapped on the shoulder for administrative positions?

Principals can encourage teachers to combine teaching and administrative responsibilities as a way of expanding their mobility without sacrificing their expertise with children. Teachers can serve on committees and task forces, where they will have decision-making roles and be acknowledged for their contributions. Adults at this period can also be encouraged to serve as mentors for younger colleagues.

The role of mentor is so developmentally important that schools with veteran staffs should consider "importing" young adults to create opportunities for mentor relationships. Schools can establish programs for interns or apprentices. Other institutions, such as colleges and businesses, can serve as resources for bringing young adults into a school. Such associations also create career exposure and development opportunities for the young adults who participate.

Providing opportunities for expanded responsibility can have immediate and long-term developmental benefits. Without concurrent organizational supports, such as increased pay or status, teachers and administrators can become angry and frustrated. Schools must respond to the complex and interrelated needs of adult workers.

Middle Adulthood. Following the midlife transition, adults begin to build the structures of middle adulthood (ages forty to sixty-five). At this time, it is important to know that adults are modifying the Dream of early adulthood, dealing simultaneously with the inevitable sense of loss that accompanies the recognition of one's limitations. Adults at midlife also begin to fashion a legacy or vision of what they now want to accomplish and how they want to be remembered. Staff development activities can help adults articulate their newly formed visions and translate future hopes into specific plans. One effective and engaging staff development activity involves asking adults at this phase of life to complete the stem: "After I leave the school, I would like to be remembered for _____." Building upon the legacies of midlife adults can be a source of individual motivation. As a collective activity, the articulation of legacies can be a resource for clarifying a school's mission.

It is helpful to know that adults at midlife are also dealing with the four major polarities Levinson has identified, as well as with other realities and paradoxes of living. Adults at midlife want and need varying, sometimes contrasting supports and working conditions. They need to feel young at times, experienced at others. They need time and space alone, as well as opportunities to be with children and colleagues.

During the culminating periods of middle adulthood until the time of retirement, adults gradually refocus their energies. They look back over the years to see what has been left out of their lives and try to incorporate missing elements. For most men and career women, this is often a time for giving fuller expression to the nurturing sides of themselves. Older adults, particularly staff who work alone or in relative isolation, can expand their contacts with children by supervising clubs or by teaching. This staff development strategy has the added advantage of freeing time for the classroom teacher. In one school, a principal regularly takes over teaching responsibilities with the provision that teachers leave the building and engage in a nonschool, adult activity. Some attend professional-development meetings, some read, and some simply take a walk or go shopping.

During their final working years, adults become increasingly occupied with issues of health and retirement. These and other concerns of midlife and later adulthood can be directly addressed in staff development sessions. A principal in one school initiated a staff development series on financial planning, investment, and health care. Staff were invited to participate with their families. Not only was attendance at the sessions higher than at other staff development activities, but participants rated these sessions as the most valuable, interesting, and relevant professional-development activity in recent memory.

By the time educators reach the latter phases of adulthood, they are likely to have been working in schools for many years. It is not uncommon for veteran educators to be weary of their work and looking forward to cultivating some of the interests they have had to leave behind. Motivating aging staff members can become a chronic problem. Building staff development activities around the age-specific developmental issues of adulthood can be one source of motivation. Faculty meetings can be organized by age, career phase, or specific adult development issues. Encouraging aging staff members to incorporate their ongoing or planned leisure interests into their worklife can be a way to bridge the gap between work and retirement. An older adult with a passion for traveling was encouraged to create a social studies unit on themes of cultural diversity. A thirty-year veteran with a love for plants was enlisted into a landscaping project to help beautify the school grounds. Both "staff development activities" renewed the waning energies of the aging staff members and offered them positive contexts for interacting with children and colleagues.

Key Points in Levinson's Phase Theory

Levinson's phase theory of development suggests an array of possibilities for working with adults in schools. It underscores the importance of taking into account the changing concerns and preoccupations of adults as they move through the phases of adulthood and the value of building upon these issues in creating staff development options. Levinson's perspective also emphasizes the tumultuous quality of changes and transitions that take place throughout the life cycle and do not abate during adulthood.

By stressing the interplay of social and psychological factors, Levinson further reminds us of the importance of dealing with the whole adult. Separating personal from professional concerns does not take full account of the ongoing issues of adulthood. Asking educators to leave their personal lives at home is neither possible nor productive. Adults bring their whole selves to work. To create work settings that respond to the complex and changing issues of adulthood, it is essential that adults know what is at issue at given periods in their development and actively plan to address the personal and professional needs that become prominent.

While Levinson's initial work focuses on midlife and derives from research on men, aspects of his conceptualization complement and extend Erikson's more general framework. Both Erikson and Levinson view development as an ongoing process of interaction between the individual and his environment, punctuated by age-related or age specific tasks or conflicts. Levinson's dualities of middle adulthood parallel Erikson's turning points. Levinson furthers Erikson's work by identifying the specific tasks that adults must accomplish as they move through adulthood. His phase theory provides even more detailed clues for educators to use in their efforts to recognize and respond to their own growing needs and the developmental issues of others.

THE PHASE THEORY OF ROGER GOULD

Mastering the Assumptions of Childhood
Working with therapy groups as a psychiatrist in California, Roger Gould began to notice that adults had common preoccupations at similar ages. He also noticed that their preoccupations revolved around shared assumptions associated with past experiences. Like Levinson, Gould identifies a series of age-related developmental tasks. During a parallel set of developmental phases, Gould uncovers specific childhood assumptions that must be conquered if growth is to take place.

Gould's model is one of mastery. Individuals have two distinct and opposing forms of consciousness – one from childhood and another that is being formed as an adult. Only as the issues and anxieties of the first are mastered can full adult consciousness be reached. Gould states:

> By striving for a fuller, more independent adult consciousness, we trigger the angry demons of childhood consciousness. Growing and reformulating our self-definition becomes a dangerous act. It is the act of transformation.[29]

Components of Adult Development
Gould's work exposes four components of adult development. First, he establishes an age range that can be used as a tangible marker. Next, he specifies the adult preoccupations that accompany a given time of life. Gould postulates that young adults between the ages of sixteen and twenty-two are preoccupied with leaving their families. He maintains that choosing work and establishing the new roles and relationships of adulthood, such as spouse and parent, are important for adults between the ages of twenty-two and twenty-eight. A period of six years between ages twenty-eight and thirty-four roughly mirrors Levinson's age-thirty transition, when adults often feel

confused and stuck. The period between the ages thirty-five and forty-five is a time of increased interest in and energy for advancing in work; it is followed by a turning inward, sometime around the age of fifty, and expressions of generativity characteristic of later adulthood.

In addition to identifying issues that preoccupy adults at different ages, Gould also describes the tone, or feeling, surrounding each phase of development. A tone of optimism, determination, and confidence is typical of young adulthood. The transitional time before midlife often brings depression, restlessness, and disillusionment. Later adulthood is infused with desire as the older adult strives to establish continuity with past and future and regain a sense of stability and commitment.

The Implicit Assumptions of Adulthood

The most novel aspect of Gould's phase theory is the identification of sets of assumptions that adults tend to carry with them at different periods of adulthood and the potential implications of such assumptions for the ways adults think and act. As one's assumptions about the world change, the world itself becomes a different place. As people interpret events in their lives differently at different ages, changes in consciousness actually alter the way events are experienced. This idea parallels Erikson's notion that prominent issues change during the life cycle and that a dominant conflict is the medium through which other issues will be addressed.

Awareness of the shifting assumptions of adulthood has important implications for thinking about the changing meanings of events in the lives of adults. If, in fact, the significance of work or family changes at distinct phases in the life cycle, understanding the nature of these changes will be crucial in determining the variety of meanings that can be given to the same task.

As meanings are transformed, an individual experiences a sense of crisis or loss similar to the process of transition Levinson highlights. Although Gould's primary association with change reflects back to early experiences of separation and related childhood anger, he, like Levinson, characterizes these periods as tenuous and problematic. Once it is recognized that adults are developing, it is essential to understand the process and impact of change. Only in this way will we be able to provide the supports that adults need from individuals and institutions as they navigate the choppy waters of development.

Gould's theory of adult growth parallels the work of Erikson and Levinson in postulating the ongoing nature of development and the importance of key life tasks at different times during the life cycle. The underlying, and often

TABLE 3.5
ROGER GOULD: PHASES, PREOCCUPATIONS, AND ASSUMPTIONS OF ADULT DEVELOPMENT

AGE RANGE	PREOCCUPATION	CHARACTERISTIC ORIENTATION AND TONE	MAJOR ASSUMPTION(S) TO BE MASTERED	COMPONENT ASSUMPTIONS
16-22	• Leaving the world of the family	• Dominance of issues of competence and independence	• I'll always belong to my parents and believe in their world.	• If I get more individual, it will be a disaster. • I can see the world only through my parents' assumptions. • Only my parents can guarantee my safety. • My parents must be my only family. • I don't own my body
22-28	• Occupational choice • New roles as spouses and parents, or inability to get into these roles • Important events: work, marriage, family	• Tone of optimism, determination, confidence	• Doing things my parents' way with willpower and perseverance will bring results. But if I become too frustrated, confused, or tired, or am simply unable to cope, they will step in and show me the right way.	• Rewards will come automatically if I do what I am supposed to do. • There is only one right way to do things. • Those in a special relationship to me can do for me what I haven't been able to do for myself. • Rationality, commitment, and effort will always prevail over all other forces.
28-34	• Being stuck • Lack of role clarity • Diffusion of goals	• Turning inward • Unrest, depression, disillusionment, questioning	• Life is simple and controllable. • There are not significant coexisting contradictory forces within me.	• What I know intellectually, I know emotionally. • I am not like my parents in ways I don't want to be. • I can see the reality of those close to me quite clearly. • Threats to my security aren't real.
35-45	• Intense discontent and urgency regarding the past and the future • Increased fervor in work (work success seen as immunity from death)	• Desire for continuity and stability, natural time for career commitment	• There is no evil or death in the world. • The sinister has been destroyed.	• The illusion of safety can't last forever. • Death can't happen to me or my loved ones. • It is impossible to live without a protector (women). • There is no life beyond the family. • I am an innocent.
50-	• Turning inward • Move toward authenticity and generativity			

Source: Compiled from Roger Gould, *Transformations: Growth and Change in Adult Life* (New York: Simon & Schuster, 1978).

implicit, assumptions that accompany adults through their development form an added dimension of his framework. This dimension provides additional clues for self-development and staff development. It suggests particular strategies aimed at identifying and supporting the conflicts of development. It pinpoints developmental tasks and their associated components. And it emphasizes the tenacious assumptions we carry with us that so powerfully influence our feelings, thoughts, and actions.

Implications of Gould's Phase Theory for the Adults Who Work in Schools
The general notion that adults carry around with them sets of assumptions about how the world should or does work and the identification of age-specific assumptions during the phases of adulthood are Gould's most significant contributions to our work with adults in schools. The assumptions that frame an adult's way of thinking, feeling, and understanding can make the world different for individual adults. If, for example, an adult believes that there is only one right way to do things, he or she will not be interested in generating alternatives or considering changes once a system is in place. When asked to consider other methods, the adult will stand fast in the belief that the way things are done now is meeting the school's needs and should be continued at all costs. If others understood how basic this assumption is to the adult's view of the world, they would think twice before shaking the foundations of his or her sense of self. When these developmental realities are ignored, the framework that keeps an adult's world view intact can be seriously threatened.

Early Adulthood. Looking systematically at the assumptions to be mastered during adulthood provides clues to the way adults may function and the supports they may require. Between the ages of twenty-two and twenty-eight, Gould describes four assumptions that guide our lives and that we must conquer in order to continue our development:

- Rewards will come automatically if we do what we are supposed to do.
- There is only one right way to do things.
- Those in a special relationship to me can do for me what I haven't been able to do for myself.
- Rationality, commitment, and effort will always prevail over all other forces.[30]

Relying on the outside world for support is common to each of the assumptions of early adulthood. There are ways the world should be, and if I do what I'm supposed to do, then my life will work. If I cannot accomplish my goals alone, there will be someone – my parents, my spouse, the school principal – who will step in to set things right.

Some of the limitations of these assumptions are evident. Those who do not share this perspective of the world understand that life can be paradoxical and quixotic. They know the importance of luck and timing. They realize they must take primary responsibility for themselves, which includes accepting their limitations as well as the limitations of others.

School people work extremely hard. One of the most persistent themes that comes through in talking with teachers and principals about their work is the extraordinary amount of time and energy consumed in teaching and administering. For some, this effort is related to the assumption that hard work will produce results (that is, rewards will come automatically if I do what I'm supposed to do; effort will always prevail over all other forces). Yet effective time management, clear goals, priorities, and realistic limits may be far more conducive to high-quality work than exhaustive persistence.

To depend only on rationality and commitment for results is likewise limiting. Schools, in particular, are organizations with a high degree of ambiguity. We know we want to educate children, for instance, but we can never be completely certain of the factors that contribute to or detract from learning in an individual's complex life circumstances – let alone for groups of students. School people must thus live with a gnawing uncertainty about the impact of their efforts. Schools are also highly political organizations, and rituals play a major part in the way schools operate. Without alternative perspectives about the workings of the world, the young adult's viewpoint is necessarily limited and rigid. In fact, the rigidity of the assumptions of young adulthood can seriously constrain the young adult's ability to generate multiple solutions to common problems and to think and act creatively and flexibly – motivated as much by experience and intuition as by reason and effort.

School principals and other figures of authority in schools may have especially problematic relationships with adults who assume that those in special relationships to them can accomplish what they cannot do for them-selves. If a principal's goal is to help teachers build a sense of autonomy, independence, or interdependence, he or she can lock horns with a teacher who encounters a situation that activates the special relationship assumptions of early adulthood. How do we help individuals take responsibility for themselves when their world view is predicated on being able to rely on others? If we are the principal, curriculum coordinator, or assistant superintendent, what do we do when *we* get stuck? This issue can become the source of tremendous stress and conflict for educators designated as school leaders when they look for special professional relationships and can't find them, or when they need to ask for help.

The shared assumptions of young adults between the ages of twenty-eight and thirty-four include:

- What I know intellectually, I know emotionally.
- I am not like my parents in ways I don't want to be.
- I can see the reality of those close to me quite clearly.
- Threats to my security aren't real.[31]

Control and certainty are two central conditions upon which these assumptions rest. Adults in the latter phase of early adulthood want to determine what they know, who they know, what they're like, and what they're not like. Supervising adults at this phase can be a challenge, requiring the supervisor to recognize the tendency to deny problems, issues, and feelings that do not fit with what the young adult wants to believe is so. If the adult at this period assumes he or she clearly perceives the realities of others, it may be difficult to understand another's discrepant point of view. Real threats to the security of the adult in his or her mid- to late thirties, such as performance difficulties or health problems, can also be hard to communicate.

Middle Adulthood. Mastering the assumptions of middle adulthood necessitates coming to terms with the illusions of earlier life and the limits of the present. Just as Levinson's midlife adults begin to recognize there are destructive as well as creative forces at work, adults at this phase, from Gould's perspective, must come to terms with the realities of destruction and death. Life combines negative and positive experiences, opportunities for protection, and times of vulnerability. Midlife adults are not innocent bystanders as they confront these assumptions of midlife:

- The illusion of safety can last forever.
- Death can't happen to me or my loved ones.
- It is impossible to live without a protector (women).
- There is no life beyond the family.
- I am an innocent.[32]

Key Points in Gould's Phase Theory

Using Gould's phase theory as a guide, the adults who work in schools can begin to explore their own operating assumptions and work to understand the assumptions of their colleagues.   Applied more broadly, the exercise of making one's assumptions explicit can support school norms of developing clear and direct communication.   Rarely do we examine the underlying bases for our actions or perspectives.   Instead, we suppose that others share our beliefs and forge ahead with our plans.   By now we should not be surprised when things don't always work the way we have hoped.   How many times has each of us been foiled by our misassumptions?   Nor do we often scrutinize the differences or similarities between what we say we believe and how we act.   Differences in our "espoused theories" and our "theories in use" often elude us and confuse others.[33]

There are a number of relatively straightforward, practical solutions to the potential problems Gould's theory highlights.   All of them involve making our suppositions known to ourselves and others. At the beginning of a meeting, participants can routinely share and examine their assumptions.   If we are meeting to discuss staff development options, what does each of us mean by staff development?   How do our different meanings relate to one another?   Do we see real or potential contradictions that may inhibit our joint planning efforts?   When we talk about giving support to the adults who work in schools, can we begin by acknowledging that support may signify something different to different individuals, depending, in part, on their particular developmental needs and assumptions?   For one teacher, support may be providing constant positive feedback; for another, it is having the space to work as *he* or *she* defines and evaluates it. Identifying the key subjects or terms we use when we work together, and clarifying their meanings, is a first step in developing a shared technical language, fundamental to collegiality and continuous school improvement.[34]

CONCLUDING COMMENTS

Phase theories offer a widened lens through which to view and understand human behavior.   They identify issues of adulthood, specific life tasks, preoccupations, conflicts, and assumptions. They also place development in context, helping to pinpoint the average times different developmental issues will be salient.   Phase theories emphasize the quality and frequency of developmental transitions, suggesting an expanded view of professional burnout.   They help to explain the emotional swings of adulthood and the predictable times of loss and crisis.

When adults learn about the life phases, they are typically enlightened and relieved. The theories put their experiences in perspective and offer a framework for thinking and talking about the cycles in their lives. Awareness of life cycle issues is a powerful tool and potential motivator for personal and professional growth. Equally powerful, but somewhat more elusive, are stages of adult growth. It is to these conceptions, particularly to the work of Lawrence Kohlberg, Jane Loevinger, and Robert Kegan, that we turn next.

4

Stages of Adult Development

Stage theorists describe development as an organic process of alternating periods of balance, transition, and reintegration, modeled upon Piaget's work in cognitive growth. According to this view, development proceeds through a series of sequentially ordered stages whose progression, in contrast to phase progressions, is *not* dependent on age. While some stage theorists have emphasized the differences between stage and phase approaches, these complementary conceptions have more to share than to dispute.

Both stage and phase theorists agree that development unfolds sequentially, that one period or balance predictably follows another. Both agree that individuals play an active role in determining the course and content of their growth and that individuals are naturally inclined toward development. Both conceptions pinpoint interactions between self and other, individuals and their environments, as the fundamental arena for growth.

Because stage theories focus on form and structure rather than content or task, they are a somewhat more elusive tool than phase constructs. Though some stages tend to emerge at general times during the life cycle, within a broad period like adulthood, distinctions may be subtle and complicated. In a very important sense, the complexities involved in precisely determining an individual's stage of development are fortuitous. This reality should help dissuade us from casting ourselves and others in rigid, overly simplified categories. Instead, both the stage approach and specific stage theories can offer broad insights into the ways adults think, feel, and act; the role of surrounding environments in supporting or stimulating development; and specific staff development strategies.

In this chapter, I will discuss the stage constructs of Lawrence Kohlberg and Jane Loevinger to delineate the issues and insights they highlight. Then I will focus in detail on the conception of Robert Kegan. In my view, Kegan's approach to development cuts through many of the differences between and among stage theories, offering what Kegan boldly believes to be a fundamental explanation of the growth process. As in the preceding chapter on adult phases, I will explore the potential implications of each theory for the lives of the adults in schools.

THE STAGE THEORY OF LAWRENCE KOHLBERG

Stage Characteristics and the Stages of Moral Reasoning

The work of Lawrence Kohlberg spans several decades of research and writing. Over this time, Kohlberg and his colleagues traced the path of moral development in largely male samples from many parts of the world. Kohlberg uncovered an underlying progression of reasoning, which he has refined into a framework for understanding moral thought.

I will not rely specifically on Kohlberg's conception to understand the teachers and administrators in this book. Instead, I will use his framework to describe the basic nature of stages, to identify a number of important questions about the stage paradigm, and to suggest some specific strategies shown to stimulate development. I leave it to readers to identify themselves and others with the moral reasoning patterns and progressions, to take a position on the issues, and to determine what, if any, approaches may be appropriate for further study and/or application.

In constructing a theory of moral development, Kohlberg carefully delineates the characteristics of stages. First and foremost is their structural nature. Each stage is a "structured whole," representing an underlying organization of thought or understanding. Stages are qualitatively different from one another. All emerge in sequence without variation; no stage can be skipped. Finally, stages are "hierarchically integrated;" that is, progressive stages are increasingly complex and subsume earlier stages. Individuals always have access to the stages through which they have passed. Under ordinary circumstances or with proper supports, people will generally prefer to use the highest stages of which they are capable.

Kohlberg identifies three broad categories of morality: the pre-conventional level, the conventional level, and the postconventional level. These categories represent a gradual shift from a self-centered orientation ("I do not steal because I might be caught and my well-being is of utmost importance"), through an identification with the expectations of others and the rules and norms of society ("I do not steal because the law prohibits stealing and I have internalized society's expectations"), to a principled morality based on abstract ideals of justice ("Stealing is unjust and I value principle as a guide"). According to Kohlberg, the preconventional level is the stage of most children under nine years of age, some adolescents, and many adolescent and adult criminal offenders. Most adolescents and adults in this society and others are at the conventional level. Only a small number of adults, generally past age twenty, reach the postconventional level.

Two distinct stages exist at each moral level, the second stage representing a more advanced and organized form. Table 4.1 presents the six moral stages, summarizing what is right at each stage, the reason for upholding what is right, and the underlying social perspective.[35]

Basic Assertions About the Stage Construct

Kohlberg's basic assertions are important for understanding adult development in schools. First, Kohlberg asserts that the development of moral thinking evolves over the life cycle and can be traced to complex, but definable, structures. Like stage and phase theorists, Kohlberg confirms that adults continue to grow and that we can identify and thereby respond to aspects of their unfolding development. Second, Kohlberg asserts that the stages are hierarchically integrated. As a consequence, he insists, later stages are not only qualitatively different but fundamentally better or more adequate.

A logical derivative of Kohlberg's belief that higher stages are qualitatively different and superior to lower stages is his belief that development should be intentionally stimulated – more particularly, that enhancing development should be the aim of education. This notion seems well matched to the objectives of schooling. Schools are contexts for the development of children, and teachers work at fostering children's growth. Extending Kohlberg's view to educational settings designed for adults also seems logical and appropriate. It is not as clear in what other settings development might be a legitimate objective. Is development an appropriate objective for the adults who work in schools?

Finally, Kohlberg asserts that his theory describes and predicts patterns of reasoning, *not* specific actions. Thoughts and behaviors are not necessarily related. Teachers might reason at the postconventional level that a rule is unjust, but uphold it, remaining loyal to conventional reasoning, because it is

TABLE 4.1
LAWRENCE KOHLBERG: THE SIX MORAL STAGES

Content of Stage

LEVEL AND STAGE	WHAT IS RIGHT	REASONS FOR DOING RIGHT	SOCIAL PERSPECTIVE OF STAGE
Level I: Preconventional Stage 1: Heteronomous Morality	To avoid breaking rules backed by punishment, obedience for its own sake, and avoiding physical damage to persons and property.	Avoidance of punishment and the superior power of authorities.	*Egocentric point of view.* Doesn't consider the interests of others or recognize that they differ from the actor's; doesn't relate two points of view. Actions are considered physically rather than in terms of psychological interests of others. Confusion of authority's perspective with one's own.
Stage 2: Individualism, Instrumental Purpose, and Exchange	Following rules only when it is to someone's immediate interest, acting to meet one's own interests and needs and letting others do the same. Right is also what's fair, what's an equal exchange, a deal, an agreement	To serve one's own needs or interests in a world where you have to recognize that other people have their interests too.	*Concrete individualistic perspective.* Aware that everybody has his own interest to pursue and these conflict, so that right is relative (in the concrete, individualistic sense).
Level II: Conventional Stage 3: Mutual Interpersonal Expectations, Relationships, and Interpersonal Conformity	Living up to what is expected by people close to you or what people generally expect of people in your role as son, brother, friend, etc. "Being good" is important and means having good motives, showing concern about others. It also means keeping mutual relationships, such as trust, loyalty, respect, and gratitude.	The need to be a good person in your own and others' eyes. Belief in the Golden Rule. Desire to maintain rules and authority that support stereotypical good behavior.	*Perspective of the individual in relationships with other individuals.* Aware of shared feelings, agreements, and expectations that take primacy over individual interests. Relates points of view through the concrete Golden Rule, putting himself or herself in the other guy's shoes. Does not yet consider generalized system perspective.

Stage 4: Social System and Conscience	Fulfilling the actual duties to which you have agreed. Laws are to be upheld except in extreme cases where they conflict with other fixed social duties. Right is also contributing to society, the group, or institution	To keep the institution going as a whole, to avoid the breakdown in the system "if everyone did it," or the imperative or conscience to meet one's defined obligations. (Easily confused with Stage 3 belief in rules and authority; see text.)	*Differentiates societal point of view from interpersonal agreement or motives.* Takes the point of view of the system that defines roles and rules. Considers individual relations in terms of place in the system.
Level III: Postconventional or Principled Stage 5: Social Contract or Utility and Individual Rights	Being aware that people hold a variety of values and opinions, that most values and rules are relative to your group. These relative rules should usually be upheld, however, in the interest of impartiality and because they are the social contract. Some nonrelative values and rights like *life* and *liberty*, however, must be upheld in any society and regardless of majority opinion.	A sense of obligation to law because of one's social contract to make and abide by laws for the welfare of all and for the protection of all people's rights. A feeling of contractual commitment, freely entered upon, to family, friendship, trust, and work obligations. Concern that laws and duties be based on rational calculation of overall utility, "the greatest good for the greatest number."	*Prior-to-society perspective.* Perspective of a rational individual aware of values and rights prior to social attachments and contracts. Integrates perspectives by formal mechanisms of agreement, contract, objective impartiality, and due process. Considers moral and legal points of view; recognizes that they sometimes conflict and finds it difficult to integrate them.
Stage 6: Universal Ethical Principles	Following self-chosen ethical principles. Particular laws or social agreements are usually valid because they rest on such principles, one acts in accordance with the principle. Principles are universal principles of justice: the equality of human rights and respect for the dignity of human beings as individual persons.	The belief as a rational person in the validity of universal moral principles and a sense of personal commitment to them.	*Perspective of a moral point of view* from which social arrangements derive. Perspective is that of any rational individual recognizing the nature of morality or the fact that persons are ends in themselves and must be treated as such.

Source: Reproduced with permission from Thomas Lickona (ed.), *Moral Development Behavior* (New York: Holt, Rinehart & Winston, 1976), pp. 34-35.

an agreed-upon convention. If thought and behavior are not necessarily related, how can the theory be of service? Responding to this and other questions raised by Kohlberg's stage construct begins to bridge theory and practice.

Questions Raised by the Moral Development Framework

Are Higher Stages "Better" Stages? Kohlberg's contention that higher stages are "better" stages has generated responses from phase and stage theorists alike. According to phase theorist Levinson:

> The tasks of one period are not better or more advanced than those of another, except in the general sense that each period builds upon the work of earlier ones and represents a later phase in the cycle. There are losses as well as gains in the shift from every period or era to the next.[36]

Stage theorist Loevinger cautions:

> Probably it is a mistake to idealize any stage. Every stage has its weaknesses, its problems, and its paradoxes, which provide both a potential for maladjustments and a potential for growth. One problem of the autonomous stage is how to reconcile the need for autonomy with dependence needs, on the one hand, and with exercise of authority on the other....To see such unresolved problems is important, lest one run to the conclusion that the person highest on the scale of ego maturity is always the best parent or teacher or therapist.[37]

Studies have shown that adults at advanced developmental stages display a range of complex behaviors associated with positive interpersonal skills, such as increased flexibility and empathy. These capacities may give teachers and administrators access to a broad array of skills and abilities in dealing with each other and with students.[38]

Kohlberg further identifies the potential of movement toward principled thinking in adults. Work experiences with a level of moral complexity, for instance, can require a teacher or administrator to take the perspectives of individuals within a system and of the system as a whole. School rules can conflict with the rights of individuals within the school.

Responsibility for resolving conflicts that result can encourage the formulation of principles that recognize and somehow reconcile the just claims of both.

Role-taking experiences, which allow individuals to take on the roles and responsibilities of others, can also stimulate moral development. Kohlberg believes that such experiences can be a central part of an adult's work, especially "when a job allows, encourages, or necessitates empathic or moral role-taking rather than non-empathic or strategic role-taking."[39]

While higher stages may be better for some purposes, it is essential to note that the higher/better formulation does *not* mean that individuals at higher stages of moral reasoning or ego development are better or more valuable *people*. Individuals may be able to reason more adequately in some instances or take more into account when they reason. In every case, the value of thoughts, feelings, and behaviors must be understood in context and with the knowledge that there are limitations and strengths at all levels.

Does Kohlberg's Model Represent a Valued Developmental Progression?

We live within a social order that requires conventions. Most adults remain at conventional levels. Principled thinking transcends conventional reasoning, substituting abstract principles of morality and justice. Kohlberg maintains that the development of fully principled thinking is rare and never reached before adulthood.[40] Loevinger has suggested that all societies are built on conformity and value conformity in the individual.[41] Principled thinking, already rarely found to be naturally occurring, could actually be dysfunctional in many organizations, including schools. If this were so, to what end might a perspective that postulates development as the aim of education prove counterproductive?

Are Some Environments More Conducive to Development than Others?

If development is to be the aim of education, and if advanced development can complicate moral reasoning and perhaps moral actions, schools might be well advised to practice the activities Kohlberg and his colleagues offer. I raise this issue for the adults who work in schools at a time when, interestingly, corporations are investing heavily in the development of human resources. In some companies, adults benefit from the availability of on-site training to enhance their professional skills as well as counseling to respond to personal needs. Frequently, these opportunities are available during working hours. Many companies believe in a strong, positive link between employee satisfaction and productivity.

Schools are very different organizations from most businesses. Lack of time and resources often inhibits similar initiatives. A focus on adult needs might detract from the attention due to children. When a teacher leaves school during the day, a substitute must be found or students may have a study period or free time. The adults who work in schools will have to weigh these issues and realities to determine whether schools can become conducive environments for adult development.

Implications of Kohlberg's Stage Theory for the Adults Who Work in Schools
The issues raised by Kohlberg's theory stimulate questions of importance for the adults who work in schools:

- If development continues throughout the life cycle, how can we understand and respond to the developmental needs of adults in schools?
- While schools may be appropriate contexts for stimulating the growth of children, should the workplace also be an arena for adult growth?
- Can the growing needs of adults be satisfied without interfering with or jeopardizing the school's primary obligation to children?
- If higher stages are better in the sense of allowing individuals to reason more inclusively or less egocentrically, what are the consequences of this perspective?
- Can we determine what modes of thought and action are most valuable in schools?
- What strategies for enhancing adult development are suitable for use in schools?

Understanding and Responding to Ongoing Developmental Needs. Kohlberg's framework provides a window through which to see and understand adult moral reasoning. An individual's responses to authority and evaluation or style of decision making and collaboration may be more clearly understood as a result. The distinct reasoning of two teachers about a colleague's impending dismissal illustrates this point:

> I can't see how the system can do anything about it. Evaluations are given three times a year to a teacher on probation and if you don't show improvement, you're out.

I know what the rule book says, but I believe everyone can change with proper support. I'd like to see the teacher get another shot. People ought to be treated with dignity. Nobody should be disgraced.

Here, two teachers have discordant views. In one case, conventional reasoning dictates a decision. The system has put a procedure in place, and it is right to abide by it. Kohlberg's stage-four orientation to social order and civic duty may shape this teacher's respect for authority. A colleague reaches the opposite conclusion through a belief in the value and potential of human nature. Guided by a universal, ethical principle, this teacher's reasoning supersedes the system's conventions and supports a different response. With Kohlberg's model as a framework, these teachers and their colleagues might have a better understanding of their reasoning and the actions that relate to or contradict the way they think.

Schools as Arenas for Adult Moral Development. We know some of the ways that moral development can be stimulated. We also recognize a potential relationship between the advanced development of adults and their increasing effectiveness with each other and with children. Making use of these methods is a promising result of understanding Kohlberg's framework. Schools can consider initiating discussions among adults around moral issues and conflicts as well as providing opportunities for role-taking experiences. Kohlberg and his colleagues have generated a great deal of material, including a large number of moral dilemmas, aimed at revealing, and sometimes provoking, individual and group thinking.[42]

Adults in schools can use or adapt such materials. Instead of the well-known Heinz dilemma, where a man must decide whether to steal a drug he cannot afford for his ailing wife, a teacher or administrator might need to choose between his loyalty to work and family, decide whether to search a student's locker, or determine if he or she will look the other way when a favorite student is cheating. According to Kegan, the value of such discussions lies in their ability to reveal how a person is reasoning. Kohlberg would not be looking for "right" or "wrong" answers.

Making Kohlberg's framework explicit for teachers and administrators might also broaden the language with which adults in schools talk about and analyze the ongoing decisions and dilemmas of school life. Kohlberg's theory has been successfully applied by educators and clinicians working with children having behavior problems.[43] It has also been used to establish "just communities" in schools and other institutions.[44] Similarly, it might be a useful tool for professional development.

Stage Theory as Hierarchical. The idea of higher as better or more important is already well established in schools. Higher test scores are better; higher levels of schooling are better and more important; higher salaries are better; higher positions in the school and the system carry more status. Chances are, this mode of thinking in schools will be applied swiftly to adult development theory and its potential applications. Yet, there is an alternative vision. Each stage can be seen as having both strengths and weaknesses. Each person's integrity can be acknowledged and celebrated by honoring the present, as well as looking forward to the future. Allowing people to be themselves is a direct consequence of this position.

Where, then, is there room for growth, and who should take responsibility for development? It is possible to respect and respond to individual differences *and* support the natural inclination toward growth. Further, there are many times when challenging a person's world view or creating the kind of dissonance that leads to change is appropriate. Such might be the case when an adult is stuck and needs options. Another instance where an adult's thinking might be usefully shifted is when the well-being of another adult or a child is at risk. That higher is different, more complex, and *sometimes* more adequate is a viewpoint toward stage theory that could be substituted for a hierarchical conception.

Links Between Thought and Action. Identifying ties between thought and action is a key issue and among the most complicated to untangle. Kohlberg warns of the loose connections, recognizing that particular circumstances may circumscribe a person's ability or willingness to act on his or her best judgment. Though a person may choose to reason at the "highest" possible level "under normal circumstances," will his or her actions be likewise motivated? My own research suggests that particular environments may actually place a ceiling on an individual's behavior, below his or her potential capacities. Just as development may be stimulated, it may likewise be stifled.

Loevinger also points out that constructs like Kohlberg's and her own are abstract models not always so cleanly represented in individual lives. More likely, individuals have the capacity and the propensity to think and behave on multiple levels and may, in fact, understand and act in quite different ways in different areas of their lives.

To increase the potential link between thought and action, adults can model and reward valued behaviors as well as practice them. Discussion, role playing, and, most importantly, role taking are practical methods for expanding a person's perspective. Practice with these strategies can potentially reduce the distance between thought and actions.

Attending to and acknowledging differences between what one says and what one *does* can be another professional development strategy. Not only is it essential for adults who work in schools to articulate their goals and values clearly and forcefully, but their actions must coincide with their beliefs. Thinking and acting consistently is an important skill for teachers to develop with children, as well as for adults to use in their interactions with one another.

Key Points in Kohlberg's Stage Theory

Kohlberg's stage theory of moral reasoning is important for its content. Further, it is useful in defining stage as a construct and in describing how stage change might be provoked. Equally significant are the questions and controversies the theory sparks. In fact, the persistent questioning and conflict raised by Kohlberg's stage approach mirror the processes basic to ongoing development.

Kohlberg's theory suggests a number of specific approaches to adult moral development. It suggests direct use of the framework as a stimulus for debate and discussion. It suggests the use of moral dilemmas, role playing, and role taking to expand individual and group perspectives on moral issues and moral reasoning. It suggests the importance of striving for consistency between models of thought and patterns of behavior.

Kohlberg's insistence that higher stages are more adequate, that principled reasoning is the most advanced form of moral judgment, and that development should be the aim of education all raise important questions for how we think of development and the roles we take in fostering our own growth and the growth of others. School people often talk about changing other adults. Principals want to change teachers, and teachers often want principals to be different. Whether support or stimulation is a precondition for growth is one of many vital issues raised by Kohlberg's theory of moral development. It is my view that support is a prerequisite for growth. I encourage you to take a stand and consider its practical implications.

THE STAGE THEORY OF JANE LOEVINGER

Jane Loevinger's work extends Kohlberg's by looking at the broad category of ego development and by focusing on performance and structure. It sets the stage for the later development of Kegan's process orientation toward growth.

Loevinger claims that ego development is a master trait, encompassing moral judgment as well as other areas of functioning. The essence of the ego is striving for meaning; as making meaning is central to human activity, the work of the ego is fundamental to development.

Loevinger identifies the following prominent characteristics of the ego. Foremost, the ego is a process. It strives for coherence and meaning. The ego is also a structure. It has an internal logic and is a relatively stable construction. An organism selects its environment to cohere to the deep, underlying order that constitutes its internal balance, or equilibrium. By selectively not paying attention to what can create imbalance, a person tends to recognize only what fits with his or her ways of knowing and feeling. Since individuals have different constructions, no environment is experienced in quite the same way. Since the ego is relatively stable, it forms a natural barrier to change. Finally, the ego is social in origin: Interpersonal relationships are crucial to its development.[45]

The concept of ego level brings a fresh perspective to the understanding of individual behavior and group dynamics. While its focus on functioning may transgress strict stage guidelines, it offers a somewhat more tangible approach to thinking about life in a particular organizational setting. It must be remembered, however, that each stage represents a clustering of traits that combine to form an ideal type. While these types are derived from observations, they are not directly observable. This makes individual classifications highly problematic. Originally a psychometrician – a psychologist who creates measures to assess psychological processes – Loevinger has developed a thirty-six-stem sentence completion test as a measuring device. As with all the stage concepts, reliance on measurement tools of this kind appropriately limits their facile application. To the extent that individuals show evidence of functioning on different levels, however, precise classification is far less important than understanding the underlying characteristics of the stage construct, in general, and the qualities of the ego, in particular.

Loevinger supports this perspective, explaining that every individual displays behavior at multiple levels. Like other stage and phase theorists, she believes that earlier stages are subsumed and transformed by later ones.

TABLE 4.2
JANE LOEVINGER: MILESTONES OF EGO DEVELOPMENT

STAGE	CODE	IMPULSE CONTROL, CHARACTER DEVELOPMENT	INTERPERSONAL STYLE	CONSCIOUS PREOCCUPATIONS	COGNITIVE STYLE
Presocial Symbiotic	I-1		Autistic Symbiotic	Self vs. nonself	
Impulsive	I-2	Impulsive, fear of retaliation	Receiving, dependent, exploitative	Bodily feelings, especially sexual and aggressive	Stereotyping, conceptual confusion
Self-Protective	△	Fear of being caught, externalizing blame, opportunistic	Wary, manipulative, exploitative	Self-protection, trouble, wishes, things, advantage, control	
Conformist	I-3	Conformity to external rules, shame, guilt for breaking rules	Belonging, superficial niceness	Appearance, social acceptability, banal feelings, behavior	Conceptual simplicity, stereotypes, clichés
Conscientious-Conformist	I-3/4	Differentiation of norms, goals	Aware of self in relation to group, helping	Adjustment problems, reasons, opportunities (vague)	Multiplicity
Conscientious	I-4	Self-evaluated standards, self-criticism, guilt for consequences, long-term goals and ideals	Intensive, responsible, mutual, concern for communication	Differentiated feelings, motives for behavior, self-respect, achievements, traits, expression	Conceptual complexity, idea of patterning
Individualistic	I-4/5	*Add: Respect for individuality	Add: Dependence as an emotional problem	Add: Development, social problems, differentiation of inner life from outer	Add: Distinction of process and outcome
Autonomous	I-5	Add: Coping with conflicting inner needs, toleration	Add: Respect for autonomy, interdependence	Add: Vividly conveyed feelings, integration of physiological and psychological, psychological causation of behavior, role conception, self-fulfillment, self in social context	Increased conceptual complexity, complex patterns, toleration for ambiguity, broad scope, objectivity
Integrated	I-6	Add: Reconciling inner conflicts, renunciation of the unattainable.	Add: Cherishing of individuality	Add: Identity	

*Add means in addition to the description applying to the previous level.

Source: From Jane Loevinger, *Ego Development: Conceptions and Theories* (San Francisco: Jossey-Bass, 1976), pp. 23-24. Reproduced with permission of Jossey-Bass, Inc., and the author.

The ways in which the issues at each stage are resolved influence the ways later stages will be formed and experienced.

Unlike Kohlberg, Loevinger does not make a point of defining stages as necessarily better, or more adequate. Nor does she subscribe to Kohlberg's separation of structure and function or the division of feelings and thoughts. The sequence of stages, she suggests, might best be seen as "coping with increasingly deeper problems."[46] In some sense, Loevinger continues, "there is no highest stage but only an opening to new possibilities."[47]

According to Loevinger, there is a range of stages and transitional periods, beginning at a presocial level, where symbiotic and impulsive behaviors are characteristic, and progressing to a stage of integration, when both independence and interdependence are possible. At each stage, Loevinger describes characteristics, traits, impulses, cognitive and interpersonal styles, and conscious preoccupations (see Table 4.2). Although stage and age are distinct, the levels between stages three and five, and particularly the transition from Conformist Stage (three) to Conscientious Stage (four) are common configurations for many adults.

Stages of Adult Development

The Self-Protective Stage. Though most often characteristic of younger people, the Self-Protective stage can make its way into adulthood. Here, externalization is a key trait. Persons at the Self Protective stage tend to blame others, circumstances, or parts of themselves for which they do not feel responsibility. Concerned with controlling and being controlled, they are often manipulative or exploitative. Life at the Self-Protective level is viewed as a win-lose, zero-sum game. Loevinger suggests that teachers and administrators might want to recognize this character type and think about effective ways of responding to adults at this stage. On the one hand, the Self-Protective personality can create dissonance in an organization and cause trouble; on the other hand, adults at the Self-Protective stage can be "the most charming and successful hustlers."[48]

Conformist Stage. At the Conformist level, individuals are preoccupied with compliance to external rules. Acceptance and approval are vitally important. A person at this stage identifies with and obeys authority. What is conventional and socially approved is right. Concern for the externals of life takes the form of interest in appearance, social acceptance, reputation, and material things. Belonging makes the Conformist feel safe.

Individuals oriented to life from the Conformist stage believe there are right and wrong ways to understand and do things and that these are the same for everyone at all times. They tend to think in terms of group similarities rather than individual differences, typically accepting stereotypes, such as broad statements of difference between males and females. According to Loevinger, people at the Conformist stage make up either a majority or a large minority in almost any social group.

The Conscientious-Conformist Level. The level between the Conformist and the Conscientious is the characteristic developmental orientation of most adults (that is, individuals over age sixteen). Adults at this level manifest remnants of the Conformist orientation as well as parts of the Conscientious stage to come.

At the Conscientious-Conformist level, there is a growing awareness of self and particularly of one's inner feelings. While rules remain important, they may have exceptions. In place of one right way, multiple right ways can be more easily understood and tolerated. Appreciation of varied possibilities and increasing self-awareness are the basic features of this level.

Conscientious Stage. At the Conscientious stage (I-4), self-evaluated standards partially replace external rules. Rather than relying on the criticism of others, individuals at the Conscientious stage can be highly critical of themselves. Interpersonal communications are especially valued now, and sensitivity to others continues to deepen.

Individuals at the Conscientious stage are reflective in ways that aren't possible at early stages. They can be more reflective because of their increased awareness of themselves and others. Alertness to choices, motivation to achieve goals, concern with living up to ideals, and interest in self-improvement are all additional Conscientious stage characteristics.

Individualistic Level. To continue beyond the Conscientious stage, individuals must become more tolerant of themselves and others. Tolerance grows out of a recognition of individual differences and complexities. A growing sense of individualism is thus an important quality of the transition from the Conscientious to the Autonomous stage. While individuals may no longer be dependent on others for their financial or physical well-being, they are aware of emotional dependence. During this transition, interpersonal relationships become deeper and more intense.

Autonomous Stage. Autonomous is the name given to stage I-5 in part because of the individual's recognition at this point in his or her development of other people's need for autonomy. At the same time, individuals at the Autonomous stage understand the limitations of autonomy, accepting the inevitability of emotional interdependence.

The excessive striving and responsibility experienced at the Conscientious stage begin to lessen at the Autonomous stage. Efforts to achieve are gradually replaced by a search for self-fulfillment. Individuals at the Autonomous stage look at life broadly, have a high tolerance for ambiguity, accept the existence of inner conflict, and concern themselves with social problems beyond their own needs and experiences.

Integrated Stage. Very few individuals manifest the characteristics of the Integrated level (I-6). Less than 1 percent of most social groups might be found at this stage, according to Loevinger. The Integrated stage is one at which conflicts and polarities are transcended. Individuals come to terms with the realities of their lives (cf. Erikson's phase of integrity), developing a firm sense of identity. They have high respect for themselves and others.[49]

Implications of Loevinger's Stage Theory for the Adults Who Work in Schools

Loevinger's explanation of the nature of the ego and its development offers a number of implications for the adults who work in schools. In this section, I will deal broadly with these implications and in the next section on the related formulation of Robert Kegan focus more intensively on particular stage characteristics.

First, the ego's natural resistance to change underscores the tenacity and integrity of individual world views and cautions staff developers against attempts to alter radically the foundations on which a person's sense of self is balanced. The social origins of the ego point again to the significance of interpersonal relationships and the continuing need for adults to be in contact with peers.

Loevinger's stage progression exposes a gradual increase in self-awareness as well as an expanded view of others. Until individuals reach the Conscientious stage, their abilities to reflect are limited. Yet we expect most adults to be reflective. Typically, we give teachers broad discretion for their classroom activities and principals primary responsibility within the building. We expect teachers to examine their teaching; we expect administrators to monitor instructional practices. Loevinger's stage progression reveals the potential limitations of applying blanket assumptions to adults and suggests a need to determine the degree to which individuals can be introspective, self-reliant, observant, and empathic.

That adults construct the world very differently and that these constructions may influence not only understanding but behavior is another of Loevinger's broad contributions. Loevinger suggests the divergent responses two mothers at different ego levels might have to their children, for instance. In either case, the role of teacher or colleague could easily be substituted. A typical Conscientious mother, Loevinger explains, feels obliged to prevent her child from making errors. A typical Autonomous mother, on the other hand, recognizes the need for her child to learn from mistakes and therefore allows the child the latitude to learn or not learn.

Diverse ego levels can also manifest themselves as different approaches to organizational processes, such as decision making. Typically, differences in roles or status or faulty mechanisms for communication are considered the prime factors leading to conflict and misunderstanding in schools. It may be, however, that the way decisions are actually *understood* at various levels of development is a key cause of dissonance. According to Loevinger's scheme, an individual at the Conformist level will not be capable of generating, or perhaps accepting, the alternatives that a colleague at the Conscientious stage may be able to offer or accept. The singular viewpoint such an individual displays at a meeting may not be a simple expression of contrariness or the result of differences in status. Rather, it may be a complex manifestation of how the world is known or experienced.

Loevinger's stage theory further suggests that school people will need different kinds of incentives and supports at various ego levels. At the Conformist level, a teacher's need for acceptance and acceptability makes frequent, positive feedback a key form of support. At the Conscientious stage, when standards of performance are more deeply internalized, evaluation from others alone will likely be insufficient. Instead, both personal and shared or mutual evaluation will provide a more appropriate kind of support.

Finally, Loevinger's stage theory and the characteristics it illuminates suggest the need for a wide range of staff development activities and strategies. The theory explains why adults might react very differently to teaching techniques. Presentations aimed at eliciting questions and alternative hypotheses can be expected to unsettle the Conformist, whose dependence on the one right or wrong way and on authority can be shaken by such an approach. Alternatively, a more directed teaching style, where a principal or staff developer relates information and procedures, will likely irritate individuals at the Conscientious stage. These individuals are eager to and capable of generating a range of solutions and evaluating their own effectiveness.

Self-study and the development of idiosyncratic staff development goals may suit individuals beyond stage four, where capacities to think and act independently and to value individuality are strongest. Principals and staff developers can build varied approaches into their staff development repertoires. They can plan both group and individual activities. With a knowledge of adult stage development, they can begin to understand and adjust to diverse responses to their initiatives. They can also begin to look at their own teaching and learning styles.

Key Points in Loevinger's Stage Theory

Many of Loevinger's ideas are consistent with other developmental conceptions. Development is conceived as ongoing. The individual, engaging in a constant process of active exchange with the environment, constructs meanings, strives for competence, and protects the self from changes that threaten to undermine the assumptions or inner logic with which the self-system is maintained. Changing relationships between self and other are the interpersonal arena for the activity of making meaning.

While phase conceptions recognize the importance of this interactive approach, stage theory offers a level of analysis previously absent. As both self and other are diversely experienced at different ego levels, the nature and quality of interpersonal relations alter. Relative to these changes are shifts in the criteria used to determine self-worth. At the Conformist level, worthiness is tied to group acceptance. With the gradual acknowledgment of one's own wants and needs at ego stage four, the locus of value shifts from the group toward the self. While some theorists have identified the persistent motivation toward competence and underscored the link between feelings of effectiveness and self-esteem, Loevinger further refines this relationship. Just as environments are known differently as individuals actively strive to construct meanings out of experience, so, too, are there shifts in the conception of the self. Along with the knowledge that feelings of self-worth are central to growth, an understanding of how the self changes is vital. Changes in the self transform the meanings of competence and worth.

Loevinger's theory thus recapitulates and elaborates the themes of

Chapter 3 on phases of adult development. In addition, the concept of ego development pushes against the limits of Kohlberg's construct. It preserves the structural components of the moral judgment paradigm but broadens it to encompass both form and function, cognition and affect.

Loevinger's construct and its translation into specific character traits, interpersonal styles, preoccupations, and thought patterns offers both a broad framework for thinking about adult growth and a guide to identifying behaviors or clusters of behaviors characteristic of different stages. Remembering that stages represent ideal types and that individuals manifest characteristics at multiple levels, adults who work in schools can constructively use the framework as a general guide, establishing the range of behaviors possible among adults in the school and examining their own styles. The framework can help explain or predict the reactions that may result at meetings, during conferences and within the classroom. One teacher's interest in debating a controversial issue may be in sharp contrast to another's need to replace conflict with agreement. One teacher's dependence on being liked by her students may be clearly distinct from others' preferences for divergent reactions, assessments and opinions.

Loevinger's stage theory expands and complicates our understanding of adult development. It reveals the complexity of individual world views and the differences in understanding and behavior that may result.

THE STAGE THEORY OF ROBERT KEGAN

Kegan's conception of development focuses not only on the characteristics of individual stages but on the process by which individuals make meaning. The activity of making meaning is the basic activity of growth. According to Kegan, growth unfolds through alternating periods of dynamic stability, instability, and temporary rebalance. Kegan claims this process is universal, that it is shared by everyone regardless of culture, class, historical time, or sex.

Table 4.3 presents an overview of the developmental process as seen from Kegan's perspective. As the stages evolve, what has been associated with the individual, such as his or her needs or interpersonal relationships, shifts so that it becomes part of a larger environment. The shifting of self and other is the motion of development.

Kegan's Stages of Preadult and Adult Development

Because changing relationships between self and other are the substance of what is growing from Kegan's perspective, I will use S (Self) and O (Other) to illustrate Kegan's stages. Some aspects of these stages relate to stages that other theorists have identified. Like the stages of Jane Loevinger, Kegan's stages three, four, and five are generally typical of adults. Although Kegan's stage two, The Imperial I, most frequently manifests itself prior to adulthood, its characteristics appear to have implications for understanding the lives of adults in schools. Not only do many adults who work in schools identify with this stage, they see aspects of schools mirrored in its structure.

A key point to be made before I begin to describe Kegan's stages is his effort to understand how individuals make meaning: of themselves, of others, and of the world. While Loevinger focuses on traits and behaviors, Kegan emphasizes the meanings that lie *beneath* behaviors. This crucial distinction means that the same behaviors can have very different roots. To understand the way you or colleagues relate to the world demands more than cataloguing what you see; it requires discovering how you and others construct or build a world view. The description of Kegan's stages that follow will distinguish some of the world views you and colleagues can bring to work.

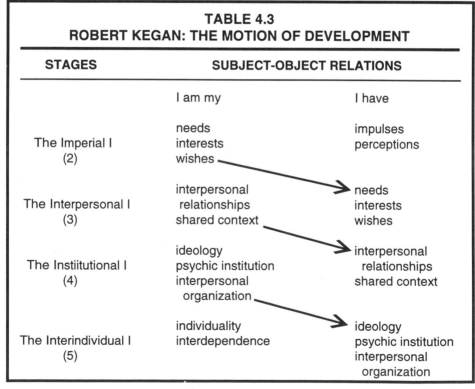

TABLE 4.3
ROBERT KEGAN: THE MOTION OF DEVELOPMENT

STAGES	SUBJECT-OBJECT RELATIONS	
	I am my	I have
The Imperial I (2)	needs interests wishes	impulses perceptions
The Interpersonal I (3)	interpersonal relationships shared context	needs interests wishes
The Instiitutional I (4)	ideology psychic institution interpersonal organization	interpersonal relationships shared context
The Interindividual I (5)	individuality interdependence	ideology psychic institution interpersonal organization

Source: Compiled from Robert Kegan, *The Evolving Self: Problems and Process in Human Development* (Cambridge, MA: Harvard University Press, 1982).

FIGURE 4.1
THE IMPERIAL BALANCE

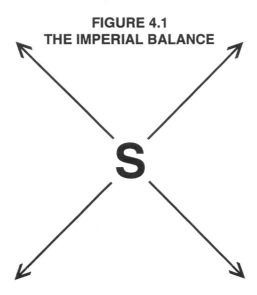

The Imperial Balance (Stage 2).   From the Imperial balance, individuals orient to themselves and the world through their needs.   Rather than having needs as objects in the world to be coordinated with the needs of others, these individuals' needs are ultimate.   In Figure 4.1, I portray the Imperial I as the individual directing energy away from the self, since at this balance outside input discrepant with my needs is not merely annoying or disrupting.   More fundamentally, it threatens to unravel the very fabric of myself.

At the Imperial balance, the self is built on meeting its own goals, orienting to others as means to ends, and becoming partners, not for the sake of mutuality, but for mutual advantage.   Adults at the Imperial I stage may become opportunistic, deceptive, and preoccupied with control and advantage in their relationships.   For these individuals, life may be a win or lose proposition.   Individuals at the Imperial stage work hard to maximize their gains and minimize their losses.

A strength of the Imperial balance is the ability of the individual to delineate a sense of self, albeit not necessarily coordinated with the needs of others.   Individuals oriented from the Imperial I stage can experience a degree of stability, control, and freedom.   Conflicts between the needs of the self and the needs of others test the limits of this balance.   In these situations, individuals at stage two will do what is best for *them*.   How others will feel is not taken into account.

What makes this balance imperial, maintains Kegan, is the absence of a

FIGURE 4.2
THE INTERPERSONAL BALANCE

shared reality. When colleagues attempt to interact with individuals balanced at the Imperial I, they can feel left out. Then, there is often no O, no other, in the stage-two configuration.

The Interpersonal Balance (Stage 3). At Interpersonal stage three, there is no self independent of other people's liking. Figure 4.2 indicates that the missing other from the Imperial I's world view is not only found at the Interpersonal level, but *bound* to it. Here the arrows point only from the other to the self, leaving the self completely dependent.

Because individuals at the Interpersonal stage are inextricably tied to others for their sense of self, they rely on niceness, compliance, and doing what they should for approval's sake to keep themselves balanced. Anger or conflict, which might put a relationship at risk, is avoided at all costs. When more than one person or more than one opinion are simultaneously present, dissonance and confusion can result. If one can feel imperialized and manipulated by the individual at the Imperial stage, Kegan maintains, one can feel devoured by the person at the Interpersonal stage.

The Institutional Balance (Stage 4). A new sense of self, self-dependence, and self-ownership are characteristics of the Institutional balance. As you see in Figure 4.3, the self is no longer so directly tied to a single other, but can relate to multiple others. Nor does one's sense of self derive only out of relationships. Symbolized by arrows going between the self and others in both directions is the new-found potential for mutual instead of one-way interaction.

Though interpersonal relationships are no longer the central arena of self-definition for individuals at the Institutional balance, it is important to understand that Kegan's framework does not diminish or disregard relationships as development progresses. In fact, there is increased access to relationships as adults grow. At issue is not whether other people are known or valued at any given balance, but *how* they are known and valued.

At the Institutional stage, individuals build and then identify with a complicated set of relationships. According to Kegan, they become adminis-

FIGURE 4.3
THE INSTITUTIONAL BALANCE

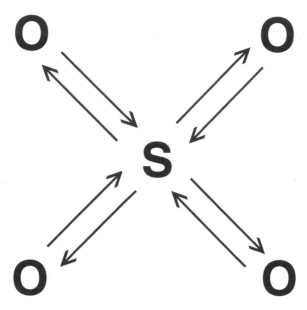

trators in the most narrow sense of the word, determined to keep the organization they construct intact and running. A person's sense of self-control is a strength of the Institutional configuration. Individuals at this balance begin to separate from the group and generate standards and values of their own. This is a stage where personal achievements, competence, and responsibility are prominent. Multiple views can be tolerated, generating alternative strategies, and mutual communications are prized.

The Interindividual Balance (Stage 5). At the Interindividual balance, individuality and interdependence are prominent. Able to take a more distant view of the organizations they constructed, individuals at this balance are now freed to run the various organizations that make up their complex lives.

At the Interindividual level, the individual begins to draw back from a high orientation to achievement and to move toward an unfolding of his or her own psychological being. A preoccupation with individuality and fulfillment replaces a focus on the administration of a complex web of connections between the self and others. Characteristic of this stage is a high degree of autonomy as well as a new capacity for interdependence. Both

FIGURE 4.4
THE INTERINDIVIDUAL BALANCE

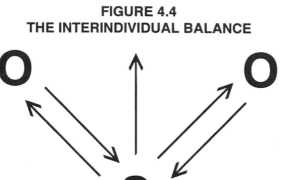

intimacy and independence are now increasingly possible, and one's definition of self includes a sense of inevitable connection to others.

Key Developmental Characteristics of Kegan's Theory
Growth as Continuing Motion.   Kegan's framework highlights several key developmental points. First and foremost, his emphasis on the motion of development is in sharp contrast to the static quality of the stages. One of the reasons I have depicted the stages diagrammatically has been to underscore their abstract and theoretical nature. In a sense, these are slides made from a motion picture, or, as William Perry has suggested, perhaps development is "all transitions and 'stages,' only resting points along the way."[50]

Opportunities and Limits at Every Developmental Point. While it is true that advanced stages enhance one's ability to engage with more aspects of the self and the world, every stage has both strengths and limitations.   The strength of the Institutional stage, for example, lies in a person's newly evolved capacity for independence. Instead of being tied to the other for a sense of myself, I have the flexibility now to bring myself to and take myself from a variety of contexts and relationships. At the same time, my very sense of self is tied to the institution or organization of others for which I am now chief administrator. My self is identified with the organization I have created, and I am invested in keeping the organization together. If individuals at the Institutional stage are freed from dependence on others, they are now tied to the organizations they have created.

The Particular Pain and Sometimes Exhilaration of Transition. Development is ongoing, requiring constant renegotiations between self and environment. Parts of the self and the world are thus continually gained or lost. Seymour Sarason has stated, "[A person's] desire for change is more than matched by his ingenuity in avoiding change, even when the desire for change is powered by strong pain, anxiety, and grief."[51] Growing is likely to be a painful expression of loss.

If something is always lost in growth, something else is always gained. Individuals in transition from the Institutional to the Interindividual balance lose their previously inextricable connection with the organization. At the same time, the self-sufficiency and solitariness of the organizational construction gives way to expanded possibilities for intimacy, exploration, and experimentation. Discovery of these new capacities can balance the sense of loss with feelings of freedom and exhilaration.

Implications of Kegan's Stage Theory for the Adults Who Work in Schools
The Imperial I. Many adult educators breathe a sigh of relief and nod their heads in recognition when they hear about the characteristics of the Imperial balance. Here an individual's needs are of primary importance, and coordinating one's own needs with the needs of others is discomforting, if not untenable. Since the Imperial I is an atypical configuration for most adults, how does one explain this reaction? A number of teachers and administrators recognize this pattern of behavior among their least amicable colleagues. A few more of them reluctantly admit that they sometimes adopt such a position, especially when they feel besieged. Others suggest the parallel between the Imperial orientation and the self-contained classroom structure of most schools. Do schools reinforce this pattern because of the way they're organized and because of the powerful norms of separation and competition?

All of these observations and questions unearth valuable points. Individuals have access to all prior stages of development, explaining why the remnants of a preadult stage might surface during adulthood. Conditions of stress, fear of disclosure, or concern about failure may likewise cause primitive behaviors and defenses to surface. The structure of organizations can also support or inhibit particular developmental patterns.

Importantly, feedback can be ultimately threatening to the person who brings the Imperial I to work. As the figure of the Imperial I reveals, there may be no room for any "other" in this configuration, especially when the others' needs are discordant. Communication can become unidimensional, with little or no opportunity for outside input. Yet feedback and open communication are central educational ideas. They underlie work with children, with teachers, and among administrators. Taking a developmental perspective adds an important qualifier to this value.

It is reasonable to question the viability of the Imperial balance for adults in schools. Even if these adults create their own empires by closing their classroom or office doors, their interactions may become strained when conflicts arise and they are unable to take another adult's or a child's needs into consideration. While we expect and accommodate the egocentricity of children and adolescents, where this stage is most frequently found, we may not be as prepared to allow for this orientation in adulthood.

Finally, it is important to say that some of the defensive behaviors seemingly associated with the Imperial stage may not indicate the Imperial balance. Anyone under siege will close the doors to the classroom and the self. Anyone seriously threatened will protect his or her needs and interests. These realities appropriately complicate stage theory. They make categorization complex and inexact. They serve as a vital reminder that we must pay attention to the meanings that give rise to thoughts, feelings, behaviors, and attitudes.

The Interpersonal Balance. On the one hand, a certain degree of adherence to external rules and regulations is vital to the smooth functioning of organizations. An orientation toward conformity can also contribute to shared goals and cooperation. Blind acceptance and excessive dependence, on the other hand, can constrain not only the individual at the Interpersonal balance, but those to whom he or she is inextricably tied. Children do not ultimately benefit from sustained and suffocating protection. Nor do teachers and administrators have the opportunity to develop their own thoughts, feelings, and behaviors when they are similarly constrained.

The Interpersonal orientation can speak loudly in a staff development session or supervisory conference. The teacher either has a sense of what is expected and cannot deviate from it or is so caught up in being liked by the supervisor that self-approval, rather than professional scrutiny, is the primary focus of the interchange. Two brief excerpts from conferences between a supervisor and a student teacher bring the Interpersonal orientation to classroom life:

Excerpt I

STUDENT TEACHER: I'm really glad you're here. I don't know what I'm supposed to be doing. My cooperating teacher never tells me how I did after class. She just sits at the back of the room with absolutely no expression on her face. And I can't tell yet whether the kids like me. So I can't wait to hear what you think.

SUPERVISOR: I can see you're really eager for feedback. What do you want me to look at today?

STUDENT TEACHER: Everything! Just tell me how I'm doing and whether you like it.

Excerpt II

STUDENT TEACHER: Hi, Mrs. Black. I'm glad to see you. I spent two hours last night preparing this math lesson, and I think I have it exactly the way you want it now.

SUPERVISOR: It sounds like you put a lot of work into your planning. Remember last time, we were working on trying to define what it is you want to get across to the kids?

STUDENT TEACHER: Right. I know that's what you wanted, so that's what I'm doing. I'm really nervous, though, because I want you to like it, and I hope my cooperating teacher, Mrs. Lemmons, stays away, because I know she would never approve of this way of teaching fractions. I'll change the lesson plan the next time she observes.

An Interpersonal orientation may be well suited to the principal or teacher who values compliance. If the adults in charge are themselves bound to an Interpersonal world view, the difficulties of coordinating the needs and opinions of diverse constituents are likely to be overwhelming.

An Interpersonal orientation has frequently been ascribed as a typical configuration for women whose focus on nurturing others, it is said, can interfere with the development of an independent sense of self. The experience of a school principal taking a year off to reflect upon and recover from twenty-six years of continual practice provides a dramatic example of this phenomenon. Living alone for the first time, she learned how closely she had affiliated herself with the needs of her family, on the one hand, and her school, on the other. Left to herself, she discovered she did not know what to cook when the only criteria for the decision were her own desires and inclinations.

The Institutional I Balance. Just as some aspects of the Interpersonal world view are suited to organizational life, many characteristics of the Institutional stage are well matched to life in schools. Adults oriented to the world from the Institutional I can coordinate the many components and relationships of their personal and professional lives. Two-way communication is relished in its own right. Individuals at the Institutional stage can engage in discussion and debate, have the capacity to evaluate themselves, and can set their own goals and standards. From this point of reference, a supervisor/student interchange might sound like this:

Excerpt III

STUDENT TEACHER: Hi, Peter. I'll be with you in a minute. I just want to finish correcting Leslie's paper. She's having trouble with the assignment, and I want to give her some help before she gets more angry and discouraged than she already is.

SUPERVISOR: Fine. Can I take a look around the room while you're finishing?

STUDENT TEACHER: Of course! Take a look at the bulletin board in the back on creative writing. I'm not very satisfied with how I have it arranged. Maybe you can give me some help rethinking the organization. Then let's get to work. I have a lot of ideas for this new social studies unit, and I can't settle on the best way of presenting it to the children.

This student teacher behaves quite differently from her counterpart at the Interpersonal stage. At the Institutional level, the student teacher is able to delay the supervisor in favor of the student – a different and temporarily absent other – to whom she chooses to give momentary precedence. The student teacher wants to address Leslie's homework, not because she fears Leslie's anger or disappointment with her, but because she understands the student's frustrations and wants to allay them for the student's sake.

Unlike Excerpts I and II, where the student teacher appears bent on receiving positive reinforcement, the student teacher in Excerpt III both recognizes and acknowledges her own judgments and invites outside help and criticism. This orientation may deprive the principal or supervisor of some degree of authority. In its place, the teacher at the Institutional level prefers collaboration and joint problem solving. Rather than expecting the supervisor to give her the right answer, she hopes that she and the supervisor together can devise a method of introducing the social studies unit that will work best for the students. Different "others" come up throughout this brief interchange. At the Institutional level, there is room for them. There is also room for the self to move back and forth among multiple demands and obligations without getting lost in the process.

Stage four's Institutional I is an especially interesting conception for thinking about an individual's relationship to work. Most work environments are structured to support the ideological orientation of the adult at the Institutional balance. When individuals internalize the ethics of the workplace, their loyalty is not only strengthened but personalized. They have quite literally organized themselves to maintain the purposes and structure of the organization. Such loyalty taken to the extreme at the Institutional balance can sometimes manifest itself as what we have come to term "workaholism." Kegan explains:

> The picture of the workaholic – with his or her all-consuming invest-
> ment in the exercises of achievement, self-esteem, independent ac-
> complishment, self-discipline, and control – looks like that of the
> evolutionary truce of institutionality in peril, working overtime lest
> it fall apart.[52]

Issues of evaluation take on heightened significance for individuals at the Institutional balance. For the educator at this level, the school has a powerful influence on the definition of the self. If I *am* my performance, rather than I *have* tasks to perform, evaluations threaten not only loss of job, but potential disruption of self.

Only at Interindividual I, stage five, can the individual extricate the self from this orientation. With the emergence of a more highly differentiated individuality, less tied to what one *does* than to who one *is*, the meaning of work is significantly transformed.

If one no longer *is* one's institution, neither is one any longer the duties, performances, work-roles, career which institutionality gives rise to. One has a career; one no longer is a career. The self is no longer so vulnerable to the kinds of ultimate humiliation which the threat of performance-failure holds out, for the performance is no longer ultimate....The self seems available to "hear" negative reports about its activities; before, it *was* those activities and therefore literally irritable in the face of those reports....Every new balance represents a capacity to listen to what one could only hear irritably, and the capacity to hear irritably what before one could hear not at all.[53]

This developmental insight has direct and immediate applications to schools, where communication is so important. First, it offers a fresh understanding of irritability. Beyond its usual meaning of annoyance, irritability may express a more basic lack of understanding. Second, the insight suggests a different understanding of hearing. Once you may have questioned your speaking or writing skills or wondered about the fitness of a colleague – stemming from a nagging sense that someone simply doesn't hear what you are saying. Now, you may realize a more psychologically grounded explanation.

The Interindividual Balance. It is not unusual in developmental theory to find that the most inclusive stages of growth are the least well defined. Whether this reveals something about our own developmental levels and limitations is not clear. Likewise, few other than the theorists are able to clearly articulate the nature and characteristics of the most complex stages. Just as a large proportion of the population never reaches formal operations in Piagetian terms, few appear to reach Kohlberg's level six, and many adults cluster in the middle ranges of Loevinger's and Kegan's schemes. Just as the more advanced phases of adulthood are only now being extensively investigated by researchers who themselves are entering or inhabiting later periods of adulthood, it may be that the more complex stages of development will be relatively unexplored until they are more heavily populated.

Two questions come immediately to mind when thinking about the Interindividual stage in the context of school life. Will independent or even interdependent behaviors be adaptive to schools? If it takes an advanced level of development to understand and describe the complexities of the later stages and phases of growth, to what extent is an advanced developmental level necessary to support the complex stages and phases of development? More often than not, when the developmental progression of adults is described to groups of teachers and administrators, a teacher will ask: "What if the principal is not in tune with the developmental needs of the faculty?" Or a principal will question: "How does an autonomous principal work with a conformist superintendent?"

The developmental orientation of a person in a helping relationship may, in fact, need to be both distinct from and more advanced than the developmental level of the person he or she is attempting to help. In this way, the issues and boundaries of the helper may more easily keep from bumping up against the issues and boundaries of the person being helped. A principal can extricate herself to some degree from reliance on a teacher's views of her performance, for instance, if she is not bound to the teacher's assessment of her.

Individual insight can guide one's feelings, behaviors, and decisions. Peter Samson recognizes the importance of understanding himself in order to know when and how he comfortably offers support and where his efforts to do so are hampered by his own developmental limits. Trying to help a teacher become more assertive with parents, he finds himself getting increasingly angry at the teacher. As they talk, he notices the source of these feelings in himself:

> I can think of one teacher who I would always like to be more assertive or more aggressive with specialists. The person is a good teacher, but I think she tends to abandon herself rather quickly with a specialist. She'll sort of hide behind me to do it for her, to take command. And it angers me – one, because I'd like this person to do it, and two, because it may be a little scary for me too. I mean, just because I'm the man or because I'm the principal, I don't have all the answers and I don't always feel well equipped to fight all the battles.

Kegan does not explore in depth what a workplace might look like if the culture could support interindividuality as well as institutionality. He imagines that individuals could reflect together on how they work, how they make decisions, and how they determine goals. At the same time, work would get accomplished, goals achieved and decisions made. Kegan concludes realistically, "it is an enormous challenge, and relatively uncommon, for the domain of work to sponsor development beyond the ideological."[54] It may be difficult to transcend the limits of the Institutional balance.

Periods of Transition. Periods of transition can be times of heightened emotion, upheaval, and unrest. Can a teacher or administrator struggle with such developmental turmoil and still carry out the day-to-day demands of the profession? Some argue that school people should park their outside lives by the curb before they enter the school building. Even if they could, I wonder what we would be losing. As early as 1932, Willard Waller declared, "For let no one be deceived, the important things that happen in the schools result from the interaction of personalities."[55] And it is certainly true that the educator's personality is an important tool of the trade. Yet Waller goes on to suggest that the particular nature of school work and constant exposure to children may, in fact, stifle an adult's development.

> Many who fail as teachers have more merit as persons than most of those who succeed, and some of the most valuable human qualities of successful teachers are sacrificed to their academic success.[56]

Growth, as we have seen, implies change and uncertainty. Yet schools demand stability and knowledge from the adults who serve as teachers and administrators. Might the demands of the profession be incompatible, or at least in tension, with the needs and realities of adult growth? Should adults expect to be growing in a setting designed for children? Will a context compatible with the growing needs of adults be a provocative or a disruptive environment for students? These are the kinds of questions that surface when school is considered as a context for the development of both children and adults.

Key Points in Kegan's Stage Theory

Kegan's stage theory of development has many broad and specific implications for thinking about the growth of adults in schools. If development is movement, and stages only resting points along the way, principals and staff developers will have all they can handle monitoring their own growing, not to mention keeping pace with the development of others. They will have to focus their attentions on providing support for adults in a setting very capable of creating large amounts of dissonance.

If developmental stage affects the degree to which we can hear ourselves and colleagues and the level of irritation that can be evoked by discrepant world views, principals and staff developers will have to listen hard to their own voices, talk with and listen to colleagues, and monitor the range of responses that individuals manifest. When an individual displays signs of discomfort or irritation, thinking about the source of the disruption in developmental terms may add a new layer of insight to one's understanding.

More specifically, the related characteristics of Loevinger's and Kegan's stages provide a rich context for greater self-understanding and increased empathy toward others. Rather than looking at and labeling individual pieces of behavior, teachers, principals, and staff developers can embrace the complexity of the stage construct as a challenge to be met by observing, speaking with, and listening to colleagues. They can use these frameworks as a resource for recognizing persistent patterns that may provide clues to individual motivation, feelings, attitudes, and understandings.

Shared knowledge of the details of stage theory can offer a common language for talking and thinking about personal and interpersonal behavior. At the very least, knowledge of Kegan's formulation and other stage frameworks demands a recognition of the complexity of adult development. Used to its fullest, it can provide an additional tool for enhancing the well-being and effectiveness of the adults who work in schools.

CONCLUDING COMMENTS

Stage theories raise a number of important issues and questions for educators. Should development be the aim of education? What is to be the balance between the amount of support we provide and the level of dissonance and stimulation we create? Is it appropriate to focus on the growing needs of children and adults? Should one's workplace be an arena for development? Do the demands of schools, in general, and of working with children, in particular, stifle the development of adults? How might independent thinking or autonomous behaviors blend with the school organization's conformist norms?

I begin with the premise that the development of the adults and the children in schools is vitally linked. When teachers are excited about life and learning, they transmit that excitement to their students. When the development of the adults in schools is inhibited, the learning and growing for students is correspondingly blocked.

Stage theories reveal the structures and processes of human development. Perhaps the most basic implication of knowing about the stages of adult development is the need for a keen understanding of oneself. Our ways of knowing the world and understanding ourselves and others circumscribe our capacities.

Adults in schools can be encouraged to increase their self-understanding by participating in professional development activities and, more generally, by paying attention and responding to their own needs for support, nurturance, and challenge. Given the ladderlike configuration of most staff development models, with principals or central office personnel left largely on the top, it is especially important to acknowledge the learning and growing needs of those expected to hold their positions because they are *already* experts. Once it is accepted that adults continue to grow and learn, there must also be learning and growing space for those at the top. Principals' centers and leadership academies are two formal structures that have recently surfaced to respond to the needs of school administrators (see Chapter 12). Opportunities for all the adults in the school to learn and grow *within schools and districts* are equally imperative.

Personal insight is also important as a basis for change. Developmental theories remind us that people learn and grow when the need for learning and growth start from within. Yet the traditional theme of training, staff development, or any teaching is that of getting *other* people to change or to learn. In schools, teachers work at helping children to learn and grow; principals work at getting teachers to change, and central office personnel, school committee members, and professional organizations see an important part of their roles as helping school people enhance their performance. A developmental perspective insists that individuals value and work toward change in themselves before they expect change in others. Principals need to value and work toward change in themselves before they can expect changes in teachers; and teachers need to value and work toward change in themselves before they can expect change in administrators. A principal makes this developmental insight explicit:

> Human beings change from the inside, not from the outside. We gain new insights that lead to changed behavior only when we see a need for change in ourselves. The irony is that we don't model change for those from whom we demand it – all the while wondering why our demands aren't met. Change will start with us. We'll worry about staff development later.[57]

When staff development is a central issue, stage theories point to the importance of understanding how the individuals with whom we are working understand themselves, their world, and others. This understanding helps us to recognize an individual's major preoccupations and assumptions, as well as to anticipate his or her interpersonal style, affect, and motivation. Talking with the adults in schools, listening to their responses, and observing them inside the classroom and within the school building are essential to gaining this level of knowledge and understanding. While these behavioral implications of stage theory may seem self-evident, it is surprising how infrequently the adults in schools talk with each other about how they see and understand themselves and their work, how inadequately most people attend to what others are saying, and how even a stated goal of frequent classroom observations is rarely put into operation.

Just as adult development is continuing, staff development can be perceived as an ongoing process as well as a formal and time-limited event. We can plan moments of staff development – such as workshops and professional days – but we must also be aware that staff development can happen any time adults in schools come together. Every opportunity can be used as an occasion for staff development. A teacher might express frustration about working with a parent. This occasion can be used to encourage the teacher to look at the way he or she conveys information, listens, and responds to criticism.

"The geranium died, and the teacher went on talking." This saying relates to the loss of a teachable moment in the classroom. A similar statement could be made to dramatize the lost moments within the school day for adult development.

Perhaps most importantly, stage theories appropriately complicate our understanding of ourselves and each other. What we may have taken for granted as a shared conception can no longer be taken for granted. Adults who work in the same building with the same principal may have very different experiences of the school and very diverse perceptions of the person who sits in the principal's office. The following story illustrates this point:

Late one Thursday afternoon, four principals are sitting together at what has now become a monthly group meeting. It is a time for sharing and problem-solving that has evolved in an effort to reduce the loneliness of the principal's position. Dick Chasen, principal from Lakewood Elementary, is explaining his frustration at not being able to satisfy the needs of all the teachers in his building. Not only does he feel that everyone is always looking to him for something, but he is confused by the fact that no matter how consistently he acts, someone is critical of his actions. He goes on to give a concrete example of what he means.

As a result of teachers asking for more support, Chasen has set aside one hour each week to visit classes. Knowing the importance of constructive feedback, he purposely writes long notes with a variety of reactions and comments. After two months, he has learned that several teachers are very grateful for this input. Two others, however, have expressed dissatisfaction. Tom Seymour, a veteran teacher of sixth graders, welcomes questions, but resents the principal's suggestions for changes. And to Chasen's surprise, Jessica Robbins, a second-grade teacher with more than fifteen years of classroom teaching experience, has seemed completely devastated by some mildly critical comments. Chasen exclaims: "I just don't get it....I think I treat everyone fairly; yet some teachers see me as supportive and others find me heavy-handed. To hear the way teachers in my school talk, you'd think there were ten principals in the school, not just one."[58]

Just as we are accustomed to thinking that there is only one principal of a school, we are also in the habit of assuming that the general terms we use to describe important components of school life, like support or feedback, have shared meanings for everyone. Stage theory underscores that these terms and others can be very differently experienced and interpreted. As we saw in reviewing Kegan's stages, feedback can be a welcome contribution (Interindividual I), a necessary nutrient (Interpersonal I), or an unwelcome intruder (Imperial I). Similarly, support may mean allowing for autonomy (Interindividual I), providing critical input (Institutional I), giving only positive reinforcement (Interpersonal I), or staying out of sight (Imperial I). The stage framework provides important information about how an individual is experiencing various components of school or home life and about how we are being experienced as we go about carrying out our professional responsibilities.

Educators persistently speak of the importance of recognizing and re-sponding to individual differences among children. Yet group teaching methods are most persistent. If stage theories underscore the significance of adult difference, will we continue to provide only professional develop-ment opportunities aimed at "group growth?" Responding to adults as the unique individuals they are – and recognizing that even when we respond similarly, they do not necessarily experience our responses as we mean them – may remind us of the importance of providing opportunities for individual and group learning to correspond more closely to the ways growth and learning are taking place.

5 *Men's and Women's Development: How Are They Different?*

Within seconds of asking the question, every hand in the room is raised high. Fifty teachers and administrators from a wide range of schools agree without hesitation that men and women are different. "How many of you have noticed differences between the men and women with whom you work?" the staff developer asks, narrowing the question to focus on adults who choose specific occupations. Perhaps the adults who elect to be educators are more alike than different. Once again, however, all hands are raised. "What have you noticed about men and women in their forties and older?" the group leader queries, since the majority of participants are veterans. From around the room comes a flurry of comments:

"Women are more enthusiastic."

"Men like to work alone."

"Men over forty are tired."

"Women are challenged."

"Women are emotional."

"Men are more stable."

In fact, we are only just beginning to understand something about the development of men or women in adulthood. Further, the vast majority of research on human development has been conducted by men on largely male samples. Most of Lawrence Kohlberg's theory of moral development, for example, derives from studies of males. Levinson's initial developmental study isolated the seasons of a *man's* life. Though researchers are beginning to turn their heads in the direction of women and seem to be uncovering some important areas of difference, the number and range of systematic studies of women's lives necessary to establish a firm research base are still lacking.

As we begin our explorations, it is important to note that researchers are not all in agreement about the existence or origins of male/female differences. It is argued, for example, that differences in behaviors and attitudes are primarily shaped by cultures. According to this view, emerging research is speculative and runs the risk of attributing broad cultural influences to basic gender differences.[59]

Without conclusive data, individual perceptions and individual case histories become increasingly important. If the fifty teachers and administrators gathered for an in-service workshop on one afternoon all believe men and women are different, chances are their beliefs influence what they think, what they feel, and how they act toward male and female colleagues. If an individual's life experience contradicts a prescribed formula for adult growth and change, such differences among men and women merit particular attention. They merit attention not because they point to deviance, but because they establish and clarify difference.

This chapter explores the issue of gender differences. It draws upon the perceptions of male and female educators and the experiences of Archer's teachers and principal. It reviews recent and emerging research. Because so little is known in this area, the chapter also points to important gaps in our understanding and suggests the potential implications of this area of inquiry for schools. Perhaps the most important point to be made in this chapter and the next is the value of *transcending* differences, whatever their origins.

PRACTITIONER VIEWS

How are men and women different? Are men and women in education different? For months, I asked these questions wherever I went. I asked teachers and administrators to talk with me about their views and experiences and to write down their thoughts and feelings. I asked men and women at all ages and stages in their lives and careers, at all school levels, from public and private schools, and from various parts of the country. I even asked some children, to see how deep impressions of gender differences run.

From their initial responses, I formed several impressions. While it is stereotypically believed that men are dispassionate and women emotional, this area of inquiry seems to bring out the passion in everyone. Not a single man or woman I asked answered without emotion. Men, in particular, displayed strong feelings – especially in response to many of the more widely accepted generalizations about males. Next, everyone had an opinion and no one denied the existence of difference. From "Vive la difference!" to "of course there are differences between men and women, as there are differences among all people," no one believed that men and women are the same.

A number of practitioners began their replies with a disclaimer. By acknowledging the complexity of human development, they hoped to avoid oversimplifications. Nevertheless, each spoke of broad differences. One woman characteristically began:

> My thoughts on male and female teachers and principals are based on twenty-three years of working in schools, and they do involve generalizations. I don't like talking in generalizations because there are so many exceptions, but having said that, I'll try to outline my overall impressions.

While individual responses were worded differently, there were definite commonalities. Listening to men and women educators voice their perceptions reveals a number of themes and suggests potential solutions. A veteran administrator from an urban parochial school comments:

> Many men seem to be so task-oriented that they ignore the human interaction or feelings of persons. Many operate from a hierarchical structure, passing on decisions or placating individuals rather than involving persons in cooperative decision making. In most situations, it seems, they feel a collaborative process is too time consuming and not "cost effective." These men need to feel secure enough to become learners in an educative process that will challenge them to go beyond their hierarchical perception of reality. Only when the present inculturation process is recognized and changed will there be any hope for a cooperative, collaborative process that enables women and men to share equally in decision making.

An orientation of women and girls toward relationships and of men and boys toward tasks is a characteristic perception.

> I've found myself to be much more intent on bonding and forming relationships than my husband or my adolescent son. My daughter expresses the same tendency. She is constantly on the phone, she pairs up with friends for school projects, and she likes doing her homework in a room with others or with music blaring. My son, in contrast, is a loner. He works silently in his room, he rarely talks on the phone, and he gets together with other adolescents at *their* initiation.
>
> Friends and relationships are critical to me; they are not so to my husband. I am really his best and only friend. Not only couldn't I imagine not having relationships outside of my marriage, but I couldn't imagine working in the absence of those relationships. Whenever I get into a tangle at work, my husband reminds me that I should not try to mix personal and professional relationships. I'm never quite sure what he means by professional relationships since it seems to me that all relationships are inevitably personal.

Reporting what he is learning about the ways men and women respond to complicated moral dilemmas, a young male teacher confirms this perception of male/female differences:

> It seems that women respond more often than not out of care and concern for relationships, while men tend to respond out of a conception of what is just or right.

He goes on to raise questions about the possible extension of these differences beyond moral choices to specific aspects of schools:

> Are there differences in conceptions of curriculum? Of supervision? Of evaluation? Do men and women view the process of learning in different terms? How does each define success? Will these differences affect how and what children learn and how their learning is judged?

Asking and responding to questions like these is just one of the potential benefits of raising issues of developmental differences.

One teacher finds the characteristic orientations of men and women toward tasks and relationships in the behavior of adolescents:

> Two students are running for a student government leadership position. The boy recites a list of his accomplishments. The girl points to her ability to get along with others. Listening to these speeches, I am struck by the differences. One is talking about the fact of doing, the other about the process of doing – one about tasks, one about relationships.
>
> What's really interesting, I think, is that both seem unaware of the dichotomy they are perpetuating. Nor are others in the room aware of it. We have learned to take these fundamental differences for granted. Even the way we listen is likely to be shaped by whether we are male or female.

A tendency to emphasize relationships appears to have both positive and negative implications for school work. One teacher/administrator describes her preference for team teaching with males. In her experience, male partners focus on the main issues of teaching without becoming distracted by peripheral details. More importantly, when disagreements arise, they are quickly resolved between this woman and her male partners, who "do not allow professional differences to spill over into the social domain." In contrast, female partners have been less willing to find solutions and have carried professional differences into personal relationships. These tendencies can then make subsequent work and nonwork interactions problematic.

In her role as an administrator, this educator has watched these same characteristics manifest themselves as diverse and gender-related leadership differences. To the extent that men can be less reliant on external input and opinions, some male administrators appear more comfortable with a "top-down approach to administration." From this vantage point, they are able to make decisions and take action. Women, on the other hand, often "adopt a more democratic approach, asking for feedback and seeking information." She concludes: "The male administrators that I have known seem to be more at ease than women administrators directing the traffic of opinions, setting priorities, and making decisions."

Just as this woman's judgments evolve from her experiences and perceptions, so, too, do the perceptions of others influence their opinions. A middle-aged male teacher explains: "Of course there are differences between men and women. Some of the differences are within the person, and others are in the eyes of the beholder." Subsequent comments reinforce his view of the importance of individual and gender-related perceptions:

You know, come to think of it, those women principals who tolerated more rule bending and whose attitudes toward students seemed to be more genuinely understanding seem to me to behave more like men than I perceive women to behave. I wonder if even this point of view is a function of my maleness?

Not only may men and women, boys and girls feel, think, and behave differently, but variations in the ways they perceive themselves and each other may themselves emanate from basic gender differences. Likewise, an individual's particular developmental phase or stage can affect his or her response. A young male teacher's reaction to the question of gender difference is colored by the idealism of young adulthood. Recognizing this himself, he explains: "I must say this issue irritates me in my idealism." Continuing to respond with a noticeable degree of anger, impatience, and indignation, he urges us to accept and appreciate differences without judging them, to work together, capitalizing on each other's strengths and compensating for each other's weaknesses.

If individual perceptions as well as ages and stages of development can sway our judgments, what are the effects of socialization? Along with researchers, many of these educators wonder if differences between boys and girls, between men and women reflect basic and universal distinctions or merely represent the potent forces of society. One woman teacher shares: "Aside from their distinct roles in procreation, men and women are basically alike. Society has made them different."

Another respondent also believes in the power of external influences. Her experiences as mother and teacher, however, have exposed her to "subtle, yet definite, predispositions that most boys and girls are born with that merely get molded and channeled by the environment." She describes the evolution of her thinking:

I am a product of a fifties "you can be anything you want to be" mentality combined with a sixties early-women's-movement emphasis on and criticism of sex role stereotyping. Then in the seventies, I began having children, and my theories, along with my sense of control, went up in smoke. The truth about what I have observed in my own children and others' is that there are real and basic differences between most boys and girls.

I am amazed at how often I see preschool boys gravitating to large motor activities and spatial-arrangement play: blocks, climbers, guns. (In my house, where toy guns are outlawed, graham crackers and twigs are invested with power.) Girls in my first- and second-grade classes were, as a rule, noticeably more "mature," better able to concentrate for longer periods of time on fine motor tasks, more verbal both orally and on paper, and able to direct their conversations, stories, and play sooner.

Differences in innate tendencies between boys and girls must imply differences for men and women. As time goes on, however, initially innate differences must become environmentally reinforced.

From a developmental perspective, where growth implies complex and ongoing interactions between the self and the environment, distinctions between culture and heredity are unclear and inexact at best. How individuals view themselves *and* their worlds is the primary context for understanding human similarities as well as differences.

Interestingly, children note the same kinds of distinctions between boys and girls and men and women. The children I talked with described these differences and traced them primarily to learning. Since adults have had more time to be molded by society, children see themselves as more alike than men and women, who have had a longer time to settle into their differences. While it is believed that girls are generally "more sensitive" and "more open," tending to get hurt more easily than boys both physically and emotionally, "they're both the same in plenty of ways." Boys and girls can be smart, and they can become good at the things they try to do. "They can be as good at anything as they want."

One shared observation of children relates to the idea that girls and women are more sensitive than boys and men. This is a view that girls and women are typically "more open." One early adolescent believes: "When girls are all together, they talk and spill out everything. Boys, they never talk to each other; they just play basketball." A slightly older adolescent boy confirms: "Women are more open; men tend to close up."

Reviewing these and previous comments, an interesting – perhaps surprising – trend seems to be unfolding. Where much of the literature on women's development points to the ways in which women's tendencies have often been labeled inferior and sometimes even deviant,[60] these comments appear to cast women's predispositions in a more positive light. Some respondents did share the more characteristically heard view that women are overly emotional while men are more rational, more reliable, and more stable. On the whole, however, the perceived characteristics of women are largely positive. Perhaps qualities commonly ascribed to women are particularly adaptive to educational environments. This is one of the gaps in our knowledge that systematic study might address.

A male administrator with more than twenty years of administrative experience says, "To me, women administrators are tougher, smarter, and more patient than men administrators." An equally seasoned educator concludes:

> There certainly are differences between men and women that surface at work. I should preface this by saying that I was the third female high school principal in the state, and at the time I was especially sensitive to differences, as were my male colleagues. Four differences stand out for me. Women are more consensus oriented, more invested in the happiness and well-being of others, and less self-centered than men. Women's decisions are also more often subject to questioning and must be well explained and defended.

From another state, the comments of a longtime teacher and administrator in a large urban system reflect similar sentiments. Although many female traits seem to be of value, being a woman – especially at the administrative level, where men predominate – seems to carry certain liabilities. "In my experience, fundamental educational changes initiated by a woman are rarely given the same value and serious consideration as those prescribed by males." Describing a controversy over the distribution of contraceptives to high school girls, this educator goes on to say that a decision to give out birth control devices to adolescent girls through the schools was "made by three males, two of them bachelors." While the two women on the school board were opposed to the practice, they were not consulted at the time of the decision. Nor were any provisions included to distribute contraceptives to males. Her conclusions extend beyond her feelings of inequity in this particular situation to the potential implications for the development of future female leaders and to the ways women may be recognized or discredited in public meetings.

Even on issues clearly gender related, men apparently feel the authority and power to make major decisions unilaterally. For this and other reasons, many women seeking positions of prominence may think that they have to act like men to succeed. This "acting" may include being cold, objective, hard-line, and inhumane. In turn, men may feel more comfortable with women who fit into this thinking pattern rather than women who combine efficiency with gentleness and flexibility.

I've watched the way women are recognized to speak in a public forum where a male is presiding. The second time around, women who are "precise" on the point are afforded the floor again. Women who voice an interest in bringing in "the human element" find their comments less welcomed and perhaps subsequently shut out.

Of course, not all educators are strident about male/female differences; nor do men and women in education necessarily believe that female characteristics are more functional in an educational setting. In a number of cases, educators are unaware of differences, have not thought about them, or act on unexamined assumptions. One male teacher says he never really thinks about gender differences because working in schools leaves so little time to reflect on practice and because the issues are too complex. A young woman teacher assumes there are differences even though she has rarely thought about them. When pressed on the topic, she shrugs in dismay: "There must be differences beyond the obvious. But what are they?" A male mathematics teacher, likewise puzzled by the question, concludes:

> Sure, there are differences between men and women, but I have been naive to them in education. I have worked for men and women principals, housemasters and department chairs. My only criterion for judging them, however, has been their level of competence. I suspect I've probably approached them differently, but I have assumed my reason for this has been personality rather than gender. Now that you ask, I think I'll pay more careful attention. I know sexism occurs in schools as well as in society, but I'm not conscious of it as often as I should be.

If these conversations with educators are at all typical, discussions of gender differences can disclose assumptions as well as raise awareness. More fundamentally, discussion and debate about the possibility of human differences is central to the educational process and promises to inform and enrich the way educators understand and respond to each other as well as to children. From a research perspective, systematically collected data are essential. Until long-term studies of the lives of men and women are compiled and examined, our knowledge of adult development will remain limited.

WRITING AND RESEARCH ABOUT MEN AND WOMEN IN SCHOOLS
For the most part, writing and research about schools does not address differences between men and women. Dan Lortie's references to men and women in his book on teachers are uncharacteristic. Talking to teachers, Lortie discovered that most young teachers do not consider classroom teaching a permanent or complete occupation. Men often combine teaching with other jobs and typically want to move into administrative positions. Many women have marriage and family on their minds and, at the time of Lortie's initial study, thought about leaving or interrupting their teaching. If neither promotion nor marriage is realized, these teachers can experience a general feeling of incompleteness or loss. This is certainly the case for Janet Kramer.

When women believe they will remain unmarried, they often expand their work commitments. Their level of satisfaction, however, varies. Married women, on the other hand, both devote less of their "life space" to teaching and derive more satisfaction from it. Lortie concludes that there is an inverse relation between involvement and satisfaction for these women. Job satisfaction increases with less rather than greater involvement.

Research on women's motivations for and interests in school work reveals distinct patterns. Examining the motivation of women in seeking administrative positions, researchers discovered women's interests focused on developing new skills and having an impact on the organization. More responsibility, higher salary, and job security were all secondary factors.[61] In a related series of workshops, researchers learned that women were very uncomfortable vying for power and even more uncomfortable achieving it. Central to their concern was the loss of relationships and the isolation that might result. Some workshop participants even described power as "lonely," emphasizing the importance these women place on relationships.[62] If men and women have different attitudes toward financial gains, work satisfaction, and the attainment of power, these attitudes are likely to affect their work.

Although research on male/female differences among educators is limited, studies that have been conducted do reveal differences of importance. A recent study of women administrators in schools points to a particular female organizational culture created by women leaders. This study contends there are differences in the ways male and female administrators spend their time, in the ways they interact day-to-day, in the priorities that guide their actions, in how they are perceived, and in the satisfaction they derive from work. Men and women administrators appear to lead differently, to communicate differently, and to have different decision-making styles.[63] There is certainly a need for additional research.

Notably, the wave of school reform reports in the 1980s paid little attention to male/female differences. One important exception was Lightfoot's study of the good high school.[64] It is not surprising that all of Lightfoot's schools had male principals. One of the most novel aspects of the education profession is, in fact, "the dominance of women in the pool from which leaders traditionally emerge and the absence of women at the top of the hierarchy."[65]

Examining the characteristics of the leaders in each of six good high schools, Lightfoot pointed to an unusual integration of male/female characteristics. All of these principals exhibited some of the stereotypical qualities embodied in male leaders. They could display the impeccable and cold rationality of the military man, the strength, energy, and enthusiasm of the coach and the wisdom and strength of the father figure. Rather than stand alone, however, each principal recognized intimacy and support as essential ingredients of effective leadership. Each needed an intimate colleague, someone to trust and to turn to for advice, counsel, and criticism. Lightfoot explains: "In the most compelling cases, the leaders have consciously sought to feminize their style and have been aware of the necessity of motherly interaction with colleagues and staff.[66] In addition to their typically masculine characteristics, these effective principals "reveal many tendencies more in keeping with the feminine principle of relationship – a sensitivity to the cultural forms already embedded in the institutions, a need for expression of feelings with trusted intimates, and authority partly shaped by dependence on relationships."[67]

These kinds of discoveries invite additional research. Not only may they reveal the need to integrate traditionally dichotomized human qualities, but they appear to hold the promise of more effective school leadership. Further transfer of these school-wide qualities to the classroom will provide children with new models of leading, learning, and living.

RESEARCH ON MALE/FEMALE DIFFERENCES

Studies of Sex Differences in Boys and Girls

In their comprehensive review of studies designed to test for differences in boys and girls, Maccoby and Jacklin discovered that many popular beliefs have little or no factual basis. Common notions that girls are more social than boys or that boys have higher levels of self-esteem than girls do not hold up to testing. Ambiguous and inconclusive findings have resulted from studies relating to anxiety, ability level, competitiveness, dominance, compliance, and nurturance. Only in four areas are differences confirmed. Girls appear to have greater verbal ability than boys. In turn, boys demonstrate advanced visual-spacial and mathematical abilities and greater physical and verbal aggressiveness.[68]

Maccoby and Jacklin's generalizations are based on the analysis of a wide range of studies. An assessment of their validity, however, must be tempered by the knowledge that the scope and methods of the studies often differ. Further, few of the studies include data on adults. In the area of self-esteem, both sexes appear very much alike in their overall self-confidence and satisfaction throughout childhood and adolescence. There is little information about adulthood, however, and evidence that does exist reveals no sex difference. There are important differences among boys and girls in the area of self-confidence. Girls generally rate themselves higher in areas of social competence, and boys more often see themselves as strong, powerful, and dominant. These findings do appear to be related to more recent research on adults.

Maccoby and Jacklin take a view earlier expressed that efforts should be aimed at minimizing rather than exaggerating sex differences. A combination of typically male- or female-typed characteristics may be important for an individual to function adequately at varied tasks. Masculine power may help a man establish credibility with his peers, but it may prove counterproductive in his role as husband or father. Diverse and typically sex-typed behaviors may also be needed together to perform a task adequately. Taking effective care of the young, for instance, requires both nurturance *and* assertiveness. Socializing a girl to the traditional feminine norm of passivity or nonassertiveness may, in fact, impede her ability to care for others.[69]

Two final points made by Maccoby and Jacklin are relevant to a discussion of sex differences as they inform the growth and development of adults in schools. First, differences *among* boys and men and girls and women may be just as important to study as those between the sexes. Maccoby and Jacklin point out that men and women *both* tend to take a tougher stance toward children of their own sex than toward children of the opposite sex. This point underscores the need to have both women and men involved in the care and education of children. They explain that

> when boys need control, men can probably provide it more effectively than women; when boys need support for independent action, they are more likely to get it from women. The reverse situation probably applies for girls: close control from their mothers, indulgence and/or encouragement in adultlike behavior from their fathers. The major implication of these considerations would appear to be that a healthy balance of focus is best maintained when adults of both sexes are involved in the care of children of both sexes.[70]

The authors also raise a relevant issue with regard to men and women and the teaching profession when they ask if there are particular sex characteristics that make men or women more or less suitable for certain occupations. Responding in the negative, they conclude there is no reason to establish job affiliations on the basis of sex. They do, however, raise an important qualifier about women:

> Perhaps the traditional assignment of certain jobs to men and others to women has come about not so much because men are in jobs that call for aggressiveness as because women, being slower to anger, are less likely to protest onerous assignments. We have seen that girls are more likely than boys to comply with demands that adults make upon them; although it has not been demonstrated, it appears likely that in adulthood as well they will "take orders" from authority figures with less coercion. To put the matter bluntly, they are easier to exploit.[71]

The need for both male and female role models in education is expanded here to include specific and explicit teaching of gender differences. Such teaching must be designed to help teachers as well as students understand long-standing and deeply ingrained differences between the sexes that will take time, recognition, and practice to mitigate.

Additional Evidence

While there has been a tendency to generalize the growth processes of men to all adult development, researchers and practitioners in psychology and psychiatry have repeatedly identified sex differences in their male and female subjects or clients. Freud's theories of sexual development are well-known examples of sex-linked developmental differences. More recently, Erik Erikson has described differences in male/female growth and acknowledged the need to study girls and women in their own right.

Erikson is relatively well known for his observations of differences in the ways boys and girls use space. Observing children's play at the University of California, Berkeley, Erikson noted that the constructions of girls emphasize interior-space configurations as opposed to the dominant exterior-space constructions of their male counterparts. From these observations, Erikson builds a case of acknowledging basic differences in the ways boys and girls experience themselves and others, related in large part to the "ground plan of the human body." The conception of woman's "inner space" is reflected in her orientation to both family and interpersonal relationships.[72] Archer's women teachers focus on marriage and family in their conversations about work. Often they express feelings of urgency or conflict in ways not commonly heard from the male teacher or the principal. For these two men, personal interactions seem less immediately significant than professional relationships. The opposite is true for their female colleagues. Nevertheless, both Don Bolter and Peter Samson place a high value on family and contend that family is an important part of their lives.

In plotting the course of human development, Erikson notes a difference in the ways males and females develop a sense of identity. The identity of boys and men is formed by establishing independence and autonomy. The development of identity in girls and women is tied to relationships. Establishing one's individuality is *not* part of the process of identity formation for girls and women. Erikson explicitly states:

> [T]he student of development and practitioner of psychoanalysis knows that the stage of life crucial for the emergence of an integrated female identity is the step from youth to maturity, the state when the young woman, whatever her work career, relinquishes the care received from the parental family in order to commit herself to the love of a stranger and to the care to be given to his and her offspring.[73]

Perceptions among school people of women's orientation toward relationships and men's focus on task is thus corroborated by Erikson's research. According to Erikson, female development progresses from one set of relationships to another. For both girls and boys, the initial phase of trust is grounded in establishing a firm and positive relationship between a child and his or her primary caretaker. Once established, development for boys passes through successive phases of separation until the time of young adulthood. While identity is formed for boys by developing a sense of independence, girls' identity seems to be fashioned through interdependence.

Although Erikson acknowledges these differences in his writing, his scheme for development reflects only the growth path for boys and men. Omission of the unique experiences and developmental characteristics of girls and women, here and in other dominant theories, has made it difficult for females to find themselves in these conceptions.

An emphasis on affiliation and an orientation to family have been prominent themes in female development noticed by other theorists. Tracing the growth patterns of two men and one woman, Robert White notes that issues of family, childbearing, and interpersonal relations are initially tied to the woman's sense of self-worth. In contrast, the two men look to advancing in their careers and establishing their independence to attain self-esteem.

Unable to have children immediately after marriage, Joyce Kingsley, the woman in White's case analysis, begins training to become a social worker as a temporary substitute. Later, she experiences conflict around getting more education and raising a family – a conflict neither of the men expresses, although both marry and have children. In reviewing the life patterns of the two men, White concludes: "[I]t is interesting that in both cases...the interests of careers tend to take precedence over those of family,"[74] while for Joyce, "her family is the central concern of her life."[75]

Roger Gould also points to differences between the development of men and women. Deciding whether to have a child is seen as one of the most important choices a woman can make. Whether it is made early or late, it has a potentially significant impact on a woman's orientation toward work. A woman may postpone childbearing until her thirties. At this point, Gould believes, when men are forging ahead with their careers, women will struggle with a decision that can no longer be put off. Gould concludes that when career and child raising are combined,

almost all women feel some pull toward their children and away from work....The pull toward motherhood and away from work saps a woman's energy and attention in both areas.[76]

How do women teachers and administrators experience or cope with these possible ambivalences? Do men in schools feel similar pulls? Can concerns for family diminish the energy and commitment available for work? How can we help men and women balance their multiple commitments? A forty-year-old female assistant superintendent, married and the mother of two children, shares:

> Probably the greatest career obstacle any woman faces is marriage; I love my husband and children, but let's face it: I can only accomplish so much. So my career has been a series of tradeoffs. I don't believe it *is* possible for any woman – or man, for that matter – to give one's all to a career and still be fair to a family.[77]

Perhaps this view expresses a "truth" for men and women, as this educator suggests. Perhaps her view is affected by the very fact that she is a woman. These are the kinds of issues and questions raised to be explored by talking with men and women in schools and pressing for more systematic research.

In either teaching or mothering, the intensity with which women embrace their roles may have further consequences for their personal development. Gould describes the intense pressures on young mothers:

> A degree of selflessness and merging is essential to good mothering, but all young mothers are under tremendous pressure to sacrifice their own development to the physical and emotional needs of their children.[78]

Can teaching have this same impact on women? Is the pressure more or less acute on women without children? How does it affect men?

Emerging Research

Issues of family and other interpersonal relationships form the core of what researchers and practitioners have recently discovered about adult development. Jean Baker Miller's work sets the stage for later theorists.

> There is no question that the dominant society has said, men will do the important work; women will tend to the "lesser task" of helping

other human beings to develop. At the onset this dichotomy means that our major societal institutions are *not* founded on the tenet of helping others to develop. All people need help in development at all stages, but it has been made to appear as if only children do.[79]

Miller's statement has implications for men's and women's development and for the work of schools. If men do the important work, then the labors of women are inherently diminished. If helping others to develop is a task left primarily to women, opportunities for adults and children to benefit from both sexes are limited. Nor is the growth of adults deemed important when only children are seen as needing help with their development. Do women or men feel valued as educators?

Miller suggests that the development of men and women proceeds in very different terms. While men tend to value doing, women more typically honor giving. Primary to the sustenance of women's psychological well-being are attachments and affiliations. Primary to the sustenance of men's psychological well-being are mastery and achievement. Where boys and men develop a sense of autonomy characterized by increasing individuation, young girls and women develop what has been variously called "a being-in-relationship,"[80] a "relational self,"[81] or an orientation toward responsibility for the care and inclusion of other people.[82]

One of the most forceful and articulate spokespersons for the expansion of developmental paradigms to include the experiences of both men and women is Carol Gilligan. Working in the area of moral development, Gilligan initially aligned herself with Kohlberg's views, accepting a model of growth based on increasingly complex and abstract reasoning. In this model, justice is defined by principles of right and wrong, independent of context.

In a study of women struggling to decide whether to have an abortion, Gilligan discovered that the language of selfishness, responsibilities, and obligations, rather than the expected terms of fairness and rights, framed their constructions. Moral dilemmas typically used in Kohlberg's research were not considered as hypothetical abstractions. Instead, the issues were consistently put in a context where the consequences for potential participants could be weighed and considered before offering a possible – though rarely absolute or conflict-free – resolution. In contrast to Kohlberg, who has found a relatively low stage of moral reasoning, in which judgments are interpersonally based, well-adapted to the needs and circumstances of women, Gilligan insists upon a link between the existence of this category and an implication of developmental inferiority. Such classification, she concludes, has far less to do with the quality of women's moral reasoning than with the standards that have been used to measure it.[83]

Gilligan's ongoing work with adolescents and adults continues to reinforce her conception that male and female development can be different. Other researchers have also uncovered differences. Mary Belenky and her colleagues have recently discovered different and distinct patterns in men's and women's thinking.[84] In a study replicating an aspect of Levinson's work with men, Wendy Stuart learned that women's growth does not always proceed through the "universal sequence" Levinson has postulated. While her study of women aged thirty-one to forty confirmed the centrality of motherhood and family to the emerging female identity, the tasks that confront women at different times during the life cycle can vary depending upon whether a woman chooses to marry and start a family in her twenties or to remain single and/or pursue a career during this time.[85]

Both men and women develop a Dream: a vision of themselves in the world that guides and motivates their development. Most men's Dreams focus on themselves and usually express hopes for success in their area of work. Women's Dreams typically include more than the dreamer and frequently form around desires for marriage and children.

Levinson has postulated the existence of a mentor as a crucial part of men's early development. Mentors help young male adults form and modify their Dream. Whether a mentor is developmentally significant for a woman depends on whether she chooses work or family as a primary task. For those women whose life structure centers upon becoming a wife and mother, mentor relationships are found to be less significant than for single or married women who devote themselves to forming an occupation. For women who marry and have a family before entering the work force at middle adulthood, the guiding role of a mentor may have a later place in a woman's life cycle than in a man's.[86] In either case, creating the conditions in schools for older adults to nurture younger adults and for veterans to support novices is developmentally important.

One significant aspect of Gail Sheehy's work has been to point out the areas in which the developmental sequences for men and women may follow divergent, asynchronous rhythms. During the first half of the life cycle, she explains, women generally experience more outer restrictions and inner contradictions than men. From midlife on, there is a reversal of this pattern. When men begin to turn inward to reclaim the aspects of the self that have been rejected on the road to career advancement, women, whose children may now be grown, begin to think about striking out in the world to make their fortunes.[87] The following poem by Ric Masten captures this point perfectly.[88]

Coming and Going*

I have noticed
that men
somewhere around forty
tend to come in from the field
with a sigh
and removing their coat in the hall
call into the kitchen

> *you were right*
> *grace*
> *it ain't out there*
> *just like you've always said*

and she
with the children gone at last
breathless
puts her hat on her head

> *the hell it ain't*

coming and going
they pass
in the doorway.

Midlife adults invariably laugh and applaud when they hear this poem. Then, one by one, they share the ways in which they find themselves in relationships where one partner is coming and the other going. Halfway through an intense summer institute, a middle-aged male principal stands up and confesses: "Now I know why I've been sitting here wishing I were fishing. I only came because my wife was going to a conference!" Another male educator at midlife shares:

I have been married for sixteen years. My wife is a reading teacher and I am a high school principal. We both are intellectually curious and

*"Coming and Going" from *Deserted Rooster* by Ric Masten (Carmel, Calif.: Sunflower Ink). Reprinted by permission of the author.

career-oriented. Moreover, neither one of us believes being career-oriented excludes being family-oriented; we believe both are possible.

In the early years of our marriage, we worked to establish our-selves, supporting one another in our respective careers – I as a social studies teacher and she as an elementary teacher. We shared the common need to grow professionally, achieving a deeper understanding of our craft. I forged through the mire of a master's program and continued into the realm of the Ph.D. At the same time, I moved professionally from the confines of the classroom into the arena of building administration.

During this time, my wife and son's mother became absorbed with parenting. Soon, she found herself in a professional void. By the time my professional development began to slow down, her latent desire for professional growth was just beginning to reemerge. I found myself walking in the door of family life only to discover my wife walking out to renew her career interests. We were out of sync.

Just as Miller's and Gilligan's expanded insights into adult development necessitate new language and fresh perspectives, Sheehy believes that some of the basic terms of adult development must be redefined to adequately describe men's and women's experiences. Erikson's concept of generativity, or helping the younger generation assume responsibility for adult life, matches the need of mature adults to nurture children and young adults. It is important for most men in midlife to have opportunities to teach, serve, and nurture others. Since serving others is what many women typically do up until midlife, their task may call for a period of assertiveness and self-declaration. Providing mid-career women with leadership and professional development opportunities is likely to match their developmental inclina-tions so that both the school and the midlife adult can flourish. Providing mid-career men with opportunities to teach or to take responsibility for training may optimize men's developmental potential during this time of life.

Describing the characteristic orientations of girls and women to relationships, Miller, Gilligan, and others are careful to distinguish attention and responsiveness from altruism. Attending to the experiences of others and caring for and about relationships are basic to women's growth and to all human experience. Giving oneself up to another, however, can be an unproductive and unhealthy form of self-abandonment.

Nancy Chodorow's work in the area of adult development specifically distinguishes mature from immature dependence. Like other theorists – particularly practicing clincians who generally work with adults whose self-system is failing or problematic – Chodorow points out that getting lost in relationships can be just as debilitating as cutting oneself off from others in a bid to establish independence.[89] One woman describes what it is like for her when her former husband returns to visit their children:

> I get smaller and smaller when he's around. It's like his needs and feelings fill up the room. All I know is how he thinks about every-thing. He gets bigger and bigger and I start feeling his feelings and thoughts....I can't even figure out what I feel or think. My whole life has been taking care of other people's feelings, so I don't even know my own.[90]

Marriage, mothering, teaching, and administering motivated by a sense of inescapable connection and responsibility can be both unsatisfactory for adults and problematic for the partners and children they seek to help. Instead, relationships initiated from a firm sense of self and a clear idea of values allow for both individuality and interdependence. Interdependence, rather than dependence or independence, may be the form of relatedness men and women will find most positive and productive. Emerging research pushes us to ask: What opportunities do the adults who work in schools have to interact? What are the nature and quality of adult interactions? Can we do more to increase and enhance interdependence among the adults in schools?

IMPLICATIONS OF THINKING ON MEN'S AND WOMEN'S DEVELOPMENT FOR ADULTS WHO WORK IN SCHOOLS

Theories of adult development reveal that men and women are continuing to grow and change throughout the life cycle and that individuals will have particular issues and concerns at different points in their lives. Theories of adult development further disclose differences between and among men and women that educators can use as a resource for understanding themselves and for responding to the adults who work in schools.

Differences in the developmental orientations of some men and women underscore the importance of having both male and female teachers and administrators in schools. The predominance of women as teachers and men as administrators presents children and adults with limited and stereotypical role models of both sexes. Schools can consciously work to bring men and women into a variety of educational roles, with initial emphasis on putting males in direct contact with children and affording women increased leadership opportunities This will allow children to see men and women in a variety of roles. It will also give adult educators expanded opportunities to express their individuality.

Educators must continue to minimize rather than maximize sex role stereotypes, both inside and outside the classroom. Materials and activities for children can be screened, roles and responsibilities for adults can be varied, and communication to parents or the community can be sensitive to these issues. A notice home about an upcoming bake sale, for example, is more appropriately addressed "Dear parents" than "Dear mothers."

The nature of relationships in schools can be particularly informed by emerging theories of developmental differences. Relationships need not be fashioned on extremes where, at one end, a sense of self is lost or, at the opposite end, abstract principles of right and wrong are allowed to supersede consideration for the needs of individuals. Instead, decisions and actions can be mediated by a perspective that includes taking responsibility for others *and for oneself* and considering the specifics of each person and situation. This approach seems especially well suited to the emphasis of school improvement programs on site-specific solutions. Only on this level can solutions respond to variations in individual contexts.

A propensity to give oneself over to the care and nurturance of others is manifested by some women and may be a particular liability of development to which women and men educators are especially vulnerable. Teachers who depend on their students for self-definition and worth will eventually discover that externally derived self-worth is inevitably finite and ultimately disappointing. Individuals invariably give precedence to their own needs; and children, no matter how devoted to their classroom teacher, move on each June.

Educators who describe themselves as "burned out" frequently say they feel let down by others and devoid of personal resources. Aside from the real-life forces that can wear down men and women in education and other service professions, individuals can be worn down or burned out from the inside by persistent efforts to be nurtured from without. When individuals constrain or suffocate the growth of others, they often reinforce relationships of negative or excessive dependence, rather than creating bonds of interdependence and encouraging a sense of positive self-worth. In these kinds of relationships, men, women, and children – parent and child, teacher and student, employer and employee, care provider and care receiver – need more and develop less.

The intense interest of many women in marriage and family has a number of implications for school life. Gould says women will inevitably feel torn between their allegiances to home and work, and women teachers often talk about these issues. Unmarried women, like Janet Kramer, can feel incomplete without such a relationship. Married women teachers without children frequently frame their current or future decisions about having children as a conflict. Lortie has maintained that the structure of teaching makes it possible for women to take periodic leaves and return without loss of salary or position. Yet with an increased emphasis on career for women as well as economic pressures requiring women to work, these structural factors are less relevant. Paid maternity and paternity leaves are one possible solution. An equally viable and longer-term remedy might well exist in the creation of on-site day care facilities for teacher/parents. Such facilities already exist in some business settings and are believed to decrease parental anxieties and increase productivity. Schools seem like an obvious and appropriate context for similar efforts, particularly where school enrollments are declining and there is available classroom space. As experienced educators retire and young adults enter teaching, such facilities will have increasing relevance.

The structure of school administration makes it hard for women and men to combine work and family obligations. Perhaps this is, in part, why many women who choose school administration do not have families, or wait until their children are grown. Pressures on men to achieve do not always make waiting possible. Many male administrators simply do not have the time to spend with their families. One male high school principal explains that he spends an average of four nights a week at meetings. He is grateful to his wife for managing life at home.

If teaching and other social-service professions are especially well suited to women's affiliative style of development, how do men who choose teaching as a career adapt? For some, it is not an issue. Don Bolter, one of two male teachers at Archer Elementary, describes his feelings about working in a predominantly female environment:

> Rarely do I think about working in an all-female environment. Except for summer jobs, I've always worked in environments like this, so I really don't think about it. Other people think about it more than I do. People ask me about it, and that's the only time it ever comes up. It's not an issue for me at all.

In sharp contrast, a male high school teacher explains why he went to night school to get a law degree:

> I knew why I'd wanted that degree, and it had very little to do with any desire to become a lawyer. I had wanted to prove something to myself. In a society that has a low opinion of the teaching profession – especially of the men who enter it – I wanted to show that I could be "more than teacher." But once I'd proved that, I could let go of it. I could do what I wanted to do, which was to teach.[91]

In another system, male teachers have formed a group for men to give each other the support they feel they need to maintain a sense of dignity about their work. A woman teacher responds with both empathy and criticism: "I can certainly understand why teachers feel a need to support one another, but I think that's a need all teachers have – independent of being a man or a woman."

Initiating support groups for men, for women, or for both men and women educators is, in fact, a viable staff development option that results from an understanding of developmental patterns and differences (see Chapter 11). In the example above, the overlap between personal and professional issues is obvious. Teaching's low status is complicated by sex role stereotypes. Providing educators opportunities to talk about the personal and professional issues important to them is a way to diffuse individual uncertainties and build a sense of community among the adults within a school or system. Most meetings among adults in schools focus on responding to the needs of others: central office, parents, children. Focusing on *staff* needs can be a refreshing as well as an energizing variation.

Though the developmental patterns and issues for some men and women may be different, adults in schools have a great deal in common. Many of the solutions that acknowledge the needs of one sex, like the support groups described above, have relevance for everyone. Explicit efforts to help the adults in schools learn about their similarities and differences can encourage appropriate responses to individual needs and concerns.

6   *Practitioner Reactions*

One way I continue to emphasize the importance of paying attention to the adults in schools is to include the thoughts and feelings of practitioners. This chapter is made up of four essays by educators who have read the chapters on phases and stages of adult growth and possible gender differences and used the ideas as a springboard for writing about their own experiences. Their writings breathe life into the theories.

As you will see, each adult and each piece is distinct. Yet they share the theme of integration. Whether the subject is the life span or the influence of gender, the underlying message is the need to adopt a broad and inclusive perspective. When the whole life cycle is understood, the complexity of individuals can be embraced. When men and women balance their needs for achievement and affiliation, the debate about gender differences can be replaced by a discussion of human potential.

The essays that follow are written by adults who have been teachers and administrators. All their names and experiences are real. I begin each piece with a biography of the author, describing his or her background and identifying the key life issues each is facing.

Understanding the Wholeness of the Life Span
MARGARET LOEFFLER

Margaret Loeffler is director of the Primary Division of Casady School in Oklahoma City and an adjunct professor in the Department of Education at Oklahoma City University, where she teaches courses in language development and the psychology of learning. She has taught at the primary level for over thirty years, served a broad range of professional organizations, and given numerous workshops and presentations.

Margaret is trying to decide what she wants to do with the rest of her professional life. At age sixty-five, she is considering staying at a school, spending her time teaching adults, writing, and doing research. What does not interest her at the moment is thinking about retirement.

I read the ideas regarding life cycle phases that have been drawn from the thinking of developmentalists such as Erikson, Kegan, and Levinson. I was struck by how important I believe it is for people first to grasp an understanding of the wholeness of the life span, with all its rich diversity of opportunities and perplexities, before focusing in on the particulars of their own developmental phase. The importance of the life span perspective, I believe, is to get a view of the span of issues that present themselves at every phase and to develop a growing appreciation for the ways in which people, at different ages, are handling their own developmental dilemmas. Adults in schools might have a more sympathetic understanding of each other through a growing awareness of the life cycle tasks; students in schools should benefit from the adults' richer view of children's development and their more complete understanding of the tasks that face youngsters at each age. The effect that the milieu of the school has upon the resolution of developmental issues, for both adults and children, should be an area of deep concern for every thoughtful educator.

As a mature woman educator, entering one of the later phases of the life cycle after many years in my present school setting, I find myself reviewing the various phases of my past through a somewhat different lens than before. I am much more interested now in examining the values that have accrued from what I once perceived as the negative elements in each phase of the life cycle. Previously – in reading Erikson, for instance – I felt that the negative residue from each developmental crisis, to use an

Eriksonian term, was an emotional burden to be carried throughout the remainder of a person's life. Consequently, the goal at each phase of the life cycle should be to have as positive a resolution as possible to the developmental crisis of that phase. Now, I am not sure.

Whether this change in my thinking is the result of my own personal life experiences, or whether it is the outcome of a seminar with Joan and Erik Erikson in 1987, I'm not certain. It's probably a little of both. What I do know is that I'm beginning to understand the importance of a little leaven of distrust, of shame and doubt, of guilt, of loneliness and alienation, and of self-pity in the nurturing bread of life. Not only are these vital ingredients, but they provide the necessary contradictions to an overidealized view of what we believe the world should be like for us. If we didn't develop, as children, a measure of distrust along with our basic trust in the goodness of the world, we would be excessively vulnerable and open to the wiles of every fast talker whom we meet. Consequently, we would not have the necessary caution to discriminate, to recognize the ugly from the beautiful and the evil from the good.

Joan Erikson has created two weavings that provide a dramatic and graphic illustration of the important and necessary balance that must be achieved between the positive and negative aspects of development. These weavings also reflect the continuing flow of development and the relative duration of the various phases in the total life span. In her first weaving, Joan Erikson has included a handful of gray threads that appear at each phase and wind through all of the bright colors that have been used to represent the positive aspects. Joan characterizes these as the dystonic, or negative, elements that are a part of development, in contrast to the syntonic, or positive, aspects of each phase.

Through her selection of colored yarns, using eight strands for the warp and eight for the woof, she has been able to weave a fabric with eight vertical columns and eight horizontal rows. In each row, one square appears as a pure color forming an ascending staircase of pure colors on a diagonal from bottom left to top right. These brightly colored squares dramatically represent each of the successive phases in the life cycle that have been delineated by Erik Erikson. They also demonstrate the interweaving of these phases into each other, and the gray threads, woven through all of the strands, remind us of the traces of negative outcomes that we carry throughout life as remnants of the resolution of the developmental issues of each phase. These gray threads, I'm beginning to appreciate, also represent critical and necessary ingredients in the development of our personalities and our characters.

The weavings of Joan Erikson are not only aesthetically beautiful, but, more than any words, they convey in a graphic way the interweaving of the phases and the importance of the gray values in the fabric of our lives. They also lead to a compelling recognition that one is never finished with trust and mistrust or with identity or with initiative and guilt, but rather that these have their initial ascendance during a particular period and then continue to influence and to be modified by experience during each subsequent phase of life.

There is a further point that is beautifully and graphically made in Joan Erikson's second weaving. This concerns the relative lengths of the various phases of the life cycle. In our focus upon the importance of adulthood, I believe that we often forget that this period is only one act in the drama; it is not the whole play.

Joan Erikson's second weaving is an effective reminder that the years prior to adulthood and subsequent years are as vitally important to the total life development as the middle span. Through her weaving, she forces us to acknowledge that no one phase totally dominates the span. She has chosen a particular color for each phase of development, and she has carried these horizontally across the weaving in broad, colorful stripes. Eight horizontal rows of differing widths are thus created, indicating the approximate years of duration of each phase. As one moves vertically through the rows from bottom to top, one gets a strong sense of the relative durations of these phases and their relationships to each other.

I believe it is especially important that educators understand the strengths and positive values evolving from each life cycle phase and the role of each phase in total development. This is important to remember when we think about the individual in a particular phase, for we do sometimes forget that Erikson stresses the role of the individual in the society or culture and the roots of cultural values, rituals, and institutions that arise in these different phases. It is important, too, that we not view older or younger individuals only in terms of their relationships to adulthood. If we do, then each younger phase of development is seen only as a staging area for the next phase and is measured not by what is emerging but rather by what is not yet there. In the same way, if we compare all development to adulthood, those past this phase will be seen as no longer developing and, in fact, will be viewed as diminishing in their capacities, although research tells us that development continues unabated.

I believe it is vital that educators appreciate the equal importance of each phase of the life cycle, that we acknowledge our ignorance regarding many aspects of the development of the students in our schools. Few of us are developmentalists, although many recognize a need to have a better understanding of the students with whom we interact on a daily basis. Our tendency is to divide the student into several equal parts, and we deal only with the intellectual portion. We send the physical child to the physical education teacher or the doctor, the emotional child to the counselor or the psychologist, and the moral child to the minister or priest. If we are to embrace a life cycle perspective, we must recognize that the child is an integrated individual, just as we are integrated adults, and we must perceive our students and ourselves as developing individuals who are dealing with the developmental issues, continuously, in whatever setting we find ourselves. When we begin to view students and teachers and yes, even administrators, in this way, I believe we will find that the school will become a promising setting for developing adults – in fact, an enabling and supportive environment for everyone.

In introducing the life span perspective into a school setting, however, I have one fear: that there will be a superficial embrace of the approach leading to facile overgeneralizations by those with only a partial understanding. I believe that a comprehensive understanding of the life cycle perspective is essential if it is to provide a firm base for understanding and practice. This will require time and study by all who are involved. Just how this can be done within the time restrictions of in-service programs is a problem that must be solved, but I believe that its solution is critical to the effective use of the life span perspective within the school.

Becoming a Woman Administrator
EUGENIA M. NICHOLAS

Eugenia (Jeannie) Nicholas teaches seventh-grade English, as well as team teaching outside the English Department, at Day Junior High School in Newton, Massachusetts. Her focus is the teaching of writing. In fact, writing has become central to Jeannie's life. She is working on a children's book and has an idea for a novel. One of the reasons she is not currently pursuing an administrative position is her desire for time to write. Jeannie has been a middle school principal and assistant principal, a high school guidance counselor, and a teacher of grades five through nine.

At age forty-six, Jeannie finds herself at a "relaxed time" in her life, a time when she feels capable of using rather than questioning her skills and creativity. Teaching and writing provide a nice balance of solitary and group activity. Now that Jeannie has proven herself to herself and others, she is ready and willing to ask herself what *she* wants to do and to seek experiences that give expression to the skills and talents she chooses.

It was an austere room, with nothing on the walls. The window was long and narrow, stretching from ceiling to floor. The sun was the only welcoming official, giving hope that the room could be transformed to reflect its warmth. I was not surprised by the look of the room. It had been stripped appropriately by the previous resident. The surprise I felt accompanied the knowledge that I, as the new principal, would be the one to transform the room into a warm and inviting space.

The years since I had been a novice teacher passed with unforgivable speed. My thoughts wandered back, reconstructing the circuitous path that led me to the principal's office. Twenty-two years before, the role of principal would not have fit the feminine image I had accepted. I had grown up believing that those lucky enough to live in the United States had many choices unavailable elsewhere. Nonetheless, Horatio Alger was a man, and I had never read or heard anything about Mrs. Alger or Ms. Alger. I believed that some choices and opportunities were appropriate for men and others were appropriate for women. Women would most likely become the teachers. Especially at the elementary and middle school levels, teaching required specifically feminine traits. It required sensitivity, nurturance, a willingness to teach the alphabet coupled with a desire to provide a warm environment, making the home-to-school transition first bearable and later intriguing for the youngster. Men would most likely become the school principals. Especially at the secondary level, the principalship required specifically masculine traits: independence, strong-mindedness, a willingness to assume broad responsibilities, and a clear desire to be in charge.

When I started working in 1964, it made perfect sense that my job choice was teaching. I had already attained a goal of great significance for anyone who, like myself, comes from a working-class family. I had completed a Bachelor of Arts, had earned a Master of Arts in Teaching, and was starting a job. Yet I did not think of my job as a career. My lifetime work would center upon the growth and development of my own family, mirroring the models provided by my mother and aunts. Until I had my own children, I would care for the children in a community's family. Teaching was an acceptable and worthwhile occupation from which I would gain valuable nurturing experience. I had no long-range professional objectives or personal ambitions.

So I began to teach, and very quickly I discovered that the role of the junior high school English teacher expanded the boundaries of nurturing to include a vast number of skills. Those that I had learned from the women in my family – for instance, how to care for others within the home – transferred directly to the workplace. Creating and maintaining a healthy, productive classroom, where caring and warmth were as important as intellectual pursuits, was my response to students' social and intellectual needs.

The day-to-day business of running a classroom, however, involved much more. I was the person in charge, the one whose daily decisions included setting clear limits, planning activities to promote classroom cooperation, selecting units of study, finding materials to illuminate an idea, and developing assignments to engage students in a thoughtful learning experience. I was exploring a multifaceted definition of "nurturing" in which decision making, problem solving, intellectual strength, and assurance became more than assets; they were everyday necessities. Weaving through and strengthening my decisions was a sensitivity to and an anticipation of individual needs. What a wondrous feeling to have the emotional and intellectual freedom to create a setting in which students and I could grow.

I do not believe what followed was either predictable or automatic. It had simply become possible. The tangled web of thought and experience is not easily unraveled. Which one shapes the other? Are the shaping and reshaping mutual? Do they occur simultaneously? I do not know. What I do know is that my personal vision had already started changing.

During the next twelve years, the notion of a career slowly emerged from a patchwork of job experiences. I worked in five different schools in three school systems, taught grades five through nine, and spent two years as a high school guidance counselor. There were summer curriculum-writing workshops and team-teaching projects. Mostly there were kids: Brian, who barked like a dog until he decided he wanted to talk with humans; Nancy, who refused to wear shoes in school and poured her painful life into writing; John, a physically handicapped boy, who joyously discovered that his brain was not limited by his body.

Looking back, it seems as if there were a tape recording in my head, repeating the same question: What do I want to do to have fun with kids and learn more about them? There was a strong "here-and-now" orientation to my yearly decisions. I did not envision the frequent changes as heading toward a distant goal but rather as expanding my repertoire of skills, generating a continuing sense of excitement and growth. However, these exploratory years provided more than valuable and interesting experiences. They supplied information that enabled me to extend my personal boundaries. I could observe the demands and responsibilities of the principalship from a distance while working for five different principals. Each one made the job seem manageable. It became evident that the personality of the principal and the position itself combined to give each school an individual aura. One of the five was a woman, and this was as true for her school as it was for the schools of the male principals.

As I reflected on the woman principal's situation, I began to realize that I could move from teaching to administration. I came to view this step less as a gender issue and more as a personal choice. I knew that I could do the job as well as my female models did. I had grown comfortable making decisions and being in charge in my classroom, and I felt no conflict showing the masculine "character traits" required by my job. My focus always had been on the students. Now I was adding a private ingredient to my work: I wanted the power and influence to shape the school. Certainly this was for the kids; but I also wanted it for myself. The questions on my internal tape began to shift. The "should" questions (e.g., Should I, a woman, want to be in charge of a school?) gave way to quality-of-life concerns about such a choice. Would I become too career-oriented? Would there be too many trade-offs with my personal life? Would my relationships suffer?

I grappled with these questions for some time, weighing one imagined scenario after another in a risk-free game of "if then," which had great appeal because the possibilities were endless. Since I was the only player, I got to make the rules, change the rules, or break the rules as I wished. I could do a mental role-play, imagining the demands of a job and the demands of my personal life and creatively satisfying both. The Horatio Alger story became entwined in these fantasies, but with a critical new dimension: I was creating Alger's missing feminine counterpart. My initial thought that there *could* have been such a woman gave way to the startling thought that there *should* have been. These thoughts became too powerful to be contained by a make-believe game.

Again and again, I heard this message: "Is this fantasy or vision? Whatever you call it, the fact is you can't stifle it, ignore it or erase it. Isn't it time to explore it?" What I needed was real information about myself in a leadership role, as well as *real* information about the role itself. I had learned all I could by observing administrators and by fantasizing a new role for myself. Yet, I still wanted to know whether I could succeed as an administrator, and I still wondered whether I would enjoy a leadership position. The time had come to find out. My short-term goals became long-range plans, and these plans unfolded over the next decade as I became an assistant principal and then a principal.

In retrospect, my decision brought with it both excitement and fear. I had neither close female friends nor family members for models. None of my professional associates seemed readily available mentors. Any exploration and map making were up to me. My background was a powerful counterpoint to my decision, forcing me to face some critical questions. Yes, I could choose a position of leadership and responsibility. Could I, however, do the job well *and* retain my femininity? Would I have to become "masculine" in order to fulfill my ambition?

Like all new administrators, I learned by doing, making some mistakes and having some success. I learned that teachers, parents, central office staff, kids, custodians, secretaries, specialists, and virtually everyone else have expectations about what school administrators should do and how they should do it. I responded to these expectations using every bit of ability I could muster and without a single thought about what was masculine or feminine. I had no time to spend thinking about how a man might have handled a particular situation or, for that matter, about how another woman might have. I tried to make decisions that were in the best interests of the school community and took into account the needs of its various constituencies. When these needs were in conflict, I tried to listen very carefully and to sort out the issues clearly. Most of all, I tried to make decisions in which I believed.

My fear of becoming masculine evaporated. It was an unwanted tag-along from the days when I had little experience with which to confront or measure it. I no longer thought in those terms. Even if I *had* wanted to model my decisions on a definition of male or female behavior similar to the one I accepted at the beginning of my career, it would have been no easy task. Stereotyping male and female administrative behavior was only possible as long as one's knowledge remained extremely limited. Everyday experience was showing me both the unfairness and the *inaccuracy* of such predetermined ideas about the way men or women would function as leaders.

For example, I found some male administrators confrontative and some not. Some listened to their faculty, some didn't. Some had a vision of the way schools should be and worked toward it, while others saw only the facts of the present. Some shared decision-making, others did not. There was a phenomenal range of behavior in male administrators and the same vast range in female administrators. Both the men *and* the women could be pliant, straightforward, elusive, responsive, pedantic, abrupt, caring, creative, or conforming. Members of either sex might try new behaviors, growing as they expand their repertoire of responses. Or they might rigidly define their personal boundaries and never challenge their self-imposed limits. They could be excellent, mediocre, or ineffective administrators regardless of their sex. They could not, however, be divided into neat and predictable categories based on sex.

Who can pinpoint the specific moment when we see a familiar scene in a new light? Everything appears the same, and yet we know something fundamental has shifted. This happened to me when I realized how much harm is done by assigning character traits exclusively or "more appropriately" to one sex or the other. This stereotyping inhibits both men and women and wastes creative potential. My own ideas of masculinity and femininity have merged into a broader conception of humanity. The seeds were planted by work experiences and took root slowly, blossoming when I recognized that character traits belong to one sex or the other only as long as we foster such narrow ownership.

There is astonishing freedom and power in the knowledge that I can draw upon the strength and wisdom of my *human* heritage as I explore new jobs and new behaviors. Human beings can be dependent *and* independent, nurturing *and* needing nurture, giving *and* taking, assertive *and* submissive. I look back and see that I created my own invisible boundaries, which were as rigid or as porous as I allowed them to be. I chained myself, and also allowed others to chain me, to crippling perceptions of femininity and masculinity. My fight for freedom was long, painful, and mostly fought on a battlefield inside my head. The fears played and replayed on the internal tape have not been erased. They catalogue one woman's experience of the struggles and the possibilities of being human. How deceptively simple and easy this sounds when written in one sentence. How unlike the experiences that led to writing it.

The austere principal's office has become a memory. The barren walls have come alive with students' artwork, the display of color and imagination, warm and welcoming. Students seeing my office for the first time look around and their eyes widen a bit. They had, perhaps, expected the principal's office to be stern and imposing. They show surprise and pleasure as they appreciate the work of their peers: "Oh, I've never been in here before. This is really awesome." In addition to the students' work, they notice a Mexican rug that has become a wall hanging. Bold splashes of red, orange, cream, black, and brown show two children, a boy and a girl, walking away from us. Hand-in-hand they walk, pausing for a moment to look back over their shoulders. It is as if they, too, realize every step is part of a merging of past and present, leaving the future open for new and unimagined possibilities. After a brief pause, they move forward, continuing their journey.

One Man's Path to the Principalship
MARK KAUFMAN

Mark Kaufman is Director of Curriculum and Instruction for the Hamilton-Wenham Regional Schools and Superintendent of Schools for the Essex Elementary School District, Massachusetts. He has been principal of K-6 and K-8 elementary schools, a curriculum developer, educational consultant, and second- and third-grade teacher.

At age "thirty-eight-and-a-half," Mark describes himself at a period of developmental "consolidation." He has come to enjoy the role of facilitator on behalf of other people's development, rather than the person in charge who typically exercises power. He attributes this shift to having taken time away from work to reflect on himself and his practice. Unlike other men in administrative positions and nearing forty, Mark sees himself moving away from his family and back into the arena of career. Having climbed the career ladder quickly, he now feels "perched." In the next three to five years, he anticipates another climb, perhaps to a full-time superintendency. In this essay, Mark responds to my question, "In an occupation dominated by women, how do men experience themselves as teachers or administrators?"

I never planned to become a teacher. Although I worked in youth recreation programs during college, my goal was to choose a field more closely related to social change. Through my youth work, however, I came to appreciate the excitement, energy, and warmth that came from working with children. I also began to see teaching and education as potential vehicles for social change.

While I did not major in education, my university had a program that enabled me to become certified during my senior year. My teaching experience in a small, urban, blue-collar neighborhood proved to be as rewarding as my other work with children. I lived close to the school and was able to become involved with my students during school hours as well as after school and on weekends. I was sold on teaching as a career. In my first job as a primary-grade teacher in an alternative school, I found that my style and attitude matched the expectations for my role. Teaching, particularly at the elementary school level, is a nurturing activity, and I could comfortably express feelings in my work. As a young adult, I had boundless energy and time to give to my students, and my early work years were marked by an abundance of emotional and physical giving. The women around me shared and supported my approach to working with children. Nurturing and caring come naturally to women drawn to the teaching profession, and I did not feel out of place behaving like them.

In contrast, I observed more differences among the men in elementary teaching. Many male elementary teachers do not have a perspective on their work that allows for an integration of their "feminine" and "masculine" sides. For some, teaching means exercising control over students. For others, it meets a need for approval or recognition. For another group, it is a way to help children grow by giving and caring. For all men, however, there is a strong pull toward the masculine and away from feminine characteristics. There is seldom support from other men to share or develop their female sides. As a result, men are reluctant to express these characteristics in their work. As Levinson suggests, "The great majority of men in early adulthood form an identity suffused with 'masculine' images, desires and values...." A man, he believes, "must feel some anxiety about the feminine and must control or repress it to some degree. He must give greater priority to the masculine as he understands it. He can make room for the feminine, but he cannot fully integrate the two."[92] While I enjoyed teaching, I, too, struggled with the two sides of myself.

After teaching for five years, I began to feel less capable of putting out the constant emotional energy, of giving on a daily basis to twenty-five children. I developed other interests outside of school and had less time to dedicate to planning for so many individual needs. The classroom became a limiting environment with little adult contact and almost no flexibility to arrange my time. I wondered how I could continue to work with children, express the caring, feminine side of myself, but remove some of the limits imposed by the structure of teaching. I reflected back to college, where I had administered several youth programs, and began considering school administration as a way of meeting my personal and professional needs.

There were, however, other influences that affected the direction of my career. Levinson presents several qualities of the masculine-feminine polarity that relate directly to the experiences of men who enter school administration. Manliness is embodied in toughness, stamina, achievement, and ambition. Confronted by a conflict between power and weakness or thinking and feeling, men are expected to exercise control and get things done in a logical, analytical fashion. The "unifying theme in the masculine pattern is a concern with *doing, making, having.*"[93] The principalship seemed to offer the opportunity to resolve some of the personal conflicts presented in teaching.

Levinson also talks about two significant components of early adult development. The first is forming and modifying the Dream.

> In early adulthood, a man has to form a Dream, create an initial structure in which the Dream can be lived out and attain goals through which it is in some measure fulfilled. In middle adulthood, his task is to modify or give up the Dream.[94]

For me, school administration addressed my Dream and helped resolve some of my masculine-feminine concerns. Becoming a principal responded to my needs for power, ambition, achievement, and accomplishment. It enabled me to develop some masculine characteristics that were a part of my Dream and not a part of my teaching.

The second component of early adult development identified by Levinson is forming and modifying an occupation. Here a man "tries to define a work enterprise and ladder which will carry him to the culmination of his youthful strivings."[95] In teaching, I had chosen an occupation that did not appear to have any ladder. The decision to seek the principalship was a move to climb a ladder within my chosen field.

Shortly after becoming an elementary principal, I experienced the dilemma of how to maintain the "feminine" values that had been cultivated during my years of teaching. There was a conflict between my self-image as a nurturing individual and the demands of becoming a "manager" of a school. While the male teacher can be nurturing, it is frequently assumed that male administrators will be more detached and objective and less involved in the personal lives of their staff. Although the stereotype of male behavior is generally well suited to most occupations, there are aspects of the principal's job that are inconsistent with this view.

The task of the principal is much greater than building management. At the heart of the principalship are the responsibility and opportunity to nurture and support a group of adults. However, nurturing adults differs from nurturing young children, and the lessons of teaching may not serve principals well. Children often respond spontaneously to people who assist and support them. Their joy at having accomplished a goal spreads to all around. On the other hand, adults take a much more guarded approach to expressing their feelings or celebrating their accomplishments. Teachers expect their rewards to come from their students. They seldom experience adult support or praise and therefore respond cautiously.

As a result, principals cannot always predict the impact of their actions or know how their efforts will be received. A principal must have a strong sense of personal identity to nurture a staff despite uncertain or resistant responses. If a principal can maintain both the managerial and nurturing sides, it conveys a powerful message about his values. The principal validates an essential ingredient of teaching while still performing the role of school manager. In particular, this poses an additional problem for the male principal. A man who reveals his emotional side, shares his feelings, and responds to personal as well as professional adult needs is taking a substantial risk. If he is unsuccessful as a "manager," he risks having his failure attributed to being too "feminine" to lead a school.

As a principal, I tried to model some of the behaviors and values that I felt were important to share: "caring, individual attention to details, the importance of the workplace, and the feeling that resides there,...qualities most often attributed to women."[96] For example, the males in my school took little responsibility for quality-of-life issues. Rarely did they help organize staff coffee hours or social events. If they did volunteer, it usually meant that their wives would do the work or they would pay for one of the women teachers to pick up some pastries. Although I never minded mixing up a batch of brownies and regularly volunteered to help, I always wondered what people thought about this man whose wife didn't do the baking! When the sign-up list for cleaning the teachers' room was posted, mine was frequently the only male name. Everyone shared equally in the benefits of community life, but the women seemed to be the only ones attending to making it happen.

My hope was that by modeling a different type of behavior, some of the men might feel free to try it themselves. I even put some gentle references to differences in male and female behavior in my weekly staff newsletter. In a late September newsletter, I thanked the people who volunteered for our in-house committees (they were all women) and pointed out other committee openings. I ended by asking the question: "Where are all the men on the staff?" I received no response to the question, no male volunteers, and there was no change in the prevailing behavior. I felt like a voice in the wilderness and was dismayed that none of the women responded to the issue or raised any concerns with me. Perhaps the idea was too threatening to *their* self-images as well. The ethos of the school may have been identical to their life circumstances, and to object to the behavior of their colleagues might raise issues about the behavior of the other men in their lives.

In addition, there was another male-female issue that had a major impact on my administrative perspective. I became the father of a baby girl and within a year began to take major responsibility for her daily schedule. By the time she was two-and-a-half, I was bringing her to and picking her up from child care five days a week. Later I took a turn every third week picking up the midday nursery school carpool. While I did not make this an issue with my staff, I did share my situation with several women teachers who had young children. As a result, I began to view the circumstances of women teachers with children in a new light. Because of our family situation, I was often playing the "mother" role. I soon discovered, however, that my parent perspective could come into conflict with my administrative needs.

For example, when a teacher received a call in the middle of the day saying that her child was ill, my first reaction was that she should attend to the child and we would arrange coverage for her class. Often there were no substitute teachers available on such short notice and other staff were busy with their responsibilities. That left me with the task of covering the class and ignoring the remainder of my day.

A second issue proved even more difficult for me. One of the teachers with whom I had shared my situation had a son starting nursery school and saw no way to get him to the baby-sitter at midday. She asked if she could take her lunch break and an extra fifteen minutes three days a week to pick him up. My heart said yes, but my head wondered what type of predicament I was creating. While I was not truly comfortable with the procedure, I wanted to avoid asking the teacher to choose between her job and her son. After four months of pressure-packed madness, the teacher arranged for her husband to change his work schedule and pick up their son. I was glad that I had supported her and given her the time to solve the situation herself.

I believe that most principals would respond in a similar manner to these situations. They recognize that teachers have outside demands that are almost impossible to address during the school day. I always wonder, however, if other men in my position would feel the same way about their decisions. There are few places for male administrators to share these kinds of questions, concerns, and feelings. Most professional meetings deal with practical issues and problems and do not provide the opportunity or security to share personal concerns. From a stereotypical male perspective, these concerns would be viewed as weaknesses to be overcome. In reality, they represent the dilemmas that men confront as they try to integrate their masculine and feminine sides.

The world and the workplace are changing, albeit more slowly than I would like. Husbands and fathers must assume a greater share of the responsibilities of day-to-day family life. Wives and mothers must be prepared to share these responsibilities and to expect men to rise to the challenge. To confront these changes, male principals also must recognize and enhance their "female" characteristics and help make schools a reflection of a world where children and adults can grow to become complete, integrated individuals.

One Woman's Development:
A Path away from the Principalship
ANGELA JAVORA

Angela Javora is based in Texas and Louisiana. She is serving as Co-Director of the Principals' Center at Harvard for a one-year period designed to reflect on the Center's long-range plans. The has been an educational consultant, a public elementary school principal, assistant principal, curriculum coordinator, and teacher. She has worked at the university level supervising student teachers and has been actively involved in the principals' center movement.

Angela is forty-three years old. Developmentally, she is focused on creating an internally derived sense of herself. Questioning the way things are and wondering about the way they could be, dealing with issues of family health, and trying to balance the work and nonwork parts of her life are all central life issues for Angela.

It is difficult to sort out all of the factors that have influenced the direction of my life and my choices, both personal and professional. However, I do know that it is no longer important to me to "play to the roar of the crowd" or to try to "make everybody happy." Both factors are usually very prevalent in a principal's belief system, particularly for a woman principal. At one time, both beliefs directed my behavior.

I am increasingly aware that I am breaking out of old behavior patterns and limiting beliefs about myself. My internal growth has catapulted me out of my box and spurred me to explore dimensions of myself that before went unrecognized and unattended. My urge to break out was not a conscious choice at first. It was born of a combination of internal stirrings, life experiences, and myriad adaptations I made with varied degrees of success as I attempted to wend my way through my life and my career.

At first, change was subtle. It became most apparent to me at a time when both my husband and I were firmly grounded in our respective careers. Both of us had lots of formal education, good jobs with status and responsibility, and a life-style that mirrored the blossoming of "The American Dream." We lived in an upper-middle-class neighborhood in a big city, owned a lovely home, a beautiful weekend lake house, a boat, and two cars. On the surface, we "had made it."

Below the surface, life seemed transitory, illusory, and artificial. It was a world of appearances, where form and protocol were strict rules necessary to sustain the proper image. The image was civilized, polite, and rooted in decorum. The image took on a life of its own. It was not as socially acceptable to vacation with one's family at home, for example, as it was to travel to Lake Tahoe or Europe. It was considered more elite to ski in Colorado in the winter than to visit with relatives in Des Moines. Life's meaning and personal worth seemed to be defined by the size of one's investment portfolio.

The personal transformation process I am about to relate is not a tidy one. It is a growth process punctuated by alternating periods of confusion, pain, anger, sadness, awareness, insight, and joy. Though change is complicated and often difficult, I do want to emphasize my belief that no matter what one's early life and previous adult experiences, no matter what one's choices at any time in one's life, it is very possible at any point to stop, reexamine, and redesign one's thinking to claim the joy and depth of living to which one aspires. It is never too late.

The growth process is a learn-by-doing one. I believe that it was only when my personal world was tilted off-balance that I had the impetus to reevaluate, reshape and redefine my sense of purpose. The reshaping involved a profound process of letting go that depended to a large extent for its success on my willingness to rely on a deeper feeling and intuitive state that operates beyond the reality we normally perceive.

In my personal world, my husband and I were experiencing similar stirrings. He, too, was feeling an amorphous discontent with life, career, and goals. His anger erupted into explosive episodes that conflicted with his basic gentle nature. In addition, one of my older brothers died suddenly at the age of forty, leaving me and my siblings with deep regrets over not having taken more time out for family events. Simultaneously, it seemed that I discovered my parents were elderly and were rapidly deteriorating. Thus, the caldron for personal change was brewing.

In my professional world, as a public school principal responsible for an elementary school that drew its population from eleven countries, I gradually grew painfully aware that my role did not allow my staff, students, or parents to perceive me as a person with needs, feelings, and frustrations. The public wants its heroes and heroines and does not want to see clay feet.

The new education reform law in the state where I worked had elements that were deeply troubling to me and were demoralizing to all educators. However, the working climate and motivation of a staff were of prime concern to me, so I felt the need to be positive. My pep talk to the staff conflicted with my real beliefs about what was happening.

At the school district level, there was declining school enrollment and the need to close four schools. The public was upset. The political home front was hostile, volatile, and polarized. The more I attempted to accommodate continuing pressures, demands, and expectations, the more I sensed a drift away from the core of my being, where an unverbalized sense of what was meaningful in life existed. I found myself becoming more deeply entangled in an ever thickening and suffocating web of games, where dodging the clash of diverse ego needs and unreasonable state mandates dominated the arena of human behavior. The core of me eventually pushed forward into my consciousness where I could no longer deny that the games I allowed myself to be drawn into seemed utterly meaningless against the overall scheme of life.

Somehow I grew to believe that there must be a higher purpose to my life than continually contorting myself to fit through hoops created by others whose belief systems included defining their life's purpose in terms of power and control. I came to understand that this game can exist only with the passive compliance of the participants. Somewhere along the way, I had crossed over the line from educator to peacemaker at all costs—in other words, a dancing puppet who changed tempos every time someone else said it was time to dance faster, longer, and harder. A characteristic of flexibility that had formerly been defined as an asset had become a liability.

As a principal, I felt that my role was to act as a buffer for the staff from excessive pressures while attempting to nurture a collegial, supportive, progressive climate in the school. However, there were no buffers between the principals and the central office and between the school district and the state mandates. I maintained a positive public stance in support of the district's efforts. The stance was inconsistent with my feelings and with my beliefs about the moral dilemmas the law created for administrators. Without a buffer zone for the principals, we stood in a zone of pure pain.

What is interesting to me now about my behavior then is that, as much as I valued support and personal growth for my staff, students, and community, I neglected my own. Somehow I never considered it one of my personal rights. This is reflective of female socialization, being geared toward people-pleasing and always serving others, regardless of the cost.

At my current stage, I am no longer content to accept beliefs or behavior associated with an unrealistic set of cultural expectations that women should perform their duties obligingly, cheerfully, and unquestioningly at all times. Although the expectation of being a peacemaker is a general expectation of men *and* women principals, I did perceive a double standard.

Women principals were expected to let more things go in order to maintain harmony and were expected to question less.

To compound my perceived harness, I felt an additional pressure as a Hispanic female to perform my duties flawlessly in order to serve as a model minority administrator. As a lone minority female administrator, I was cognizant of many eyes watching, waiting, and judging.

From my present vantage point, not only do I recognize that my old lenses were self-limiting, but I also recognize that everyone wears lenses that are culturally imposed and that severely limit one's ability to relate to others at   the most meaningful level of all: the human will to care.

I perceive old lenses as equally limiting to men, who are not permitted to demonstrate their nurturing side for fear of being considered unmanly, weak, or effeminate. Many men are constricted by cultural expectations of achievement, power, and invincibility, especially when they are exposed to women as peers in leadership positions.

I believe we need to encourage men to move out of their boxes and allow the warm, feeling, nurturing side of themselves to be celebrated as evidence of wholeness rather than as a sign of weakness. The price men pay to mask their feelings is losing touch with who they really are. Losing touch through desensitization also involves losing access to depths and potentialities within the self that can only be tapped through refinement and attunement to one's feeling nature.

Essentially, I am moving out of the female box and proudly taking with me all of my sensitivities and nurturing nature, which before I had considered unprofessional. Now I see them as strengths that need to be honored and shaped so that I can feel comfortable as well as be professionally effective while incorporating them into my style. Rehoning these qualities is not easy. It means undertaking the task of re-forming myself. It means being willing to make mistakes in public as many times as it takes to master myself. This is no small task for a woman who prided herself on her "perfect image."

I have become aware that questioning the direction of one's life involves conflict – lots of internal conflict with one's previous level of awareness. When one chooses to act differently, then the conflict moves from the inner world to the outer world, where any change will be met with resistance. Any time a life script is to be changed, it leaves the other players in one's life in a surprised and reactive position, which generally turns out to be resistive.

Prior to making noticeable changes in my life, I had embarked on a personal investigation of other dimensions. I began reading philosophy books and attending workshops, seminars, and lectures whose focus was on developing one's potential. Through the association of new acquaintances in these courses, I found validation for myself and for the nature of my inquiries from like-minded people in all walks of life. The urge to know and to change moved me into what I call the first stage of my growth. I enrolled in a clandestine fashion in a few basic courses. The secret nature of my actions was to protect my public image and avoid being thought inappropriate or unstable. The exploration of new ideas, concepts, and issues in a safe setting opened new vistas to dimensions of my inner self. My newly found "classmates in life" were intelligent, sane people of both sexes who were responding to similar internal stirrings.

Hence, the second state of growth had begun: the validation of the new feelings, stirrings, and questions, as well as the validation of my newly discovered right to grow. To explore new pathways to growth was exhilarating, frightening, and addictive.

Just as in Plato's allegory of the cave, once I stood in the light of my own possibilities, I knew I could never go back to being a mere shadow of the person who was unfolding. I didn't want to go back. I sensed I was undergoing a transformational process. The process did not point out a clear way to go; it just erased the road behind.

For me, the road ahead meant risking everything I once defined as essential elements of my world. I resigned my job as principal of a public school. This also meant jeopardizing a standard of living my husband and I had grown accustomed to as a dual-career couple. It further meant putting my marriage at risk, because not only did our financial status change, but the marriage script was being rewritten. That involved my writing a new chapter daily and placing my husband in the position of ad-libbing. (No one was writing his script.)

At the present time, consulting to many different schools rather than working in one school allows me the freedom to continue to grow while staying involved professionally. Continued growth for me involves further discovery of my old beliefs and structuring new ways of thinking, feeling, and behaving for myself.

I believe the hope for the future lies in breaking out of old patterns of thinking and feeling regarding sex-related roles, expectations, and behaviors so that creativity can be released within everyone and a more androgynous behavior pattern can emerge. Such behavior can create an environment that will permit individual talents and abilities to emerge, potentially releasing the multifaceted capabilities latent in us all.

Part Three

Theory into Practice

Four Teachers in Developmental Perspective

With an introduction to adult development theories as background, we return now to the four teachers whose portraits initiated this journey. What can be learned from listening closely to teachers talking about their school, about their experience of teaching, and about themselves? Will their individual impressions of the school be consistent with how the school is generally perceived? What will each find most important? What will each want, and need, to feel successful? What will be needed for each to feel comfortable with him- or herself and with others?

Judy Cubbins, Janet Kramer, Don Bolter, and Nan Johnson all teach at Archer Elementary. Judy is a ten-year veteran. Janet and Nan have each taught for twelve years. Don started his teaching career eleven years ago. Judy and Nan are both married; neither has children. Don is married and has young children. Janet is single. All are in their thirties.

One might initially say these teachers are very much alike: veteran educators, roughly the same age, with ten to twelve years of teaching experience. Were these teachers more superficially distinct, differences among them might easily suggest varied professional development needs and strategies. Surface similarities, however, can easily mask basic differences. These differences begin to reveal themselves through attentiveness and with the help of a broad framework through which to make sense of adult experiences. Creating conditions for school people to talk about their work and listening carefully to the adult voices in the school can provide the needed source of attention; theories of adult development can offer a useful frame of reference.

I begin this chapter by focusing on each of the four Archer teachers in order to understand their individual needs and circumstances. I point to similarities among the teachers as well as differences. As reference points, I use particular developmental stages and phases. These expand our understanding of the teachers' capabilities and limitations and suggest appropriate professional-development responses.

JUDY CUBBINS

For the past ten years, teaching third grade at Archer Elementary has been Judy Cubbins' exclusive work experience. During the first three years of her teaching career, she was married. Then, after a stormy divorce, she remained single until recently, when she married for a second time. In an important sense, both Judy's personal and professional development revolve around the school. Neither Judy nor the school has remained unchanged.

Judy speaks of the changes in principals during Archer's unsettled history. Her impression of the first principal is colored by her position as a novice. Without experience, she did not have the standards to evaluate his performance. As both a new teacher and a young adult, she had a high and unquestioning regard for authority. "[N]ot having experience with other principals, I thought Sam was the end-all and the be-all." Blinded by her adulation for the principal, Judy could not reliably delineate his strengths and weaknesses. Sam Ellis' fear of parents, for instance, was something she "didn't realize at the time."

During the early years, Judy was particularly threatened by parents. Other teachers confirm that Sam Ellis was not a strong leader, that during his principalship the school was "run by the parents." Judy's inexperience as a teacher and the reality of the times combine to explain her initial experience of work.

Judy underscores the links between self and other, person and context, as she describes the comings and goings of Archer's next two principals. Bob Slater, a "gruff, short-tempered, and didactic man" with a stern, authoritarian style "came at a good time for the school." Suffering from a lack of discipline, Archer seemed to need Slater's authoritarianism. Likewise, when Peter arrived, "we were really ready for him." Parents, teachers, and children had come together and were ready to substitute gentle support for mandates and tensions. Had Samson come earlier, his style and demeanor might not have fit the times. The need for a suitable match between leader and setting are thus inherent in these descriptive statements.

Both the principal's role and his or her personality are important to Judy. This ability to distinguish role and person provides an initial clue to Judy's developmental orientation. Here and elsewhere, she tells us that she can understand the complexities of people and things. Initially, she saw the principal as "the end-all and the be-all." Initially, she brought her "whole self to teaching." Now, she is able to enter into and leave different environments and relationships with different people. Judy recognizes competence, consistency, intelligence, and fair-mindedness as essential personal and professional qualities for the principal. She is also aware of the need for a role that supersedes responsibility and allegiance to an individual classroom.

Just as Judy is able to differentiate role and person, she separates her needs for affirmation from her desire to feel a sense of accomplishment. At her present developmental level, both are important. Though Judy loves to teach because she likes to create materials for her classroom, she does not believe she would be fulfilled as a curriculum developer. Interactions with people, thinking that she is "doing something important," and seeing the results of her efforts are all parts of the reasons she feels positive about teaching.

Judy provides numerous examples of the close connections between her personal and professional lives. When she first started teaching, school was her whole life. While this level of immersion is typical of beginning teachers, it is also true that the troubles Judy was having with her first marriage were an additional incentive for burying herself in work. Likewise, when she went through a stormy divorce during her fifth year of teaching, she used her school relationships for validation and the school for a sense of stability.

> Especially when I've gone through hard times in the other parts of my life, teaching here has been a guarantee that tomorrow was going to come and that I would be able to do something organized and productive so that I would feel like a worthwhile human being.

For a number of years, Judy taught with a partner. Now she is teaching alone. Though she feels lonely teaching by herself and misses many aspects of the partnership, the time she has for her life outside of school is more important to her now that she is remarried and thinking of beginning a family. Her decision to forego a teaching partnership is thus motivated by considerations extraneous to work.

Judy describes herself as someone who is willing to take initiatives. She also believes she has a high level of self-confidence. Both of these characteristics reveal aspects of her development. Judy can interact freely with others and is not generally constrained. She has a strong sense of self and uses it to accomplish what she believes is important. Within her classroom, Judy feels free to make changes. When she disagrees with a school-wide decision, she is neither afraid to voice a dissenting opinion nor unwilling to translate her convictions into actions. Though she has not ventured beyond the school to change system-wide policies or practices, such as the report card program, *she* has decided not to pursue this avenue of change, opting instead to put her energies into teaching.

As Judy reflects on her ten years at Archer, she traces a path in her development: From a self-centered teacher, she has become more student-oriented; at the same time, she has also expanded her sense of self. This makes it easier for Judy to separate teaching and nonteaching, teacher and children. Initially, Judy and her external environment were inextricably combined in much the same way that Loevinger describes a Conformist developmental position and Kegan portrays the Interpersonal I. Judy explains: "[M]y identity was always dovetailed to whatever environment I found myself in." Over time, a strengthened sense of self has given Judy increased freedom. She says: "Now I shed my environments like skins."

Not only does this shift toward the Institutional I give opportunities for expression to the many different sides of Judy's self, but it releases her from extreme dependence on external approbation. Not only is it important to know that Judy's sense of confidence has increased over the years – as might be true for many veteran teachers – but identifying the *source* of her increased confidence is significant.

> When everyone else is telling you that you're good, you have to keep going to prove to yourself they're right. But it's a nice day when you realize that you're competent. That was a lot longer in coming, you know, really believing it…*really* believing it!

With a more clearly defined sense of self, Judy is better able to distinguish others. In the classroom, she sees the children as individuals. She feels more comfortable with children and "far more outgoing." She concludes, "You feel much more comfortable with anybody when you feel comfortable with yourself."

At the moment, Judy feels comfortable with herself and satisfied with her career. She also recognizes both her own and others' characteristic fears of change. She does not want her teaching to "become stale;" nor does she want to become overly involved in her life outside of teaching. The one area she identifies as having the potential to pull her away from teaching is starting a family. In part, her ambivalence surrounding this issue reflects the dual aspects of her developmental orientation at Loevinger's Conscientious-Conformist stage or in transition between Kegan's Interpersonal and Institutional I. At the same time, Judy is drawn to relationships and the positive feelings she expects to derive from having a family and feelings of productivity that come from work. In teaching, she has found "a nice balance." She has opportunities to interact positively and productively with children and adults. She has structured her teaching so that she has time for outside relationships and interests.

That Judy continues to feel more challenged than complacent in her job has similar developmental roots. Of course, she would feel depleted if she thought she were doing the same thing year in and year out, she tells her husband. Instead, her ability to set boundaries around herself and others and to recognize and appreciate differences allow her to feel that people and things are changing. Because she sees the many parts of herself and others, she is also able to assume multiple roles.

> This year's group of children is entirely different from the class before them. I can be a different authority figure to them. I can be a different person. I can be a different friend. I can be a different source of information. That, to me, is why I've never gotten tired of teaching third grade. Each year is entirely different.

Judy's capacity to be many different selves and to see many different others is an important component of her development, momentarily well matched to her personal and professional life.

Staff Development Implications

Now that Judy Cubbins has revealed a great deal about herself, and adult development theory has helped put her story in perspective, what kinds of staff development initiatives would help her maintain her current level of satisfaction and offer her the possibilities of continued growth? One of the most interesting aspects of an approach to staff development that relies on paying attention to the articulated needs and closely observed behaviors of school people is how much is quite explicit. For example, Judy says that putting together curriculum materials is part of the reason she likes to teach. She likes to create, to color, to make bulletin boards, and to design learning materials. Not only can she be encouraged to exercise this love in her own classroom, but she might be called upon to contribute to the development of materials for the school and the system. Taking seriously Judy's need to economize her time so that she has energy for her life outside of teaching, acknowledging her creative efforts within her classroom and providing opportunities to expand her talents is one viable and immediate staff development option.

Given her ability to recognize and respond to individual differences, Judy might be challenged by working with third graders with particular learning needs and special problems. Perhaps she could combine this strength with her love for creating materials by designing child-specific materials.

If Judy's teaching is proceeding as smoothly as she perceives it to be, and she is intentionally working to create more time for her life outside of school, a viable option might be a staff development moratorium. Do school people need continuous engagement in professional development activities? Is it necessary for individuals to be developing in all aspects of their lives simultaneously? Who should determine the answers to these questions? Can individuals make these decisions for themselves? What is the consequence if different determinations are made by teachers and administrators? These issues themselves might generate an interesting and provocative staff development discussion.

Some supervisors would look at Judy Cubbins' position in the school over the past ten years and decide it was time for a change. After all, not only has she taught the same grade for all these years, but her practice teaching and teaching have both been in the same building! Here is precisely where a developmental framework can prove important. To know that Judy experiences herself, her students, and her position differently from year to year and is able to draw upon these differences to keep her and her students engaged in learning is potentially a useful piece of knowledge not necessarily revealed by the superficialities of her position. Talking with Judy and observing her teaching over time can be essential components of determining appropriate staff development activities.

JANET KRAMER

Janet Kramer's experience of teaching at Archer has been different from that of Judy Cubbins in many ways. She also feels differently about her job and herself. Janet is tired of her job; she is also unhappy with her life.

Janet identifies the change in principals at Archer as a significant event. For Janet, the principal is primarily an authority figure and a source of reinforcement. While other staff are important because they provide moral support, the position of the principal is critical to the attitude of the teachers, to the quality of their work, and to the way they view themselves. In this sense, a principal like Peter, who focuses on finding positive aspects of teaching when he observes in a classroom, is vital to Janet. His role as a buffer toward a mass of intimidating parents is also important.

Judy, like Janet, needs the principal's support. For Judy, however, Peter's support is largely implicit. When she went to the science specialist to modify the curriculum requirements, she did not go to Peter first. Both she and others express a sense that in most cases Peter will back them up and direct contact with him is not needed. When Janet meets an unfriendly parent in the hall, however, she needs to seek the principal out. Even though he says essentially the same things that she herself has expressed, hearing the words directly from him seems important. Nor is Janet concerned with acting on her insights. Instead, her orientation is toward acceptance and reinforcement.

Positive feedback is critical to Janet's sense of self-worth. A primary goal in her teaching is to instill in the children the importance of showing respect. This goal is not simply an abstract ideal to be learned, however. For Janet, a show of appreciation from the children helps her to feel good about herself and what she is doing; it is the fuel that keeps her able to work. In part, the insular existence of teachers working in self-contained classrooms and the fleeting rewards of teaching are characteristics of the profession to which Janet may be responding.

Researchers and practitioners have identified these occupational liabilities and reported on the tendency of teachers to respond by seeking fulfillment within the classroom through relationships to students. Nan Johnson illustrates this tendency when she explains that she does not feel isolated even though contacts with other adults in the school are limited. She speculates, "I guess it's because I get so many good feelings from my children...." For Janet Kramer, dependence upon positive reinforcement or protection from blame may be indicative of a more pervasive developmental orientation. Janet not only *has* relationships, as Kegan describes the individual rooted in the Interpersonal, she *is* those relationships. Her very sense of self seems defined or defied by the responses of others.

In speaking of her past, Judy Cubbins identifies a manifestation of a similar orientation put into fresh developmental perspective. She says, "I tried to make everyone happy, which is something you cannot do." Janet Kramer, on the other hand, is still trying: "You can't please all the people all the time, but you try, and it's nice when you can."

While feedback from parents remains an important resource for Judy, it is no longer the only form of sustenance. On the one hand, freedom from this bond may have altered Judy's relationships to parents. Alternately, continued positive feedback may provide a context from which Judy can more easily view her own strengths. In fact, Janet receives positive reinforcement from the principal, from children, and from many parents. She explains that it is only a small number of parents who exert a negative influence. Oriented from the Interpersonal I, where relationships are so vital to one's sense of self, even the slightest amount of negative input can be unsettling.

Janet sees many things pessimistically at this point in her life. She is easily overwhelmed by external forces that she feels she can neither control nor combat. Is Janet stuck because she is tired of teaching and has given up? Or does Janet's developmental perspective predispose her to burnout?

It may be that an individual enmeshed in the world of the Interpersonal I will inevitably find a professional setting discomforting. In schools, for example, teachers are often called upon to take a stand independent of whether they will be liked. They must deal with recalcitrant students and unhappy parents. More generally, it may be difficult for any adult to remain in a position of constantly needing external nourishment. The particular demands of working with young children, however, can allow a form of symbiosis to develop. A bond approximating the mother-child relationship may prove nurturing to both child and adult. While the mutuality of this affiliation can be comforting, it may be inappropriate to the student-teacher relationship. Nor may this form of mutuality be consistent with the function of schools to prepare children for independence and self-sufficiency in later life.

A pregnant teacher at Archer is confronted with the issue of parenting. She is very clear, however, about wanting to keep the roles of mother and teacher distinct. She reasons:

> I don't want to be a mother in the classroom. That's one thing I'm trying not to do. I guess I'm afraid that their image of me is going to change, and I don't want to lose our professional relationship.

Janet has not always felt discouraged about teaching. She recalls: "At the beginning...you're very, very enthusiastic. You know, the sun, the moon, and the stars are your class." Nor has Janet always responded in the same way to children and parents. Over the years, she has adopted various teaching strategies. Likewise, she traces a shift in dealing with parental conflicts:

> Now this has changed....It used to be that if I really believed in something strongly I wouldn't give in to [parents]. Now, just to make my own life easier, I might try to convince a child's parents that the way they saw something wasn't the way I saw it. But I'd probably give in just because I'd like my year to be a pleasant one. I don't want parents making my life miserable. It's unfortunate.

Janet's passive acceptance, her desire to smooth things over to make her life more pleasant and to avoid conflict are characteristic of the Interpersonal I perspective. A past ability to take a stand and to become actively involved in problems and their solutions indicates an authorship illustrative of Kegan's Institutional self. Currently unhappy in her job, Janet's work environment may be unconducive to her personal growth.

Janet herself identifies the school as a constraining environment. Whereas Judy Cubbins finds the stability of a core group of staff supportive and comforting, Janet feels locked into a closed society that she now finds stagnant. Just as Judy's life outside of school affects her attitude and performance at work, Janet, too, is influenced by external circumstances. She notes, "If I were married and had a family and had other things going on that were enough variety in my life, then I wouldn't be so overwhelmed by this feeling in teaching."

It is true that elementary schools, predominantly populated by women, do not afford a fertile context for establishing male/female adult relationships. For Judy Cubbins, this has been a reality of her work world that she has made efforts to circumvent. For Janet, this reality has become an increasingly immobilizing constraint. Working with young children can provide a transitional phase from one's family of origin to the early period of adulthood. It may also be true that failure to complete the life task of creating one's own family may be exaggerated in this context. Janet suggests this interpretation when she says: "I'm getting tired of taking care of other people's children; it would be nice to have my own kids, too."

Levinson's analysis of life phases and the importance of completing or resolving them at specific times in the life cycle points to another possible explanation for Janet's discomfort. The task of establishing a relationship and initiating a family are the work of early adulthood. Now in her mid-thirties, Janet must deal with a life task that is incomplete. She states:

It probably didn't bother me this much ten years ago, but it bothers me more now, so that must have something to do with the way I view myself. I feel cheated and I think that has some effect on [my] teaching.

Roger Gould has discussed the importance of issues of family and childbearing to women's development. Decisions around these issues, he contends, pull at women, especially as they move into their thirties and the time for having children begins to run out. Nan Johnson shares the pressures of this conflict: "Now I look at my life, I'm not sure I want to have a child. That biological clock is ticking very quickly, and we really have to decide." Do concerns for family diminish the energy and commitment available for work? For Janet Kramer, this seems to be the case.

Janet's strong developmental orientation toward the Interpersonal appears to be at work in many areas of her life. According to Janet, a relationship with a man feels essential to the completion of her self. From the perspective of an individual whose very self is brought to life by others, this position is developmentally consistent. At this point in her growing, Janet *is* her relationships. As a relationship to a man through marriage is a prominent unresolved phasic task, it is ultimately the most significant missing piece in Janet's sense of self. She concludes, "If that other aspect of your life isn't fulfilled, then you really feel like somehow it's just not complete."

In Erikson's terms, Janet has become a passive adjuster, rather than an active adapter to an environment that she no longer finds nourishing. Unstimulated in her workplace, and in a developmental position that leaves her completely "wrapped up," Janet goes around in circles. She knows she is dissatisfied staying, but she cannot break out. Locked in by the limitations of her developmental orientation, she is momentarily stuck.

Staff Development Implications

Working with Janet at this time in her life is bound to be draining. Janet will require a great deal of outside counsel and support. A major staff development challenge will be determining how to urge Janet to take initiatives and to make constructive changes, when she prefers to be passive.

If Janet is tired and frustrated with teaching, shouldn't she be urged to look for another job? Certainly this would be a realistic option if all we knew about were the external manifestations of Janet's psychological state. Knowing, however, that her frustrations are more closely tied to her life outside of teaching than to her job, it might be possible to help Janet understand the nature of her developmental conflicts and isolate the troubles she is experiencing around a basic life phase task. Though the particular requirements of teaching may exaggerate these difficulties, teaching itself is not Janet's central complaint.

Leaving teaching is certainly one option for Janet, though she remains a competent teacher and would need help separating the suggestion to look for alternative career opportunities from a negative judgment of her performance and self. Within teaching, Janet could be encouraged to work in different settings, with different people, and at different grade levels. Since she likes team teaching and enjoyed working with a male partner, creating this option might raise her spirits. Since she is interested in working in a male-female environment, she might want to consider moving to a middle or junior high school, where the faculty is typically more mixed. Janet spends her summers working at the town summer school. Perhaps she could better use this time exploring alternative work environments. Continued study might also broaden her sights.

Are there inherent conflicts in trying to help someone who cannot currently take initiatives, and who is bound to relationships, to be more self-initiating and more independent? At what point does support become overprotection? Can it ever be counterproductive? These basic staff development issues take on a somewhat different hue when viewed against an understanding of adult development. Introducing the developmental framework to Janet may be an important first step toward greater self-awareness. With firm support and increased understanding, Janet might gradually be able to make some changes in her own best interest, as well as in the best interest of students and colleagues.

DON BOLTER

Don Bolter is both different from and similar to Janet Kramer and Judy Cubbins. While adults differ developmentally, they also have a great deal in common. Needs for approval and validation are pervasive, for instance. The intensity of these needs, however, can vary depending on how one is oriented toward the world and toward the self.

While Don Bolter seeks recognition, he is not immobilized by controversy or disagreement. It is not surprising that he is one of the few teachers at Archer to have gotten along with principal Bob Slater. Slater responded negatively to all first requests, putting most teachers off.

Recognizing Slater's technique and not confusing individual style with personal judgment, Don was able to continue asking. "I didn't like it, but I didn't let it get in my way. I can't think of anything that I didn't do as a result."

Don's strong sense of self surfaces in his opening statements. He uses self-generated standards to judge his performance. Change is important to Don, and he takes responsibility for changing himself. Beyond self-scrutiny, he is open to evaluation from others.

Unlike Judy and Janet, Don's interest in teaching was more accidental than planned. He began teaching in the inner city because that's where the jobs were. His move east from Wisconsin was motivated by a desire to return to New England; where he worked was "secondary."

Don's dislike of change is not uncommon. When he came east, he was careful not to change too many aspects of his life at once. He sought work in the inner city because that was the setting he was coming from. Whenever Don makes a shift in his life, his initial reaction is cautious and negative. Gradually, Don grew more comfortable with his surroundings. Influenced, like others, by externals, his adjustment was aided by signs that he was being accepted as well as by the arrival of Christmas.

Don has a way of blending in with his environment. He traces his satisfaction with inner-city teaching to the civil rights movement, which made what he was doing "fit right in." He accepts trends in the Scribner system because they seem to parallel his own shift toward conservatism. At the same time, Don is able to step out of his environment and act independently. He does not apologize for his affinity to Bob Slater, though most teachers disliked Slater. He was willing to challenge Slater to get what he believed was important, and he is not threatened by impending layoffs in the system because of his confidence and sense of competence.

Like other teachers, Don attributes much of Archer's positive atmosphere to the current principal. He appreciates both Samson's personal and professional strengths. While he acknowledges the importance of Samson's ability to give positive feedback to teachers, he also welcomes constructive criticism. He readily accepts Samson's style of making a general observation about student behaviors and allowing teachers to determine the appropriate response. Other teachers – perhaps Janet – might feel uncomfortable without a definitive judgment from the principal. Don, on the other hand, appreciates both open communication and the latitude to formulate his own standards. Of Samson's role he says, "He doesn't set up barriers because of his position."

Interestingly, Don does not make full use of his partner as a critical observer. While he values self-improvement and appears open to scrutiny, he does not believe he and his partner have used their partnership to full advantage. Perhaps the low-key attitude of the principal and his tendency to let teachers work in their own ways has diminished the incentive for the continuous observation and critique that Don says he would find advantageous. Perhaps it is still hard for Don and others to accept critical appraisal. While his developmental orientation may give him the strength to absorb constructive criticism, the safety of his environment may not challenge him to live up to his potential.

On the one hand, Don's ability to be independent is reflected in his attitude toward his friends and toward school-based relationships. Since he has married and had children, he has had less time and need for friendships and he is content with only casual connections to colleagues. On the other hand, Don finds a strong identity in his family. Perhaps his needs for connectedness are satisfied by his relationships outside of work. Yet many of his women colleagues, and even women colleagues with family ties, seem to value and need these connections. Don's more casual attitude toward relationships emerges at several points in his description of the school and his life. Working in an all-female environment, for instance, is something he rarely thinks about. Nor is Don troubled by the team structure of the school and its tendency to separate faculty members. He comments, "I know there's a feeling of separation between the two teams as a result of the way the school's organized, but it doesn't bother me one way or another."

Just as Don does not seek connections through collegial relationships, he does not seem to want to be tied into the system-wide decision-making process. Don seems able to draw clear boundaries around himself. He accepts his place in the system's organizational structure, knowing there is room for his input and for assuming responsibility for voicing disagreement.

Like Judy Cubbins', Don's initial focus on himself has gradually shifted to encompass the needs of his students. As a young adult, his eagerness for change and experimentation complemented the social and political atmosphere of the 1960s. "Having a good time was first, learning was second." Don is now more sensitive to children's needs and more aware of the messages and values he conveys to children through his actions. Thinking about bringing two comfortable but ragged couches into his classroom in those early days, he reflects: "When I think about it now, I think about the messages I was conveying. You know, when you put trash in your room and expect kids to use it, maybe you're telling the kids that that's what they're worth." A shift from self-absorption to child-centeredness appears to be both a developmental and an occupational transition.

Developmentally, Don exemplifies many of the characteristics of Loevinger's Conscientious stage and Kegan's Institutional I. His tendency to replace external rules with self-generated standards, his ability to be self-critical, his sense of competence, and his capacity for maintaining and balancing multiple relationships all typify this orientation toward the self and the world. While Don manifests aspects of earlier stages, such as his need for approval and recognition, he does not seem to be absolutely dependent on them. Interestingly, Don's developmental needs for achievement are thus far satisfied by his classroom teaching. Particularly at the elementary school level, it is unusual to see a male teacher without administrative aspirations. Don's interest in progressing seems less outwardly directed and more closely associated with improving himself as a teacher. Don's orientation toward family and the relative subservience of work is also interesting and unusual among men, particularly in their thirties, when climbing the occupational ladder is prominent. Don's individual expression of his developmental position may, in fact, be well suited to elementary school teaching. Here, he is not pressured to advance and he has time to devote to his family. Conservative by self-definition, Don can literally conserve his sense of self in an environment that offers more developmental supports than challenges. Since this Conscientious orientation is well suited to many working environments, Don understandably feels comfortable with himself, comfortable at Archer Elementary, and comfortable in the profession.

Staff Development Options

With just a little bit of encouragement, Don seems ready and able to look closely at his teaching. He has the ability to reflect and the confidence to attempt changes. Initially, he might be urged to make better use of his partner as a source of observation and analysis. He might also be ready for other observers.

Don does not give the importance to work relationships that his three women colleagues do. While he participates in team meetings, his interest in forming strong collegial ties is limited. Such ties are important to professional improvement. Can Don focus seriously on his teaching in the context of casual relationships? Is it likely that teachers at Archer will engage in peer observation and critique? Can and will the principal take on this function?

Of all four teachers, Don gives the least indication of his ongoing professional objectives. Judy has some interest in teaching teachers and designing teaching materials; Janet wants to add some new ingredients into her work; Nan thinks about assuming a leadership role in the school or in the system. Helping Don formulate both his short- and long-term professional goals is another staff development option. At the moment, Don's interests and time seem to focus outside of work, on his family. Will challenging him to focus on his career goals be ill-timed or distracting? Can Don think about future career options without sacrificing his interest in teaching?

Don describes himself as happy and comfortable with teaching. At what point does comfort become complacency? When does a staff developer introduce challenge or dissonance? If work is not a teacher's primary focus, is it the staff developer's job to channel and intensify interests in teaching? These are some of the fundamental staff development questions raised by Don Bolter's needs and circumstances.

NAN JOHNSON

Nan Johnson describes herself as a "fence sitter." Faced with decisions, she explains, "I can easily see both sides of an issue, which can really make it impossible sometimes." She says she is torn between an adventurous side of herself and a part that she likes to remain established and unchanged. While she sees herself as an adult, she is highly identified with the ten-year-old child of her past. These pulls mirror the transitional stage of development exemplified by Loevinger's Conscientious-Conformist orientation, midway between Kegan's Interpersonal I and Institutional I. According to Loevinger, this is the stage of growth for most adults. It is not surprising that both Judy Cubbins and Nan Johnson operate from this stage of adult development nor that Janet Kramer and Don Bolter manifest precursors or remnants of this developmental orientation. Adults can expect to recognize or discover many of these same themes and traits in their own lives.

At a Conscientious-Conformist stage, an individual wants to be accepted by the group as well as to be different and to stand out. Pushing oneself toward high standards and self-criticism for failure to reach these heights are characteristic. While a strong sense of what is expected from the outside remains salient, there is a gradual development of one's own sense of "shoulds" and beliefs.[97]

In the terms of Kegan's framework, an individual shifting from the Interpersonal to the Institutional perspective will waver between an orientation in which she *is* her environment and her relationships to a position from which she can move in and out of multiple environments and relationships. As Nan tells her story, she seems to speak in the terms of this transition. At the same time she is pulled toward a desire for inclusion (best served by an Interpersonal orientation), she is drawn toward expressing a sense of autonomy and directness (most adequately served by an Institutional position).

Nan Johnson, like Judy Cubbins and Janet Kramer, reflects on the importance of the principal to the organizational climate and smooth functioning of the school. She is critical of Bob Slater because he did not seem to know what principals "were supposed to be like." When Bob Slater ran the school, it was not always clear to Nan where she stood, while Peter Samson finds ways to let Nan know she is doing a good job.

Like Janet, Nan needs to know from the principal how she is doing. His constant surveillance and input, however, are partially replaced by the high standards Nan imposes on herself. She also takes on a great deal of responsibility for reasons expressive of both poles of her development. Not only does Nan like the feeling of making other people happy, but she enjoys the sense of accomplishment. While she sometimes feels overextended, she is driven to push herself.

It has been important to Nan to prove herself to others, as well as to herself. Describing herself as a highly competitive person, she needs to know where she stands in relation to the group. She enjoys becoming involved in activities both inside and outside the classroom. A wide array of professional-development offerings in the system and opportunities to attend meetings and serve on committees provides abundant outlets. In this sense, Nan's develop-mental inclinations and the nature of the school environment are well matched.

Nan's energies and willingness to take on a wide range of responsibilities are not always viewed as an unqualified strength. While some teachers are grateful to Nan for the duties she takes on so that they are not burdened, others find her energy threatening. As one teacher described the conflict, some people in the school are known as "overextenders," and "if you're an overextender, you have to be extremely cautious. You can take on responsibilities so that other people don't have to, but you must not step on anyone's turf. Most important, you must not show another teacher up." Gertrude McPherson has suggested that extreme behavior or emotion within a school is frequently a source of discomfort. At Adams Elementary, where McPherson worked, "[E]nthusiasm was suspect. It disturbed stability and raised questions."[98]

Nan gives many examples of the pulls she feels between sitting back and allowing things to happen and standing up for herself. Even in the early days of Bob Slater's reign, she says, she first felt cowed by his presence and prayed that he would not venture into her classroom. By the time he left, however, she had begun to "stand up to him a little bit." Realizing that she did not lose her job, she felt wonderful.

A given developmental orientation represents the tenuous balance of the self in the moment. From the inside, upsetting that balance can threaten to cause not only temporary disequilibrium, but permanent loss of self. At the Interpersonal balance, when the self *is* the relationships in which it is encompassed, negative feedback from the outside or termination of a life-supporting attachment feels like an end to the self. Emerging on the other side of disequilibrium wondrously still intact is both tenuous and exhilarating. Nan continues to feel that such experiences are hard. She also has a sense of newfound strength.

Each time Nan takes the difficult step of moving toward her own beliefs, she feels like she is growing. When she became a supervisor to counselors at a childhood camp, it was hard for her to assume a new position:

> It was one of the most "growing" things I've ever done in my life: having to be able to face someone who was really not very much younger and say, "You're not doing the right thing. This is the way I think you might be able to do it better." It was really hard. It was not working with little kids anymore. It wasn't even being a counselor. It wasn't even being a teacher. It was very, very much different – a lot of meetings, a lot of decisions. And I think that what I learned, as hard as it was and as many tears as I cried that summer, I think it really helped me to grow up in terms of being able to face some responsibilities and say, "I've got to do this. I mean, that's my job."

It is interesting that Nan distinguishes between the capabilities necessary to supervise adult counselors and the abilities needed for a teacher's work. Referring to the elementary-school-age child she harbors inside herself, she also believes that the childlike qualities she possesses may make it easier for her to teach. Judy Cubbins also links her enjoyment of teaching to her desire to color, to make bulletin boards, and to create. Does a teacher who works with young children need to maintain a childlike presence in order to remain connected to her students and to her work?

It has been suggested that the happiest and most effective teachers may never have completely transcended aspects of their own childhood or adolescence. Does holding on to the child in the self impede peer interactions or, more fundamentally, arrest further growth as an adult?

For Nan Johnson, as for Judy Cubbins, Archer Elementary has been a safe, stable, and happy environment. Judy has relied upon the stability of the school to provide a base from which to make changes in other parts of her life. In some ways, it has been easier for Nan to make changes within the school than outside of it. While she describes the conflicts surrounding past decisions to marry and to move, and the difficult impending choice regarding children, she says that she is always willing to change what she does with her class. Comfortable with her teaching and with the school, she has recently been able to venture out into the larger system. The general supportiveness of the school seems to have provided Nan with a secure base from which to expand her self.

According to Kegan, a "culture of embeddedness" is a necessary foundation for growth. The bond between mother and child is an early example of this nurturant environment. A series of "contradictions," however, necessarily foster the separation needed for development. Limit setting is an example of a "benign contradiction," establishing the self as distinct from the immediate environment. Spurred on by contradictory experiences, which are gradually incorporated into a new view of the world and the self, development is characterized by movement to qualitatively new cultures or contexts. While contradictions are the impetus for growth, a supportive culture is prerequisite.

In many ways, the environment at Archer appears to offer Nan the foundation she has needed to begin to move out. Within this setting, she has begun to take some risks. It has been a gradual process, however. Her adventurous side, which she feels free to explore inside her classroom and now in the system, needs to come back to a place that feels safe. As Nan recognizes:

> [The adventurous side is] just another part of me. It comes out in small chunks, when I know that I can come back to something safe, where I don't have to be adventurous in everything. A large risk, like quitting my job and doing something completely different, is probably a little bit too great at this point.

For the moment, the context in which Nan is most comfortable is the school. When she considers what she will do after she decides – or it is decided for her – that she will or will not have children, she thinks of returning to teaching. In almost the same breath that she says she is "really ready for something new and different," she concludes that she would like to come back to Scribner. As in the past, it is hard for Nan to separate herself from an environment that has become nurturant. In addition, Archer is a setting in which she can feel worthwhile and productive. While Nan feels that she has probably proven to herself and to others that she can teach and that she is ready to move on, acting on these feelings is still problematic. Remaining on the fence in what Nan describes as an "even period," she waits for the next internal or external "jolt."

Staff Development Implications

In many ways, Nan Johnson presents herself as an ideal teacher with whom to work. She has an abundance of energy and drive and her own high standards of performance. Since she is "probably harder on myself than any supervisor would ever need to be," she would likely be able to establish an ambitious professional development agenda of her own.

Yet Nan also describes places where she gets stuck. She says she is ready to move out more into the system, to work on curriculum, to take on increased leadership. What holds her back is her parallel needs for safety and assurance. How could Nan be helped to take more of the risks she says she would like to take?

Nan's staff development plan can differ from Janet Kramer's because of her positive attitude and her expressed desire for expanded responsibilities. With a small amount of verbal support, Nan probably has enough drive and self-confidence to go a long way by herself. Creating challenges that do not force her to give up all of the comforts and guarantees of the present would probably give her enough stability to begin to take some chances. The success that she is likely to have when she does assume added responsibilities may well provide additional impetus.

Within the classroom, Nan says, she is very adventurous. She also says she is willing to try new things without direct guidance or permission. Reinforcing this strength, a supervisor could help Nan think through the kinds of changes that might make a significant difference to children's learning. Nan is also open to trying new ways of teaching and working within the school. A partnership or a mixed-age group might also be appropriate staff development options.

Like Janet and Judy, Nan is struggling with family issues. Should she have a child? If she has a child, will she take time away from teaching? What can she do when she is ready to resume working? Although Nan is asking herself these questions, she seems to be waiting to see how the decision will be made for her. Recognizing the links between personal and professional development, options concerning family decisions might appropriately be tied to discussions of a staff development plan specifically suited to Nan's personal and professional objectives. Should Nan think of making a career move while she is planning to start a family? Could she combine a partial maternity leave with a part-time position of increased responsibility outside the classroom? Are there limited changes Nan could make in her job now to see if she really wants to move into system-wide work at this time?

Nan has difficulty making decisions. Being able to see all sides of an issue and being loathe to make big changes, she more often vacillates than takes action. This is a part of Nan she already recognizes. Perhaps staff development activities could be directed toward helping Nan understand the nature of her ambivalence about issues of teaching and learning. This might help to maximize the energy she has available for continuing development. Because Nan begins with a great deal of insight into herself, these and other issues of her development will not likely surprise her. With only a minimal amount of support, Nan seems ready to explore and address many parts of her self.

COMMONALITIES AND DIFFERENCES

Commonalities

A striking similarity in the portraits of Judy Cubbins, Janet Kramer, Don Bolter, and Nan Johnson is the spontaneous emergence of the principal as a key figure in teachers' perceptions of the school. The present principal is consistently viewed as a positive influence, while former principals, whether viewed positive or negatively, are central to teachers' views and feelings about their workplace.

A second striking similarity, true for three of the four teachers, is the high degree of satisfaction they derive from teaching, in general, and from working at Archer, in particular. Nor is any of the four teachers planning on making a change. Although the literature on teaching typically portrays the difficulties of the profession, many teachers at this elementary school are happy with teaching. Only Janet Kramer describes the school with ambivalence and her own experience as less than satisfying. Yet her sense of dissatisfaction is more attributable to her personal development than to teaching.

The stories of all four teachers illustrate the close ties between personal and professional development. During Judy's divorce, the stability of the school was essential to her. When Nan Johnson's and Don Bolter's lives were disrupted by moving, they, too, welcomed the school's order and organization. Judy's shift from team to individual teaching was primarily motivated by her need for more time outside of school rather than by educational considerations. Don also likes the structure of teaching because of the time it allows him to be with his family. And Janet's dissatisfaction with the predictability of teaching is linked in part to the inactivity in her life outside of school. Not only are there inevitable connections between a teacher's life in and out of work, but these connections can influence how teachers view teaching, their attitudes toward parents, children, colleagues, and themselves, and the energy available for work.

Similar patterns toward work seem to develop for teachers that mirror their developmental patterns. At the beginning of teaching, Judy and Don describe the energy and idealism characteristic of novice teachers and young adults. A shift away from the needs of the self and toward the needs of children is also characteristic of increasing experience and ongoing development.

Though each teacher needs different kinds of support and validation from the principal, from colleagues, from parents, and from children, everyone has some need for feedback and validation. Not only is validation needed to confirm and buttress an individual's sense of self-worth, but recognition is an essential precondition of caring. Just as mothers are more nurturant to their children when they themselves are nurtured,[99] teachers and administrators need to be listened to and cared for so they can listen to and take care of others. Some teachers may need concrete, positive feedback. Others may respond best to the affirmation inherent in giving individuals opportunities to make their own judgments and decisions. The need for validation and support is persistent.

Linked to the need for validation is the positive effect of sharing in a context of support. All of Archer's teachers mentioned the importance and rarity of talking about themselves and their work. Many said they felt both a sense of relief and energy from sharing the things that weren't working as well as exploring ideas that might work. Making time for teachers to talk with one another, with the principal, or with an educator or consultant not directly tied to the system seems like a low-cost and high-gain strategy for staff development.

Though an individual teacher's needs for support can vary, depending, in part, on diverse stages and phases of development, each of the four Archer teachers agrees that support from the principal and support from the system are vital. Before teachers are willing to take risks, they must feel some level of safety and acceptance. Peter Samson and the Archer school appear to provide teachers with the different kinds of support they need to feel productive and comfortable. Is it possible that a relationship or an environment can be overly supportive, so that the impetus for movement is blocked? Can Janet Kramer's needs for external approval be continually met? Will meeting her needs prevent her from experiencing the conflicts and contradictions necessary for growth?

A seemingly minor incident involving Judy Cubbins highlights the complexities embedded in these questions. Three months into the school year, Judy asked to have her teaching watched. Although she warned that she had trouble asking for help or accepting suggestions, she listened intently to the post-observation comments and actively participated in generating alternatives. Several days later, she was ebullient. She had tried something new with a reading group, and it had worked. Reflecting on the incident, she offered:

> It's the first time that has happened to me in ten and a half years: having someone actually sit down with me and critique a class. It was good to have someone come in who didn't simply give me positive feedback, but who actually stimulated me to think about making some changes.

Then, thinking back to her sense of the supportiveness of the principal and the school, she puzzled over whether knowledge of that ongoing support was, in fact, what had allowed her to be open to criticism. "Perhaps having Peter here to give me lots of positive comments sets a stage for me to be able to accept constructive suggestions from somebody else." Interestingly, Judy did not seek out additional help. "You notice I'm not asking you to do it again," she said one day in the teachers' lunchroom. "I don't want to spoil something good, I guess. I don't want to rock the boat."

This last comment of Judy's exemplifies the general conservatism of the four teachers at Archer and their shared dislike of change. Are these traits characteristic of many adults? Of many teachers? If so, how can teachers and administrators committed to professional development establish an atmosphere of continuous improvement? Are they more likely to encounter resistance than enthusiasm? What about their own tendencies and limitations?

Differences

In many ways, Judy Cubbins, Janet Kramer, Don Bolter, and Nan Johnson have similar perceptions of the school. For the most part, they tell the same story of the school's evolution and its present status. Yet close scrutiny reveals subtle, but important, differences in how they think and feel, what's important to them and why. In the area of support, for instance, Janet requires acceptance and reinforcement. While Judy, Don, and Nan also begin from a base of affirmation, each requires somewhat different stimulation and encouragement. Judy, it seems, can tolerate a little critique from a trusted outside source. Nan is most likely to want to develop the details of her own professional development agenda with some suggestions but limited dictates. Don's acceptance of generalized critiques that he can then apply to his particular classroom situation suggests broad discussions of teaching and education with opportunities for him to make connections to his own teaching. Teachers and administrators will readily describe the kind of feedback they prefer. Colleagues must then decide whether and how to expand the repertoire of techniques that fellow teachers and administrators are willing and able to accept.

Many of the same developmental traits and themes emerge in talking with each of these four teachers, as they can be expected to emerge when talking with most adults. Yet each teacher – each adult – is unique. While Judy Cubbins and Nan Johnson are oriented toward themselves and their work from a similar developmental position, each plays out her development distinctly. Both seek a balance between affirmation and individuality; both want to be part of the group and to stand out. For the moment, the classroom is the primary area for Judy. Nan, on the other hand, expresses the various parts of herself in the classroom, within the school, and in the system.

Though relationships are vital to Judy, Nan, and Janet, Don seems less affected by them. Though his needs for connectedness may be satisfied by family at this point in his life, it is interesting to note his relative indifference to work relationships. Also different is the degree to which the women struggle with conflicts and issues around family. While it is true that none of the women has children and each has urgent feelings that time is running out, Don does not express the typical pulls that women express both before and after they start their families. Because Don's wife is a full-time mother, her availability to his children may reduce his concerns. Potential differences between men and women on this and other dimensions are worth further consideration.

Janet Kramer's experience of the school is markedly different from that of her colleagues. Though the source of her discomfort largely rests outside of work, its influence spills over into her feelings and attitudes about many things. In a setting like the Archer school, where most teachers are satisfied with teaching, what opportunities are there for teachers to express dissatisfaction? Janet Kramer was hesitant to express her negative feelings in an environment where most teachers are content. Holding a minority view made her feel even more isolated. Even when many teachers feel dissatisfied, are there constructive outlets for dissenting opinions?

Not everyone at Archer experiences the school in the same way. For Judy, a veteran staff feels supportive and comforting; for Janet, the existence of a core faculty is stifling. More broadly, Nan's interest in learning and professional advancement seem well suited to the opportunities at Archer and in the system. Don, on the other hand, does not seem to be getting the push he needs to make use of his partnership for ongoing observation. Though Janet seemed at one time to be able to stand up to parents and express opinions of her own, her current dissatisfactions have led to withdrawal and a gradual unwillingness to risk conflict and dissension.

Just as Judy says she can be a different friend, a different authority, a different source of information to children, so, too, can teachers and the principal be different sources of support, authority, and information to colleagues. In fact, they will be perceived differently by adults and children whether they intend to be or not. One of the lessons of developmental theory, this perspective can help school people understand both commonalities and differences.

The Role of the Principal and the School Environment

The centrality of principals to schools is well established. Whether the principals of Archer Elementary have been perceived favorably or unfavorably, each has made a definite impression on Archer's teachers. In turn, how these principals have been seen has directly affected each teacher's experience of the school and influenced his or her satisfaction with teaching.

Research on effective schools links the quality of the school as a workplace to teacher effectiveness. It also maintains that the single greatest predictor of teachers' perceptions of the quality of their workplace is their perception of the quality of their principal.[100] Most teachers at Archer Elementary are satisfied with the principal; they are also satisfied with the school.

How does Peter Samson establish a positive and productive work environment for most adults? Are there aspects of Samson's style or values that other principals could emulate? How much of his success is situational or idiosyncratic? What part does his development play in his effectiveness?

This chapter isolates aspects of Samson's role and personality that seem to work at Archer. It underscores the degree to which the principal's image and effectiveness can vary, depending, in part, on the developmental needs and orientations of individual teachers. The chapter also returns to the school to explore how the context or environment supports or impedes Samson's efforts.

The individual life structure is a patterning of self and world. However, self and world are not two separate entities. They are not like billiard balls that, colliding, affect each others' course but not each others' nature. An essential feature of human life is the inter-penetration of self and world. Each is inside the other....The self is in the world; the world is in the self.[101]

Growth is a process of interaction between the self and the environment. Looking at the interpenetration of self and world, we can begin to understand each more fully.

THE PRINCIPAL

Daily Activities

On an average day, Peter Samson arrives at school before 8:00 a.m. and leaves for home after 6:00 in the evening. In between, he will talk formally and informally with teachers, students, and parents; he will spend bits and pieces of his day on the phone, opening his mail, and writing memos and bulletins. He may monitor the lunchroom, supervise buses, and accompany a work crew to a malfunctioning boiler.

Except when Peter has a private meeting, his door is always open. Before school begins and after the last children have left, teachers come and go from his office, taking a seat to talk seriously about a difficult child or

---

TABLE 8.1
A DAY IN THE LIFE OF PETER SAMSON

7:55-8:30 a.m.	Office: brief meetings with teachers, aide, secretary
8:30-10:00 a.m.	Meeting at Central Office with School-Based Assessment Committee
10:00-11:00 a.m.	Open mail, return phone calls; meetings with two teachers
11:00-11:30 a.m.	Write a bulletin
11:30-12:00 noon	Observation related to formal teacher evaluation
12:00-12:15 p.m.	Office
12:15-12:30 p.m.	Lunch
1:00-1:35 p.m.	Observation related to formal teacher evaluation
1:35-1:50 p.m.	On the roof retrieving a student's playground ball
1:50-2:00 p.m.	Telephone call
2:00-2:15 p.m.	Meeting with the girls from the Upper Team
2:15-3:00 p.m.	In classroom helping with minicomputer
3:00-3:30 p.m.	Helping with dismissal and bus boarding
3:30-5:00 p.m.	Archer Cabinet meeting
5:00-5:30 p.m.	Talking with teachers
5:30-6:10 p.m.	Office work

standing at the door to share an amusing story about the day's events. During the school day, teachers pass through the front office to gather their mail, often poking their heads around the corner to exchange a brief greeting. Although lunchtime is frequently taken up with supervision duties, meetings, a phone call to the central office, or a conversation with a parent, Peter joins teachers in the lunchroom for a sandwich and casual conversation whenever he can.

In addition to formal classroom visits for purposes of supervision and evaluation, Peter enjoys spending time around the school informally. Teachers sometimes invite him into their rooms to view a special event; he also drops in to take part in whatever activity is in progress. When Peter comes into a classroom, he frequently spends time talking and playing with children. Before or soon after he leaves, he gives the teacher verbal or written feedback, always finding something positive to say. When he has a criticism, he shares it in the form of a question or suggestion.

In many ways, Peter behaves just like any other member of his staff. Within the system, he participates in professional-development courses, for example. He also takes part in activities within the building. One year, the school acquired several computers and workshops were set up to demonstrate their use. Not unlike other teachers, Nan Johnson was intimidated by the new technology and resisted introducing it into her classroom. Peter urged Nan to try. If he could learn, he told Nan, anyone could. So Nan and Peter went together. Later that same week, Nan arranged to have the computer in her classroom. Peter came to help with the lesson.

Peter's willingness to participate in school and system-wide activities may not be characteristic of all principals. In one class on large-group management, for instance, he is the only principal among a group of teachers and aides. Most of what Peter does as principal of Archer Elementary, however, is typical of principals at all school levels. In fact, whether a leader or manager is highly effective or ineffective, his or her observed activities are generally much the same. "[T]he leadership difference appears to come not from what the individuals 'do' during the day, but from how they think about what they do, how they communicate how they think, and what they 'do' while they are 'doing' it."[102] Equally important, and frequently overlooked, is the way others perceive them.

The Role and the Person

Part of the way Samson is perceived is attributable to his role. While the principal's role may not represent authority to everyone, the role connotes a school-wide allegiance that transcends affiliation with any single classroom. Responsibilities for budget, hiring, supervision, and evaluation also define the principal's role, separating and distancing the principal from other adults in the school.

The role of the principal is key to the life of a school. The principal is in a central position to effect change and to set the institutional climate. Positioned between the school and the wider community, the principal becomes a buffer, protecting the school from outside influences and pressures potentially counterproductive to growth. When Peter receives a punitive memo from the central office, for example, he does not always pass it on to teachers. Where specific teachers rather than the entire staff are affected, he will speak to individuals rather than distribute a statement to everyone. These prerogatives present themselves to Samson because of a role that positions him between the school and the wider community.

Beyond the role of the principal, the person in the principal's role is important. All of Archer's teachers single out the personal qualities of Peter Samson. Waller comments:

> The school must always function as an organization of personalities bound together in dynamic relation....[I]n a living bit of tissue, persons transcend offices; they embody offices, but they engulf them.[103]

This characterization seems to fit Peter Samson. Perhaps it explains why teachers at Archer feel he enlivens the school.

When teachers talk about Peter, they use words like "rare," "special," and "unusual." Their larger-than-life characterizations suggest that effective principals may be born rather than bred. This issue is central. If an effective leader has inherent personal qualities that cannot be learned, emphasis on selection and recruitment for the position is a logical consequence. If, on the other hand, the traits of strong leadership can be acquired and refined, more intensive professional training is justified. Like any complicated issue, this one does not have a simple answer. Inborn talent and personality as well as training play a part in the development of leadership.

Archer teachers describe Samson as "competent," "consistent," "intelligent," and "fair-minded." They say he is accessible, maintains open lines of communication, provides positive feedback, and listens. Many of these behaviors can be learned. Active listening, for example, is a basic and powerful staff development tool, integral to many characteristics of effectiveness. As a source of validation, listening both comforts and motivates. When individuals are heard, they gain a sense of recognition and a feeling of empowerment. Samson demonstrates his ability and willingness to listen by his open-door policy and through his practice of providing teachers with regular and constructive feedback. Samson's frequent classroom visits also give teachers the sense that he understands their professional skills and objectives. Because he listens, teachers trust that Samson knows them. It is for this reason that Nan Johnson believes Peter realizes that she has high standards. "Probably it's because I talk to him a lot and because he's such a good listener. Maybe he picks up on the things I try to tell him." Samson's abilities to listen help him provide responsive feedback as well as facilitate his ability to keep lines of communication open. In addition to his physical accessibility, Samson's psychological attentiveness, demonstrated by his abilities and willingness to listen, is a key component of his perceived effectiveness.

For some less experienced teachers and prospective administrators, Samson, an adult at mid-life, serves as a mentor. When Peter first transferred to Archer, one teacher requested a similar transfer to maintain their mentoring relationship. Samson's beliefs are mirrored in his behaviors. Both his words and his actions offer guidance to younger and less experienced adults in search of a mentor to support and guide their ongoing development.

Samson's ability to provide guidance and support to teachers is the most frequently cited characteristic of his effectiveness. The ways he provides support, however, and the kinds of support needed by individual teachers are varied. For Janet Kramer, support is positive reinforcement: explicit confirmation from outside to validate the self. For Judy Cubbins and Nan Johnson, support is less tangible. A strong foundation of internalized approval and validation allows Judy and Nan a broader scope of independence from which to make decisions. For them, support from the principal is increased freedom to take initiatives and to make individual determinations. Don Bolter finds support in generalized statements and questions and in constructive criticism.

Support from the principal in many different and individually tailored forms is critical to all of Archer's teachers. When the support offered is different from the support needed, a teacher can feel threatened, undermined, attacked, or abandoned. One teacher finds praise insufficient; instead, she longs for challenge and debate. Another finds questions unnerving; she would prefer specific ideas that she could simply take and implement. For the most part, Samson's perceptions of teacher needs for support are accurate. When they are not, he can adjust his response, guided by a teacher's reaction and by his knowledge of adult development. Evidence of feeling threatened can signal the need for a less aggressive approach. Expressions of abandonment may suggest a need for immediate tangible help.

Can a principal be overly supportive? At what point does support become stifling? Will complacency take the place of critical appraisal and continuous improvement? Support may be a precondition for growth, but when and how are the equally essential contradictions introduced? Can the same person provide both? This question echoes continuing dilemmas about supervision and evaluation. Can a principal be an impartial judge and a trusted confidante?

Peter Samson does push teachers when he feels it is appropriate. He describes a relationship with one teacher in which he is intentionally providing both comfort and gentle prodding. Referring to a teacher who is stymied by children with behavior problems, he says:

> I would like this particular teacher to do what, in her heart, she would like to do but can't. In other words, if you feel in your heart that you'd like to do something, I'd like you to be able to get to the point where you *can* do it and not back off from it all the time. I'd like her to be true to herself.

Then, considering his role in this teacher's development, Peter continues:

> I help her to grow, I think, by talking with her when a situation occurs and giving her suggestions or techniques. Sometimes she will say, "I know I should be able to do this, but I can't." So what I do is try to get her to tighten the belt one notch each time we talk without strangling her with the belt...nudging her, but not really pushing her with my foot.

Although Peter says he does not have ultimate or inflexible standards for teacher behavior in most instances, there are cases where he feels compelled to set institutional limits. A teacher promising a parent something for a child without going through the proper channels is an example of inappropriate use of teacher initiative. But teachers can take initiatives in many areas that are appropriate, according to Peter, and in these cases, they receive his full help and support – if they want it. "Often I help teachers to plan a project or write a grant. Of course, if it's their program, they're welcome to do it any way they want."

Peter generally takes his cues from an understanding of what teachers need and want. When teachers express or demonstrate their needs, there is a good chance that Peter will hear, understand, and respond. When teachers are reticent or ambivalent, however, they may not receive needed help. Janet Kramer's needs and wants are currently unclear. Unless Peter can formulate a staff development strategy for her or create a context in which she can gradually formulate her own, she will remain stuck. Though Nan Johnson needs similar help when she is "on the fence," a gentle push is likely to send her full-speed ahead. Don Bolter is capable of examining his teaching more closely. Judy Cubbins appears to need inside support and limited outside input.

In general, Peter feels, his style is more supportive than provocative. If a teacher wants to become more assertive, he tries to help; if a teacher cannot be assertive, but performs effectively in most other facets of her work, "I'd have to decide whether I could accept that. If I could live with it, fine. If I couldn't, I might have a hard time with that teacher." Peter Samson's broad tolerance of individual differences rarely puts him at odds with teachers. As a result, he can most often exercise the supportive, nurturant side of himself, with which he is most comfortable, and hold in abeyance his confrontational self, with which he feels far less safe.

In addition to the needs of teachers, principals have needs, beliefs, and styles of their own. Samson believes in looking for the positive. His words and actions consistently provide teachers with evidence of this belief. "You can be doing the most rudimentary lesson," a teacher comments, "and Peter will always find something praiseworthy to say about it. Even when he has a criticism, he puts it in the form of a question or suggestion, which does not make you feel awful, and leaves you with a sense that you have some choice." Peter explains:

If I want to effect change, I do it by raising questions, not by saying, "You will do this, or you will do that." I also don't give the staff any false expectations about what weight their voice is going to have. I let people know what their level of involvement should be or can be – whether or not it's really an open-ended discussion, a choice that I will have to make, or a foreclosed decision that I simply have to transmit. And if it is an open decision, I will frequently abide by what the staff says even if I may not totally agree with it.

While providing individuals with options is generally a good formula for success, some teachers do prefer definitive judgments or directives. It is interesting to speculate on Peter's ability to adapt or even violate his needs, beliefs, or style to meet the requirements of the teachers he supervises. Is his role primarily to satisfy teachers' needs and preferences, giving them the comfort and room to take increasing initiatives, or must he continually push the adults in his building to expand their competence and stretch their limits?   To what extent do teachers have to conform to the principal's predispositions?

While some principals like to work with compliant teachers, Peter prefers staff members who are willing to be independent. His behaviors reflect his inclinations. Attending a Lower Team meeting, Peter mostly listens. When it is time for him to present a concern about playground supervision, he outlines the parameters of the issue and asks teachers to generate possible solutions. Later he shares the philosophical conviction out of which this customary strategy stems:

> In general, I would like to work with people who take a lot of initiative. I don't need to make all the decisions. If teachers don't have an investment in a plan, it isn't going to work.

While Peter consistently attempts to respond to teacher needs and preferences, he, too, has personal and professional strengths and limits. Confrontation is not easy for him, and, like most adults, he wants to be both respected and liked. In describing his interactions with a teacher who has difficulty working with specialists, he illustrates this point:

> I can think of one teacher whom I would like to be more assertive or more aggressive with specialists. This person is a good teacher, but I think she tends to abandon herself rather quickly with a specialist. She'll hide behind me, wanting me to do it for her, to take command. And it angers me: one, because I'd like this person to do it; and two, because it may be a little scary for me too. I mean, just because I'm the man or because I'm the principal, I don't have all the answers and I don't always feel well equipped to fight all the battles.

In this case and many others, Peter's awareness of his own strengths and weaknesses helps him to understand, monitor, and adjust his personal and professional interactions. Awareness also lets him know when he needs to ask for help. In part, Peter's perceptiveness is a result of his experience and maturity as an educator. He has been a teacher and a principal for many years. Increased self-awareness has also been nurtured by immersion in professional-development activities and, most specifically, by participation in a three-year pilot program where he met regularly with principals from different towns and a group of consultants to share issues and concerns surrounding the principal's work. Peter describes the experience as key to his development. In fact, tracing his growth over that period, he describes what appears to be a developmental progression. According to Peter, participation in the group helped him move from a position of too easily "abandoning" himself in order to please others and reach a solution agreeable to everyone (characteristic of the Interpersonal orientation) to a place where he can more firmly bring his own point of view to a situation and stand his ground (a sense of self increasingly separate from those around him, characteristic of the Institutional orientation).

THE PRINCIPAL IN DEVELOPMENTAL PERSPECTIVE

To what degree does the principal's own developmental level influence his or her ability to lead and support others? One of the most striking findings of the initial research conducted for this study was the high developmental level of the principal relative to the teachers at the school.[104] Given Peter Samson's major influence on the quality of life at Archer Elementary, it is interesting to consider whether there is a relationship between high ego level and the capacity to create supportive and nurturant environments. In order to be effective in a helping role, leaders may need to be at a point in their own development sufficiently beyond those they are helping, to prevent their own growing edge from continually bumping up against the boundaries of the individuals they seek to help.

Research on effective leaders and good schools supports this hypothesis. A high level of awareness is described as a characteristic of effective leadership.[105] The ability to integrate masculine and feminine tendencies is likewise identified in good school principals.[106] This ability is also characteristic of advanced levels of adult development.

Within Loevinger's and Kegan's frameworks, Peter Samson manifests an Autonomous or Interindividual I orientation. Loevinger gives this stage its name because of the increasing recognition of other people's needs for autonomy. Samson's acceptance of a broad range of individual styles among teachers certainly manifests this stage characteristic. Moving from the Conscientious or Institutional position to the Autonomous level, striving for achievement is partially replaced by a search for and a capacity to support the needs of others. Importantly, Autonomous adults are able to transcend concerns for their own immediate experiences, becoming more realistic and objective about themselves and others. This last tendency is especially useful in helping Samson understand teachers' needs and concerns independent of his own. The fact that individuals at the Autonomous stage can be both intimate and independent affords them the capacity to identify and empathize with others as well as to maintain a sense of distance and personal integrity.

Whether schools and school systems can provide adequate supports and incentives for developmentally Autonomous individuals remains a question. Teachers and principals at these levels often express frustration with organizational constraints and frequently go on to less confining work (see Chapter 9); researchers have also noted the attrition of effective school leaders.[107]

Again, developmental advancement does not necessarily imply developmental superiority. Loevinger comments:

> There is a temptation to see the successive stages of ego development as problems to be solved and to assume that the best-adjusted people are those at the highest stage. This is a distortion. There are probably well-adjusted people at all stages....Certainly it is a conformist's world, and many conformists are happy in it.... Probably to be faithful to the realities of the case, one should see the sequence as one of coping with increasingly deep problems rather than to see it as one of the successful negotiation of solutions.[108]

THE PRINCIPAL AS A SCHOOL LEADER

Effective principals are said to have a clearly formulated and articulated school vision or mission. They focus their goals on student learning, create a safe and orderly environment, and provide strong instructional leadership. Effective principals are hard-working, energetic, and knowledgeable. Within the school, they are perceived as the chief initiators or facilitators of change. Effective principals are good speakers and good listeners. They are sympathetic and decisive.[109]

Certainly Peter Samson has many qualities of a school leader. Some important elements are missing, however. While Samson is a special and sensitive human being, he is not the charismatic visionary described in the literature. Nor does Samson see himself as an instructional leader, acknowledging instead the expertise of teachers. While Samson's general expectations for teachers and students are high, he allows individuals considerable latitude in determining their own goals and standards. A careful observer of the school would see a range of teaching and learning philosophies and styles.

Samson describes himself as a "clinician." He sees a major part of his role as addressing the needs of teachers, students, and parents and protecting the school from outside intrusions. In this sense, he creates the strong, safe, and trusting environment Kegan describes as essential for growth.

Samson sees support as primary and works hard to provide it. While he makes use of a principal's authority, it is authority partly shaped by a dependence on relationships. Samson pays careful attention to the needs of adults as well as children, and he treats adults as professionals by offering them autonomy and support. Beyond some of the typical characteristics attributed to effective leaders, the roles of clinician and educational supporter are special parts of Peter Samson's repertoire as principal and central components of his adult development.

THE SCHOOL ENVIRONMENT

Daily Activities

Archer Elementary is a school where most teachers feel satisfied at work. More fundamentally, many report that they are continuing to develop as adults. An abundance of literature documenting the negative aspects of the teaching profession, persistent teacher burnout, and a growing concern with recruitment make the widespread reported satisfaction of Archer teachers a surprising and unpredicted state.

In addition to the fact that teachers repeatedly speak of the school in positive terms, observations provide further evidence of high morale and satisfaction. Gatherings and meetings among staff within the school are characterized by a casual and friendly atmosphere and a high level of sharing and joint decision making. At a meeting of the Lower Team, for example, teachers alternately assume prominent roles regarding issues for which they have a particular investment. One teacher, who has received a sample of educational games, delights in displaying them and asks if others would like to have an opportunity to use the materials. A suggestion is made to create a sign-up sheet so that the games can be evenly distributed among all. Although the principal is present, he primarily listens. When it is his turn to present an issue, he does so as teachers have done before him.

Life in the teachers' lunchroom is an especially good indicator of the high morale generally exhibited throughout the building. Archer teachers move in and out of the area, taking a place at the long table without hesitating to calculate who will be occupying the next seat. In addition to the usual banter about a particularly unruly child or complaining parent, teachers frequently share stories of success with the lessons they are teaching or discuss plans for future projects, actively soliciting help and suggestions.

From time to time, birthday parties erupt; several teachers will present a cake to a colleague. On a more serious note, four teachers continue a discussion begun in the waning evening hours of one of several staff gatherings concerning the problems of the Outreach Program. One teacher spontaneously begins to take notes on the ideas that are germinating and volunteers to follow up on some of the suggestions. Nor does the tone or substance of a discussion alter when the principal comes in. On the other hand, lunchtime was stiff and formal on a day when the school received an unexpected visit from the superintendent.

Both in school and out, many teachers work and play together as colleagues and friends. One group spends an hour once a week after school exercising in the gym. This year, several staff members have arranged weekend trips, and two teachers have chosen to travel south together during the winter vacation. Judy Cubbins attributes a great deal of her satisfaction with the school to the existence of long-term, close friendships.

School and System Characteristics

One characteristic of Archer increasingly common in schools is the existence of a veteran staff. Most of Archer's teachers are tenured and have been in teaching for ten or fifteen years. The majority of teachers are in their forties and fifties. From the principal's perspective, possibilities for shared leadership are potentially enhanced when a staff is experienced. Alternately, veteran teachers may be unwilling to make changes or to follow the principal's lead. At Archer, a little of both situations has developed, creating opportunities and constraints for the school.

The team structure at Archer is another aspect of the school environment with strengths and weaknesses. On the one hand, teachers complain that teams divide the school and restrict peer interactions. Within teams, however, teachers have a chance to talk about teaching and learning, to share ideas, and to raise questions.

A special feature of the Archer School is the learning disabilities center. Designed to serve the entire system, this large space is centrally located in the building. Not only does it house a large variety of curriculum guides, books, and activities, but it brings specialists to the school, expanding the number and scope of adult relationships. The center is an important and unusual addition to the school environment. It adds resources and personnel to the school. It provides a quiet place for teachers to work. Since teachers from other schools as well as visitors come to the center, its existence also elevates the stature of the school and, by extension, the school staff.

Parents are another part of the immediate school environment, and teachers talk about them frequently with emotion. While some teachers, like Janet Kramer, find parents threatening, most speak of them as helpful and interested. All think of parents as potentially powerful and disruptive. They refer back to the early days in Archer's evolution as evidence.

Differences in attitudes and perceptions toward parents reflect, in part, varied developmental orientations. Janet Kramer's dependence on positive feedback for feelings of self-worth leaves her vulnerable to the unpredictable responses of parents. More certain of her self-worth, Judy Cubbins has learned to accept parental support as well as to confront parents when confrontation is needed. Over time, the influence of parents at Archer has diminished. Both the strong presence of the current principal and the increased involvement of women in work outside the home have combined to decrease the necessity and time for parental involvement.

Beyond the school, opportunities in the system are a source of satisfaction and stimulation to some. One teacher, in particular, praises the system for the quality and array of professional-development offerings. A sixteen-year veteran, she explains: "If it weren't for that, I'd never have lasted as a teacher for so long. I can't even imagine being able to survive and continuing to feel happy and stimulated in any other system." Another teacher describes the shifts she has been able to make in school assignments as her needs and interests have changed. She credits the flexibility of central office personnel with maintaining her excitement and satisfaction with teaching.

It should no longer be surprising to learn that not all teachers view Scribner's staff development offerings and system opportunities with equal interest. Again, it is the interaction of contexts and individuals that emerges as most important. From Janet Kramer's perspective, courses and committees no longer serve her purposes. Alternately, a teacher who has recently gone through a divorce clings to the chance to immerse herself in course work. She speculates: "I think it's a reaction to the divorce that I should be involved in so many projects." A teacher who has been in the system for many years has yet another reaction. Feeling tired and pressured this year, she continues to favor the existence of system opportunities, but she feels that participation is not always a matter of choice. Since attendance is taken, she knows she will be missed. As a result:

> You're too tired to go, but you go. You don't want to be left behind. You don't want to be one of the ones who says, "Oh, I didn't know about that." You want to be up there. I don't know, I guess I'm growing in spite of myself.

THE SCHOOL ENVIRONMENT IN DEVELOPMENTAL PERSPECTIVE

Because development is an interactive process between individuals and their environments, looking at adults out of context fails to capture the complexities of growth. Just as the different developmental orientations of principals, teachers, and parents influence interpersonal relations, the diverse needs of individuals can complement or clash with the demands of specific environments. Since the demands of environments may differ, and because individuals function in multiple arenas in their lives, it may also be that responses will vary. Evidence of diverse functioning dependent on context underscores the fluidity of development. Shifting developmental states rather than static growth stages may best capture the ways in which individuals seem to adjust or adapt to the demands of different environments.

Not only may teachers and principals behave differently in and out of school, but their responses to the same environment can fluctuate over time. This seems to be the case for Janet Kramer. While she was initially capable of taking a stand with parents, she is no longer willing to assume the same position. Instead, her strong need to be liked and to keep her life free of conflict has left her vulnerable to criticism and unable to act. Janet appears to have adjusted to a setting that she no longer finds satisfying. A diminished sense of self and arrested, or even regressed, development seem to be the results.

Environments, like individuals, may manifest developmental orientations. These manifestations may be somewhat analogous to the stages of growth. The descriptive traits identified by Loevinger as characteristics of the Conscientious-Conformist and Conscientious stages and by Kegan as the Institutional I seem to be well matched to the characteristics of the Archer School. At a Conscientious-Conformist position, Loevinger describes an orientation toward helping, an awareness of self in relation to group, an ability to set goals and to generate alternatives. At the Conscientious position, she identifies an increasing capacity to assume responsibility, a focus on achievement as measured by self-evaluated standards, and a concern for communication.

Similarly, at Kegan's Institutional I stage, the self begins to separate from the group and to generate standards and values of its own. An emphasis on achievement, competence and responsibility is well matched to the demands of a school environment. An increasing ability to be inner-directed suits the particular requirement of schools for teacher autonomy.

It is interesting that almost all of Archer's teachers manifest developmental traits that conform to the Conscientious or Conscientious-Conformist orientations. Given that the majority of these teachers also describe themselves as satisfied with their work environment, it is reasonable to suspect that the underlying traits of the organization and the characteristics of the individuals who work there are largely coincident.

Only two adults at Archer manifest divergent developmental orientations. Interestingly, both have positions somewhat peripheral to the school. One is a specialist who travels between schools and whose primary affiliation is to her district-wide department. The other is the principal, who likewise sits on the boundary between the school and the system. How might these two adults adapt to the school if their jobs were more within its boundaries?

Besides adaptation, self-selection is an important factor in considering the impact of the school environment on adult development and functioning. Just as individuals can be shaped by their role or their setting, they can initially choose contexts well suited to their personalities, styles, and interests. Judy Cubbins identifies the somewhat intangible influence of self-selection when she speculates that her inclinations toward control may have something to do with her occupational choice.

Oh, I'm sure they do – subconsciously, at least. I don't think I really planned it that way, but I like to be in control. I like to know when things are going to happen. I like to be prepared for it. It's all part of teaching.

Self-selection may not be a factor in Peter Samson's and Don Bolter's choice of profession. Family and children are important to both men. Bolter says family is the most fulfilling part of his life and that he envies his wife because of the time she has to spend at home. Describing a father as someone who spends a lot of time with his children, he elaborates next on the importance of physical affection: "hugging and telling your kids that you love them." Neither man speaks of the importance of his job in terms of advancement and achievement. One says a man's job "will hopefully be fulfilling;" the other describes the quality he likes best about himself as "my capacity to love."

In describing the men who work at Archer, many of the women use terms like "low-key," "mild-mannered," and "even-tempered." Several teachers specifically comment on Samson's nurturant qualities, particularly his capacity for caring, his gentleness, and his listening skills. It is interesting to consider the effects of the school environment and the possibility of self-selection. Elementary schools may be particularly inviting and unusual workplaces for nurturant men.

While individuals may have a primary or preferred way of holding themselves and their worlds together, they may be capable of functioning in different ways in response to particular external demands. A given setting may call out several voices. Individuals both actively select and create the worlds in which they live, and they actively or passively adapt or adjust to the constraints and opportunities of these worlds.

LEADERSHIP WITHIN THE SCHOOL ENVIRONMENT

Although we cannot personify the school environment to assess its leadership capabilities as we did with Peter Samson, we can say that aspects of Archer's school environment either stimulate or stifle the possibilities for adult growth and leadership. The availability of a wide range of professional development activities offered by the system allows teachers and administrators to engage in ongoing personal and professional development. The existence of mechanisms for effecting system-wide change also creates room for individuals to expand their leadership roles and potentials. We can say that the principal's protection of the school and his ability to tolerate and support a range of individual styles and differences provide some teachers a solid, secure context from which to experiment and take risks. These opportunities for growth provide a fertile context for uncovering and expanding the leadership capabilities of adults.

Oriented to the Conscientious-Conformist and Institutional stages, Archer Elementary and the Scribner district may place limits on the potential for the development of autonomy and interdependence, as described by stage theorists. The school environment does, however, provide room for adjustment, adaptation, and change. It does support the developmental needs of those at the Conscientious-Conformist and Conscientious stages of adult development, as well as some of the Autonomous or Interindividual stages.

The constraints and the opportunities of schools as contexts for adult growth have yet to be fully tested. Paying careful attention to the adults who fit into these organizations, as well as those at all levels of development for whom schools, teaching, and administrating are counterproductive, can begin to yield important information about both the individuals and the school environment.

CONCLUDING COMMENTS

Archer Elementary and Peter Samson are examples of a good school and a good principal.[110] They exhibit many qualities of effectiveness, but there is room for improvement. Teachers and the principal at Archer might profitably engage in more frequent and continuous talk about practice. They might routinely observe each other. They might plan, design, research, evaluate, and prepare materials together. They might more frequently and more self-consciously share their expertise on teaching and leading. While some degree of collegial interaction of this sort does exist, professional relationships at Archer could be expanded and enhanced. Perhaps Samson can provide the leadership for this increased professional intensity without jeopardizing his important role as clinician. Certainly he can empower others to take initiatives.

As school principal, Peter Samson plays a central role in creating a quality workplace that allows teachers to teach effectively. The school and the district support Samson's efforts by being largely fertile contexts for adult growth. Teacher satisfaction with Archer Elementary and Scribner is closely tied to perceptions of Samson's effectiveness. Pursuing continuous improvement, along with the risks and uncertainties of such pursuit, is a further challenge that Peter Samson and Archer's teachers can avoid or embrace.

9

Putting Developmental Theory to Work in Schools

Almost all adults find theories about their development intriguing. Quite naturally, we search for ourselves in the theories and often discover bits and pieces in many places. Making use of these insights is another question. What difference can it make to know we are at the Conformist Stage or about to weather a mid-life crisis? Will anything change as a result? Can subtle, individual development shifts have any impact on those around us? Will our work lives be affected?

The two cases in this chapter address these questions. Each is the story of a school principal dealing with the tasks of administration. The names of the principals and their schools have been disguised. In Case I (coauthored by Matthew King, superintendent/principal of the Carlisle, Massachusetts, Public School System), Ray Hamilton, principal of Randolph Middle School, is in the process of terminating a veteran teacher. In Case II, Helen Hanlin, principal of Willow Creek Elementary, is searching for ways to increase staff morale and minimize interpersonal frictions. As their stories unfold, what they learn about their development plays a key role in shaping their decisions and actions. By being aware of their development and then making specific choices based on that awareness, they gain a sense of efficacy. In both cases, doubt and struggle slowly give way to feelings of increased confidence. By listening to themselves, these school leaders are better able to deal with both personal and professional issues. Their attitudes and behaviors further influence others in the school community. Their stories are vivid illustrations of developmental theory in practice.

CASE 1: INTERSECTIONS BETWEEN PERSONAL GROWTH AND A CRISIS IN THE WORKPLACE

This is a story. Part of the story is about a school principal terminating a veteran teacher whom he has judged to be ineffective. It tells of his decision to dismiss the teacher, the reactions of the faculty and community, involvement of the local and state teachers' associations, and what finally happened. Another part of the story – often important, but rarely recognized – is about the principal's own personal development. This part of the story describes a man approaching middle adulthood and going through a developmental transition. As both events unfold, the drama lies in their intersection. Here the principal's awareness of personal issues supports a series of professional decisions leading to a resolution of the crisis, individual insights for the principal and some teachers, and a strengthened sense of community and shared purpose. For the past four years, Ray Hamilton has been principal of Randolph Middle School, a medium-size school west of Philadelphia. During this time, he has established himself as a dynamic and fair school leader, respected and trusted by colleagues and the community. Ray has worked hard to build a positive culture in the school. He is particularly pleased with the system-wide teacher evaluation plan he helped develop. Overall, teachers feel good about working at Randolph; Ray Hamilton is proud of what he has accomplished. It is against this background that Ray was surprised by reactions to a recent evaluation decision – and by his own feelings. In this case, we will relate the story as Ray Hamilton told it to us, interspersing his voice with our own narrative and comments.

The Story

> This year has been quite a roller coaster. I'd go from periods of elation and a sense of people being behind me to moments of questioning and despair. What was I doing? Was I ruining everything I had built up over the years? This crisis caused me to examine what it means to be a leader and has left me with a clearer sense of myself.

The story began several years ago, when Hamilton began to feel very strongly that there was a veteran teacher in the school not working up to the standards expected of teachers in the district. The teacher continually had problems relating to students and found it hard to manage or motivate them. Over a period of two years, Ray, two other administrators, and a consultant worked intensively with the teacher, identifying problem areas and offering specific suggestions. By the spring of the second year, after almost no change, Ray reached the conclusion that the teacher should be dismissed.

> Looking that man in the eye and telling him that I would be recommending his dismissal was the most difficult thing I've ever done. Would you believe that I actually had tears in my eyes? The whole experience leading up to this conversation was agonizing. There was observation after observation, followed by unpleasant conferences and increasing bitterness. While I didn't have any doubts that I was making the right decision, I was troubled by the feeling that once I began this process, things could get out of hand. Although I'd successfully counseled teachers to leave in the past, I knew this would be different. I like to be in control, and once I started this process, I didn't know what would happen.

After trying unsuccessfully to negotiate an agreement with the teacher and a representative from the local teachers' association, Hamilton proceeded, with the support of the superintendent, to initiate a dismissal process. When a representative from the state association held a press conference and attended a meeting of the local association, the story became public. Over the next several months, a number of teachers wrote letters to the school committee, disagreeing with the principal and supporting the teacher. Within the school, the tension was "palpable." Within Ray, a characteristic sense of optimism and self-confidence was replaced by a growing sense of despair.

Hamilton describes the situation as a crisis. Although on the surface teaching and learning continued as before, Hamilton became painfully aware that this incident had become the major topic of conversation around the school. People were taking sides, and many initially disagreed with Hamilton's decision. After years of professional and congenial relationships between himself and the faculty, Ray feared ruining the school culture he had worked so long and hard to establish. More fundamentally, he felt isolated and profoundly disappointed.

> What it raised in me was a sense of feeling very alone. I just didn't want anything to do with people around here. I felt really let down; I felt they had let me down.

In reality, the erosion of support was much less dramatic than it felt.

Some teachers privately agreed with Ray's decision, and many who disagreed acknowledged his skills as an evaluator and accepted his professional judgment.

> I pointed out to people that it didn't make sense for them to say I'm a good evaluator and then complain when I give someone an unfavorable evaluation. That's why a lot of people supported me. They said, "Hey look, that's his job, and if this is his evaluation, fine."

As the situation intensified, Ray began to think about himself: Who am I? What am I doing? Do I want another job? He brought these questions to the men in a support group he belongs to and to his rereading of *The Seasons of a Man's Life*, Daniel Levinson's book about men's development. Ever since assuming his current position, Ray has been participating in a men's group that meets every two weeks to talk about personal and professional issues. For weeks he shared the details of the crisis, looking to the group for guidance and perspective. In talking with the group, Ray began to realize he was dealing with more than the repercussions of dismissing a teacher; he was dealing with a developmental shift. Rereading Levinson's book confirmed his and the group's suspicions. In particular, Ray came across a paragraph that put into words exactly what he was feeling.

Levinson identifies a phase between ages thirty-five and forty, which he calls The Late Settling-Down Period. During this time, "becoming one's own man" is a major incentive. Part of the work of this period is to sort out conflicting desires to establish oneself as an individual and to be accepted. Ray read:

> On the one hand, a man wants to be more *independent*, more true to himself and less vulnerable to pressure…from others. On the other hand, he seeks *affirmation* in society. Speaking with his own voice is important, even if no one listens – but he especially wants to be heard and respected and be given rewards that are his due. The wish for independence leads him to do what he alone considers most essential, regardless of consequences; the wish for affirmation, however, makes him sensitive to the responses of others and susceptible to their influence.[111]

As soon as Ray read this paragraph, he felt something inside him fall into place. Mulling it over and talking with members of his support group, he began to realize that the feeling was a sign of recognition. Having words for his feelings, he began to experience a sense of relief. As his numbness was gradually replaced by understanding, he began to feel stronger and more confident.

> For the first time, I understood that I was caught right in the middle of an ambivalence. I wanted to have my cake and eat it too, and that was unrealistic. I wanted to be able to fire this person, and because of all the goodwill that we had established, have everyone feel good about it – and about me. Reading the paragraph was an insight. The insight was: This is what I'm feeling. I'm feeling numb, and the numbness is from this dilemma. After I read it, a lot of the numbness went away.

With the numbness greatly eased, Ray was able to articulate how he had been feeling. Understanding the nature of his ambivalence, he was also freed to decide which side of the conflict would guide his future feelings and actions.

> Underneath the numbness, I discovered that I had been feeling abandoned by people. I thought I'd ruined the school, that I had eroded all my support, that I was vulnerable to other people's evaluations of me, and that I was a bad person. When I read this, I became much less vulnerable to what I feared people thought of me and more directed from the inside in the belief that I had done what was right.

Armed with this powerful insight and the feelings that accompanied it, Ray devised a plan and proceeded to carry it out. He called a faculty meeting and shared simply and honestly what everyone had been experiencing but had been unable to discuss. Feeling more confident, he spoke to the faculty, never specifically mentioning the crisis.

> This has been a very tough year, and I just had some things I wanted to share with you. First of all, I really apologize, because I know this has been very hard on you. And it's been very hard on me. I told you when I started here four years ago that you can always count on me to be honest and direct. While people might not have agreed with me, they've always felt I was up front with everybody. And I feel

good about that. At the same time, there are instances when I have had to make decisions that aren't popular. I know that I've made a decision this year that was unpopular, but I believe it was the right thing to do.

Sometimes what distinguishes a leader from just a manager is doing the right thing as opposed to doing things right. In this case, I felt that I did the right thing. I guess I'm just going to have to count on the foundation of goodwill and trust we've had that you'll understand.

Then, complimenting the staff on how well things had proceeded in the school despite hard times, and expressing his confidence that they would continue to do so, Hamilton adjourned the meeting. Though he had left time for questions and discussion and urged people to speak up then and afterward, the room remained silent. At the meeting's end, several people came up to compliment him and to remark on his candidness and confidence. Over subsequent weeks, others found their way to his office to talk about the meeting as well as the evaluation decision. In each case, Ray gave teachers the opportunity to express their views, but he was also clear about his own beliefs. "My developmental insight helped me feel more comfortable talking about it. I was also able to rely on the foundation of trust and respect that teachers and I had established."

One of the first things Ray recognized, as he and faculty talked about the events of the past months, was the prevalence of developmental issues. "A number of people I spoke with about the incident had developmental issues they were dealing with, though almost no one seemed to know it." In one case, a teacher in his mid-forties told Ray he was feeling very threatened by the dismissal proceedings. Since the teacher was an outstanding one, Ray asked him how he could possibly have such a reaction. "Well, I'm getting old," the teacher replied. "Is this what's going to happen to me?"

When Ray pointed out that several older teachers had recently retired after long, successful careers, the teacher was surprised he hadn't remembered. He said he was distracted by issues in his own life, questioning where he had been and wondering where he was going. The dismissal incident was like waving a red flag in front of him, signaling that he, too, might some day lose his job. As the teacher talked about his feelings, Ray watched him begin to develop a new perspective.

Certainly everything did not suddenly go smoothly after the brief faculty meeting – not even after weeks of subsequent talking and sharing.

Local newspapers continued to publish critical letters, and there were still heated discussions within the school. Less vulnerable to outside opinion, however, Ray did not find these events as unsettling. At one point, he reasoned philosophically:

> You're judged by your friends and your enemies, and if you don't have any enemies in this business, you're not doing your job. You have to have a clear point of view, and it's inevitable that somebody will not like it.

Multiple Endings

This story has many endings. Over the next several months, a settlement was negotiated with the teacher. For Ray Hamilton, the results of this process have been immediate and promise to be enduring. Always a believer in the importance of a strong school culture, Ray has an even firmer commitment to building and sustaining a positive culture in the school. He is convinced the school would not have survived the recent crisis as well as it did without such a solid foundation. Ray intends to continue focusing on the quality of life for adults in the school.

At the same time, Hamilton wonders whether disappointment is a lurking corollary of high expectations. During the period of despair, a teacher told Ray he overestimated people, expecting more from some adults than they were capable of giving. Another important insight from developmental theory is that each stage of development has built-in opportunities and liabilities and each person has both strengths and limitations. While we often accept and respond to this reality when we work with children, we are much less tolerant of our own frailties.

Hamilton realizes he must consciously attend to both his own developmental strengths and weaknesses and the developmental issues of his adult colleagues. Personal and professional development cannot be neatly separated. Adults bring their whole selves to work when they come to school each morning, just as they carry their work lives home each night.

Less bound by the judgments of others as a result of this work crisis and developmental transition, Hamilton feels more at ease in his role. Although he has always projected a high degree of confidence, he senses a significant shift in how he feels about himself.

> I think I was pretty confident. But I'm also pretty driven, and being driven means I'm always doubting how effective I am. I

think I'm probably less driven now and more confident.

Along with confidence comes a sense of personal efficacy. Hamilton felt immediately empowered by his developmental insight, and he has found that strength sustaining.

> I discovered quite palpably through this ordeal that in a leadership position you are ultimately alone. You have support. I mean, the school committee was very supportive, a few colleagues were supportive, and my family was certainly supportive. But you're still alone. The perspective I gained through understanding what I was dealing with in my personal development was an ally, an intellectual ally. It enabled me to step outside myself. By allowing me to do that, it liberated me from feeling so constrained. I had a much better perspective on things. The insight let me take charge instead of being a victim.

Development implies complex interactions between an individual and his or her environment. Just as the strength of the school's culture was a vital part of how this story unfolded, the nature of the school and the system will help determine the degree of freedom or the constraints on Hamilton and others as they continue to develop. In this case, Hamilton had the chance to act with relative autonomy. As he continues to grow, will the setting remain open and flexible enough to meet his needs? Not surprisingly, this is the issue Hamilton now says he is facing.

> How do I remain active and forward-looking within the same job? That's an issue for me right now. Do I want to stay here? Do I need another job in order to stay active and to keep growing? I haven't so far, because the school has always changed. I have a great deal of autonomy, and I work with a wonderful group of teachers and parents.

Though Hamilton's most recent crisis has left him with many questions, he feels there is still room to grow in his present school system. He wonders about education more generally, however, and the opportunities for growth and change in the profession. As adults develop, will schools provide the ingredients of support and flexibility essential to continuing growth and change?

In Case 2, Helen Hanlin leaves the field because she believes working in a school can no longer satisfy her developmental needs. At a time when she is capable of acting with a great deal of independence, she has been held back by school system rules and policies. Finally she decides the compromises she has had to make are no longer compatible with her changing values and growing sense of autonomy. Will Ray Hamilton ultimately need to make the same decision?

People often ask how developmental theory plays itself out in everyday situations. Certainly this story is a good illustration. Further, it demonstrates the direct links between developmental insight, decision making, and action. Once Hamilton recognized the ambivalence in which he was caught, he was better able to see his choices. Once he decided where he stood, he took action. The faculty meeting he called, subsequent conversations with faculty, and the way he conducted himself throughout the rest of the negotiations were all actions directly influenced by his insight, his decision, and the norm of open and honest communication that Hamilton had established within the school.

Hamilton intends to bring the developmental perspective directly to the faculty. He has already asked an expert in the area of adult development to come to a future faculty meeting. He plans to begin the meeting by sharing his own developmental transition as a way of demonstrating how his personal development is an issue for him in his work, just as it is for all of them.

Ray is also considering the importance of his peer support group and plans to suggest similar groups to his teachers as vehicles for general sharing and more specific understanding of the intersections between personal and professional growth. Hamilton's experience attests to the potential power of these kinds of groups (see Chapter 11). In one school we know, the principal has brought in a psychologist to meet with teachers monthly, with an agenda targeted toward personal issues and away from everyday classroom incidents. Within the group, the psychologist reports a tremendous amount of personal and professional growth among the participants; within the school, the principal and teachers notice more collegiality among staff and a significant increase in the level of energy for and interest in teaching and learning.

Lessons

This story has a number of important lessons. Hamilton identifies four of these lessons himself:

The number one lesson is: You need to listen to yourself. Number two: You need a framework and a vocabulary to think about yourself as an evolving adult. If you don't have a framework, you can't listen; all you have is feelings. Once you put things together, lesson three is the need to think about what it is you should do and translate that into action. Lesson four deals with considering your role as supervisor. To work effectively, you must take into account an adult developmental perspective.

Knowing something about the way adults grow and change and the issues that are most important at specific ages can help us understand our own interests and dilemmas, as well as the issues and preoccupations of colleagues. Not only can this understanding influence our daily decisions and actions, but it can also serve as a guide for devising individually tailored staff development plans and programs.

At the intersection of the developmental and professional issues that play themselves out in the case of Ray Hamilton is another important lesson. The close relationship between personal and professional issues means that educators must attend to both strands of development. An understanding of adult development theory can provide a framework and a language to anticipate and respond to these personal and professional intersections.

Ray Hamilton's story suggests several conditions that appear to facilitate the use of a developmental framework. The context for growth must be a healthy and fertile one. This is true whether the setting is a school or a peer support group. Unless the culture is strong – to allow for inevitable transitions and crises – and supportive – to nurture delicate changes – the already rocky journey of growth may become tumultuous. An attitude of self-reflection is an especially important facilitator of the growth process, as is a willingness to engage in open and honest communication. If Ray had not sought to understand himself better, he would have been unlikely to ask himself and others the kinds of questions that led him to understand his work and developmental crisis. If he had not been willing to communicate honestly and directly with others and give them the opportunity to share, in return, the level of misunderstanding and crisis would have escalated and the degree of growth and learning would have declined.

Finally, as Ray Hamilton discovered, everybody is at a developmental point that influences how he or she feels and thinks. Few of us, however, recognize the influence of adult growth. A developmental perspective offers the opportunity to become more aware of what is going on within our own lives, in the lives of colleagues, and in the lives of students. As a result, this perspective paves the way to more satisfactory working relationships among adults and a more positive learning environment for children.

CASE 2: INTERSECTIONS BETWEEN PERSONAL GROWTH AND STAFF DEVELOPMENT

This is a three-part story. Part one is about a school principal trying to find a cure for low staff morale. It tells of her discoveries at a summer conference, her return to school, and the impact of what she learned and shared on curriculum development, staff morale, and student learning. Another part of the story is about teachers' awareness of their personal development and the significance of that awareness for the way they interact as a faculty and with children. Part three describes the principal's growth. It charts the evolution of a series of insights that change the way the principal works with adults in the school and lead to more fundamental professional and personal choices.

At age forty-two, Helen Hanlin has been a principal for six years, two at Willow Creek and four at nearby Lawrence Elementary. Formerly a kindergarten, first-, third-, and sixth-grade teacher, Helen knew from the time she was young that she wanted to work with children. In fact, she had no ambition to move out of the classroom until colleagues recognized her organizational and leadership skills and "ushered" her first into a curriculum coordinator's role and then into a principalship. Helen's story begins during the summer between her first and second years at Willow Creek.

The Story

All year long, I'd been feeling restless and uneasy. Things didn't feel right anywhere in my life. When I finally had a way to think about what was going on, the tensions gradually eased. At school, I had some guidelines for working with staff; outside of school, I was finally able to begin making some informed choices.

Helen Hanlin left for a summer conference with "an assignment" from her faculty: "Find something to boost staff morale." Though teaching and learning were proceeding relatively smoothly at Willow Creek Elementary, there was a sense of malaise among teachers that Helen couldn't seem to pinpoint or eradicate. The conference introduced Helen to stage and phase theories of adult development. She explains:

> I had read *Passages* by Gail Sheehy before I came to the conference, but I never thought of *using* the ideas in any way with adults. After I learned more about adult development, I realized I had to do something with these concepts. But I also realized I couldn't "fix" people myself. I had a responsibility as leader of the building to initiate, but then it became a joint responsibility.

Helen played with these ideas throughout the conference, talking with other administrators and exchanging experiences. Though she continued to have many questions and uncertainties, she left the conference energized. With the beginnings of some fresh insights and with a host of new information, she eagerly returned to Ohio.

Even before the school year started, Helen called the grade level chairpersons together to share what she had learned. Laying out her notes, she charted the age-related phases of development. "Oh, my," reacted one of the team leaders as she found herself on the timeline. "Have I been that difficult to get along with?" Another team leader joined in, "Now I know I'm going to be facing the 'empty nest syndrome' next year. But how do I deal with it?"

A lively discussion followed about how the staff could support each other through the predictable cycle of personal development while still working to meet their professional responsibilities. As the meeting ended, Helen underscored the need for the staff to address personal and interpersonal issues within the school. She left them to determine the way they would proceed.

Two weeks later, a disappointed but still hopeful Helen Hanlin reconvened a meeting of the grade level chairpersons. After what appeared to be a positive start, Helen had heard nothing. Though she prodded the leaders to formulate next steps, she was met with silence. Staff members told Helen they needed more time.

Once school opened, the grade chairs passed Helen's information on to teachers. Still, nothing happened. Helen checked in with her faculty every week, but they were at the talking stage and not yet ready to take action. In fact, Helen noted initial signs of withdrawal among staff:

> When I went down the hall, teachers would literally duck into doorways. They just didn't want to see me. It was as if they were readable and predictable; self-awareness had also generated vulnerability.

Several weeks into the fall term, four teachers came to see Helen. They had become aware of a number of their developmental issues but did not know how to address them. How did personal and professional issues connect? Weren't they in the school to work with children? Helen explained that personal issues are present independent of one's awareness of them. Understanding personal development can give adults the perspective they need to recognize and put personal issues in their place and the empathy to support others through difficult times.

> We need to find ways of helping each other through – like saying, "Obviously you're being distracted, but what can I do to help you finish this report?" – something that honors the person by recognizing the issues and feelings but also says we have a professional role to perform.

Another six weeks passed before a small group of teachers made an appointment to see Helen. This time they had a great deal to say as they laid out a broad plan for improving both staff morale and curriculum. Helen describes it as "the most comprehensive teacher in-service building plan I've ever seen." She also admits that it is a plan she could never have devised alone; nor could she have convinced her staff to try it if the ideas had not come from them.

Following up on a reading theme Helen had set for the year before, teachers proposed an in-depth focus on writing. "Writers Are Winners" involved children in reading and writing, listening and role playing. It was a broad-based plan making writing an integral part of the curriculum. Before long, students were checking books out of the library in record numbers; first teachers and then children started keeping journals. Helen had planned to introduce the idea of journal writing herself. A technique used at the summer conference, Helen had found it a helpful tool for thinking and sharing. When teachers discovered it themselves, she was delighted.

Keeping journals was a logical consequence of the planning and brainstorming teachers and students were doing. Realizing that ideas come at different times during the day and not necessarily at a planning session or during a forty-five-minute writing period, teachers began to carry pads around with them. In the classroom, they noted some of their ideas on the blackboard. Soon children began doing the same things. Even parents got involved, initiating a newspaper as a forum for children's writing, demonstrating creative ways to do puzzles, and introducing new vocabulary.

What started as a focus on teachers began to spread throughout the school community.

Helen believes the depth and breadth of these efforts and the energy from teachers needed to sustain the program emerged directly from their focus on personal development and Helen's explicit acknowledgment of adult needs.

> Teachers had been operating on a superficial level, but they were not at all operating that way at the start of this year. Learning about adult development, they had become increasingly introspective. They pushed themselves into looking at kids as people because now *they* had been treated as people.

Helen's role was largely confined to maintaining the positive atmosphere in the school and supporting the adults who were creating it. She wondered what small changes she might make to sustain teachers' energy and enthusiasm. Interestingly, her first ideas involved food – a literal form of nourishment. In addition to bringing doughnuts to school two or three mornings a week, Helen used money from her discretionary budget to pay for a salad bar for teachers one Friday each month. On alternate Fridays, baked potatoes were made available. Instead of a low-energy time, Fridays became "a big party day in the building." Helen reflects, "I wish I had known these little things were that important. It was easy enough for me to respond to them."

Beyond Helen's supportive efforts, teachers devised ways of sustaining each other. Along one wall of the teachers' lounge, they posted a large drawing of the developmental timeline, writing beside each phase key issues and conflicts. From time to time, they wrote each other's names on the chart, both as a form of humor and as a way of acknowledging a colleague's concerns. Now having a framework and vocabulary, they began to share their thoughts and feelings. Hanlin believes the developmental framework fostered more and better communication among teachers on many levels. With the aid of the framework, she also believes, the faculty became increasingly collegial as they adopted a school-wide, rather than a classroom, focus.

As these dynamics played themselves out among faculty and students within the school, many changes were taking place for Helen Hanlin. When Helen learned about the age-forty transition, she began to wonder if her own sense of confusion and unrest might be linked to this developmental shift. "Things just didn't seem to be fitting." So Helen, known for her direct style and willingness to scrutinize herself, decided to take stock of her life. She created a detailed inventory, listing her past and present hopes and objectives. What was it that she wanted at one time of her life that shaped the choices she was now living out? Did she still have the same goals and preferences? Reviewing the lists, she was startled by the discrepancies. She began to wonder how much of her present discomfort was related to the conflicts these lists uncovered. Intent on finding out, Helen decided it was time to make peace with the mismatch or to make a series of new choices. Caught in a developmental transition, she needed to reassess her past and determine future directions.

When Helen looked closely at her professional life, she noticed that she had developed a number of strong educational beliefs and values over the years, though she rarely had the time to identify them and apply them to her practice. Career ladders were just one of numerous "innovations" to which Helen objected. She did not like pitting teachers against one another and was, in fact, afraid that the adoption of a career ladder in the system might undo all of her staff's progress toward establishing a sense of cohesion.

After a great deal of thought and initial ambivalence, Helen decided she needed to find a setting that demanded less compromise. After six years in the principalship, she decided it was time to move on.

> I chose to leave the school I dearly loved. I loved the staff, the community, and the kids. The strong feelings I had for them kept me there. But I was not allowing myself to deal with the fact that I had changed. In some significant ways, my beliefs and values were different.

Just as Helen was feeling unsettled in her career, she was also questioning her marriage. A sluggish economy had recently resulted in her husband Frank's layoff from work. While both Helen and Frank were angry and frustrated by the situation, Helen sensed that Frank was also angry for other reasons that she couldn't pinpoint. They began to worry that they might no longer "fit." Looking closely at the developmental framework together helped them identify their individual conflicts. Gradually they recognized they had different needs, "issues we had to sort out whether or not we lived under the same roof." For the first time, Helen felt she was able to separate herself from her husband in a way that allowed them both to determine their own needs and recognize their individual boundaries.

This description of separation and individuation defines Helen's more general developmental shift: "I recognized that I have a separate identity from other people, that I can be of service and in service without being a nonentity."

Multiple Endings

Viewed through a developmental framework, all stories have multiple endings. Since each person experiences herself and her world distinctly, the "same" events are subject to numerous interpretations. In this story, Helen Hanlin left the principalship. Helen and Frank remain married, though they continue to work out the ways they can be both together and separate. Two years after Helen's departure from Willow Creek, faculty morale is reported to remain much improved. Helen keeps in close contact with several colleagues. Together they wonder whether the school environment will be able to support the choices and changes the adults there are making. Will the school's new principal give teachers the space and support to keep growing? These endings are yet to be written. Helen describes the impact of her developmental insights in broad and enthusiastic terms:

> Let me say this, and I mean it quite honestly: If I had not been introduced to the concepts of adult development, I don't believe I'd be married today and at peace with my marriage, myself; my choices, or where I'm going with my life. I here's no question about that. It was like a transforming experience. It changed my life.

Though Helen makes this transition seem magical, she also acknowledges that changes happened slowly and not without the pains and joys inherent in development.

Since leaving the principalship, Helen has spent a great deal of time talking with school groups about adult growth. She has also begun to create teacher-training materials. She likes the freedom, the intellectual challenge, and the noticeable impact of her work on people's lives. What she will do next is uncertain. At this point in her development, however, she believes she will stay in the field of education.

Lessons

Helen Hanlin's story dramatizes the powerful influence of insight and its link to decision making and action. Once Helen learned about adult development and began to make connections between the concepts and the ways teachers could be experiencing themselves and the school, she realized she had to share what she was learning with teachers and other administrators. The theories also helped her to see that she could not effect the kind of changes she envisioned alone. Not only is the principalship a lonely position, but widespread expectations of the principal's omniscience are seriously misguided. As Helen discovered, the principal can (and should) initiate change, but then the responsibility for change must be shared.

It was not enough for Helen to be empowered by her developmental discoveries. She needed to plant the seed with teachers and wait until it began to germinate. Recognizing that change is a slow and complex process and that principals, as change agents, must be patient, it is not surprising that Helen's post-conference fervor was not immediately infectious. Teachers' first inclinations to "duck into doorways" when they saw Helen coming underscore both the potency of the framework and the fragility of the adults whose lives give the theories meaning.

Though Helen continued to prod the staff, she could not make them go much faster than their own readiness. When they did finally come to her on their own terms, they more than satisfied her hopes and expectations.

In fact, once the change process takes hold, the leader may have a relatively subsidiary role. By introducing the developmental material, Helen provided the substance for change; by waiting for teachers to determine their own course of action and then nurturing them as they worked through the process, Helen created and maintained a fertile and supportive context for growth. Perhaps this is a principal's most primary function. Perhaps leadership is less pulling and pushing and more initiating and supporting. At least, this was true in Helen Hanlin's case.

Helen arrived at the summer conference tired and confused. She knew something was awry in her life, but she didn't know what it was. As she made more and more connections between developmental theory and her own life, she felt at once relieved and empowered. The relief came from finally being able to identify and talk about her concerns; the empowerment derived from the opportunity to make fresh choices. Options are an important component of both school change and personal development.

Not only did Willow Creek staff gain a new vocabulary for understanding and talking about themselves, but greater self-awareness stimulated greater understanding of others. An increasingly broadened perspective allowed teachers to see beyond their classrooms to the school as a whole. Where miscommunication and lack of sharing had been part of the interpersonal breakdown at the school, collaboration and honest communication became important parts of the solution.

Interestingly, both Helen's and the teachers' insights were spawned by conflict or crisis. Helen was "stuck and in pain" when she arrived at the conference. Staff morale was low and waning when teachers left Willow Creek in June. Using the developmental paradigm as a model, change is often a product of disequilibrium. The crises of development that Erikson calls "turning points" create opportunities for break*down* or break*through*. After a period of disequilibrium, a new balance must be established. In the school, teachers worked together through a curriculum project to restore the school's balance. To regain her sense of equilibrium, it was necessary for Helen to leave the principalship, though she was still able to work within the boundaries of her marriage.

The specific nature of Helen's developmental transition traces a familiar pattern from lesser to greater self-definition. One of the reasons it was so hard for Helen to identify where she was, or decide where she was going, resulted from her developmental tendency to overidentify with the people and things around her. As a profession emphasizing service and self-sacrifice, education can reinforce a pattern of overidentification. Helen attests to this when she recognizes: "I had made an unfortunate link in my identity to the job. Given the time and space to think about that, I was able to sort out the pieces."

On the other side of the developmental transition, Helen began to rediscover and redefine her sense of self. Once she recognized her separate identity, she was freer to help others and more able to remain true to herself.

Helen links some of the stress and pressure she was feeling to her strong drive to succeed. In part, she attributes this drive to more general societal pressures to compete and achieve. Another source of pressure, however, she believes is particular to being a woman in a leadership position. Women leaders, in Helen's experience, often feel "an amorphous kind of pressure to be much more productive than men in order to get equal recognition." This may be a cultural liability for women that contributes to their distinct experience and, perhaps, to differences in their development.

Helen Hanlin's story suggests several conditions that appear to facilitate the use of a developmental framework. First is the presence of a supportive environment. In Helen's case, the context for growth was away from her school at a summer conference. Here she had the time and encouragement to focus on herself – a luxury not often available to her at home or work. Clearly, ongoing development is best supported in a regularly accessible environment. When no such environment exists, however, a temporary context for growth (e.g., conferences, retreats, vacations) may be an important stimulus for development. An attitude of self-reflection is another condition that facilitates the use of a developmental framework. Had Helen not been willing to relate the theory to her own life, her gains from the conference would have been limited to a rich set of class notes. Helen developed the awareness she did by listening to voices both within and outside herself.

Helen's experience and her story illustrate once again that personal and professional growth cannot easily be pulled apart. Her personal development was initiated at a professional conference; her staff's professional growth was spurred on by personal insights. In fact, Helen's case underscores the importance of making personal and professional development complementary rather than competing objectives. Helen knows that personal issues will be present independent of whether they are recognized. With increased awareness comes the possibility of better understanding and more control.

Connections between the growth of adults and children's learning are striking in the case of Helen Hanlin. The energy generated from a developmental insight appears to be contagious. When adults become more reflective, they may adopt a similar attitude toward students. Treating teachers as adults may also serve as a model for the way they behave toward children.

The power of modeling is another important lesson. Its effects were evident on multiple levels around Helen Hanlin. After Helen shared the adult development material with her grade chairpersons, they did the same with teachers. When children saw teachers putting their writing ideas on the board and in journals, they also started writing. In turn, parent involvement was sparked by the activities of teachers and children.

When some people learn that development starts from within, they are initially discouraged. Changing the behavior of others often seems more palatable than changing our own. Since behavioral changes are among the most difficult objectives to accomplish, the tremendous power of modeling as a catalyst for change is extremely encouraging.

A final and hopeful lesson is how simply some significant changes can be made. From providing special lunches to treating teachers and administrators like adults, enhancing the school environment may require little cost and effort and may yield great benefits. The story of Helen Hanlin makes a strong case for attending to issues of adult development.

CONCLUDING COMMENTS

What can be learned from the stories of Ray Hamilton and Helen Hanlin? In both cases, we have seen the influence of insight and its link to decision making and action. We have seen that the developmental framework can be an important catalyst for change. Not only do these insights empower those who have them, but they lead to the empowerment of others. For both Ray Hamilton and Helen Hanlin, developmental insights paved the way for more direct and open communications. Their sharing also led to insights and changes for others.

Adults are continually growing. As Ray Hamilton discovered, all the adults in the school had developmental issues with which they were dealing. More often than not, however, they were unaware of these issues and, therefore, unable to apply developmental insights to their personal and professional lives. Awareness is an essential precondition for using this perspective. Understanding the developmental framework gave Ray, Helen, and a number of teachers the words to express their feelings and the vocabulary and confidence to talk candidly with one another.

The developmental framework has its greatest impact on individuals when the insights it offers are internalized and used as a basis for understanding, decision making, and subsequent actions. When Helen realized she couldn't "fix people," but that change was a joint responsibility, her role as leader shifted from lone and lonely miracle maker to individual and group facilitator. Not only did this shift free Helen of the heavy and unrealistic burdens she had been carrying for everyone, but it gave her the opportunity to take responsibility for herself.

Interestingly, both Ray's and Helen's insights are spawned by conflict and crisis. In Ray's case, conflicts about terminating a teacher sparked his personal development; in Helen's case, personal conflicts led to professional changes. Ray knew he felt alienated from his faculty; he understood he was isolated and in conflict, but he did not know quite why or what to do about it. When Helen arrived at the summer conference, she was looking for more than a cure for low staff morale; she was personally "stuck and in pain." She knew she had to do something, but what ailed her or what she might do about it remained elusive. Developmental theory helped Ray and Helen put their personal and professional lives in perspective.

The natures of Ray's and Helen's developmental shifts are remarkably similar. Each involves a separation of the self from others that allows for increased independence. Ray put enough distance between his own judgments and others' judgments of him to allow him to make a clear, unconflicted decision. Helen disentangled herself from her job and from her husband in order to feel more "at peace."

Both Ray and Helen link some of the stress and pressure they were feeling to a sense of drive. Ray says his strong drive always made him doubt the quality of what he was doing. Helen's drive kept her in constant motion, distracting her from paying attention to her own needs. Looking back at her most recent choices, she says:

> If someone had told me two years ago that I'd be making these choices, I would have thought: "No way. I mean, that's just not typical of me. I'm too task oriented. I've got my list of things to do; I've got my timeline." But none of these tasks included giving myself permission to take a look at me as a person. That's the competitive nature of our society and the strong cultural norms of achievement, and I'm definitely tied to both.

Part of Ray's and Helen's hesitations in responding to their own needs may also stem from the profession's strong service orientation. Educators are continually called upon to do things for others; often they run out of time for themselves.

Ray's and Helen's drives have one important difference. Helen believes that being a woman in a leadership position carries with it particular pressures to achieve just to stay even with her male colleagues. Determining whether this perspective is realistic may be less immediately important than recognizing and responding to Helen's perceptions as a force in her professional life. Clearly, issues of differences among school leaders and between men and women principals merit continuing attention.

We see in both cases that personal and professional growth are closely related. Development is a complicated, integrated process that encompasses all aspects of functioning, from one's job to one's marriage, from one's view of self to one's perceptions of others. Helen's case, in particular, points to the importance of linking personal and professional development. While teachers at Willow Creek were doing a good job with students, breakdowns in their interpersonal relationships, stemming in part from unrecognized developmental issues, impeded interactions among adults, as well as between adults and children.

The potential impact of developmental insights for adults on the lives and learning of children is an especially powerful lesson. So, too, is the significance of modeling. More than rhetoric, action may be an effective catalyst for school improvement. Likewise, the principal may make the greatest contribution to schools by supporting and sustaining the development of teachers, rather than by mandating change or pulling and pushing teachers toward a predetermined objective. Providing teachers with useful information that promises to make a difference to their personal and professional lives seems to be a first step in initiating change. Giving teachers the time and encouragement to make use of new information may come next, closely followed by continued nurturance.

The stories of Ray Hamilton and Helen Hanlin are powerful and dramatic. In addition to highlighting the individualistic nature of their experiences, both cases also draw attention to context. Hamilton insists on the importance of a positive school culture. Without it, he believes, neither he nor the school would have survived intact. In Helen Hanlin's case, the positive involvement of teachers, children, and parents is also evident. Change in schools, as in all complex organizations, is difficult to initiate and sustain. Individual, school, system, and community support and involvement increase the possibility of pervasive and tenacious improvements.

These stories are deceptively straightforward. School administrators gain insights into their personal development that spark dramatic changes for them and those around them. A number of complex conditions and qualities are needed to make developmental theories useful, however. Externally, there is the need for a supportive environment. Internally, energy, commitment, introspection, honesty, and courage are just a few of the personal qualities that Ray Hamilton and Helen Hanlin seem to have in common. Many threads are woven into the fabric of an effective school leader, and many tools are necessary to support and enhance the performance and satisfaction of the adults who work in schools. A developmental framework is one such tool, potentially serving as both an ally and a guide.

Part Four

Promising Practices

10

Writing

I want to write essays about the issues I'm involved in at work. I want to move into fictional territory. And I want to run a writing group for teachers in my school. I think all educators need to experience more of the artistic in themselves.

Hardly a day or hour goes by without some kind of writing coming from a teacher's or principal's desk.

These comments are quoted or adapted from conversations with practitioners who have become involved in writing. They underscore both the reality and the potential of writing for teachers and administrators. Not only is writing something that is required of the adults in schools, but it can also be a catalyst for self-expression and self-awareness.

When colleagues and I have looked closely at the writing process, we have discovered parallels between effective writing, professional development, and adult growth.[112] All three require reflection, collaboration, and ownership. Writing is, by its nature, a reflective activity. Professional development – such as reading and independent study or clinical supervision and peer coaching – necessitates observation and feedback. Adults gradually increase their ability to see and know themselves as they continue to develop.

Contrary to popular belief, writing is not a solitary act. Instead, writers refine their thinking and expression by sharing and receiving feedback. Most forms of professional development require internal as well as external supports. And development, as we have seen, takes place in the context of interpersonal relationships.

Finally, the effectiveness of writing, professional development, and adult growth is predicated on a sense of ownership. When adults determine their own directions for change, changes are more likely to take place – and to stick. It is a lot easier to disown something we *say* than it is to divorce ourselves from what we *write*. Professional development activities are far more likely to be engaging and sustaining when teachers and administrators have a hand and a voice in their determination. Adult development is an active process, not a passive one.

Writing and thereby professional development and adult growth can be structured for practitioners in writing groups, faculty meetings, and conferences. It can be initiated and supported by teachers, administrators, students, and parents. What follows are several examples of writing activities that have stimulated writing, professional development, and adult growth. They are drawn from work at the Principals' Center at Harvard[113] and the influence of Principals' Center activities in schools.

The chapter begins with a description of the Center's Writing Group, described by the group's coordinator. Also included are an excerpt and comments from the journal of one practitioner/participant and reflections during an interview I did with another. I go on to describe the way we have integrated writing into our annual summer institute. All of these approaches are readily adaptable for schools, districts, and professional associations. Descriptions of how writing is used during the school year reinforce this point. I end the chapter with a brief section on writing for publication, a goal that can be lofty and frightening, but also positive and productive.

Using Writing as a Means for Personal and Professional Development

VICKI A. JACOBS

Vicki A. Jacobs is Coordinator of the Principals' Center Writing Group, Instructor in Reading, and Assistant Director of Teacher Training at the Harvard Graduate School of Education.

The Principals' Center at Harvard University has sponsored a Writing Group for a number of years. Educational administrators join this group to reflect upon and raise questions about their practice and to pursue answers to those questions with the support of their colleagues.

Before I assumed leadership of the Principals' Center Writing Group, it was essentially a mini-grant program designed to support administrators who wanted to publish. The emphasis I chose to take was on writing as a reflective means for professional development. Thus, in the fall of 1983, I advertised the Writing Group as a "context for reflective dialogue among professional peers."

Over four years, the Writing Group's membership grew from six to sixteen. Members have included a variety of administrators: principals, assistant principals, a special education director, an admissions director, and staff developers. Despite their diversity, members join the group because of a common interest: to receive collegial support through writing. To meet the needs of the various members, the Writing Group serves multiple purposes: as a supportive community for administrators, as a training ground in elements of the writing process, and as a clearinghouse for publication. Similar groups could be created for teachers or for teachers and administrators.

The Writing Group meets monthly from October through May. Each two-hour meeting is generally divided into two parts.[114] The first half usually consists of a group discussion in which writing is used to generate, analyze, and synthesize ideas. The group members prepare for this discussion in two ways. First, they "freewrite," that is, take a written inventory, without stopping or editing, of whatever comes to their minds. Such writing allows members to acknowledge and then dismiss baggage from the day, to diffuse heightened feelings, to unearth biases, to discover focal ideas, and to reveal the unexpected. The time spent freewriting tends to bond the group as a writing community and allows each member to "arrive," centering his or her energy on writing and thinking.

Following the freewriting, the group continues to prepare itself for discussion by synthesizing reflections about a topic selected for discussion at the previous meeting. Members are encouraged to write about the assigned topic between meetings and to analyze the relation of the issue to their work. Together again at a meeting, members reflect upon their interim writing by summarizing how their thinking about the issue has evolved, what questions still remain for them, and what they would most like to hear addressed by others in the group.

Discussion ensues for about an hour. Issues for discussion have included such topics as using writing to investigate thoughts about administering, maintaining personal voice in administrative writing, using computer-aided instruction in writing, the role of writing in staff development and evaluation, and encouraging writing and implementing writing groups in schools. When discussion seems to have peaked, members write about how their thinking has progressed, what questions remain, and what they need help clarifying.

The second half of the meeting is usually spent in small groups where members provide each other with formative responses. The focus of formative response is just that: the formation of writing and thinking. It is thus different from summative or evaluative response, which often simply passes judgment. During formative response, respondents help writers rethink or clarify their meaning. Responsibility for the relevance of response is shared between writer and respondents. Writers are responsible for establishing where they are in their thinking and writing and where they would like to proceed, as well as establishing the kind of support they think they need. In turn, respondents are responsible for inviting writers to continue their reflection in pursuit of clarification. One kind of response involves the respondents' actively listening to text and feeding back to the writer what they hear. Writers then judge whether what was heard was what they intended to be heard. If there are discrepancies, the writer's task is to figure out why they exist and then how they can be resolved. This kind of exchange encourages writers' investment in and accountability for the development of their thinking and writing.

The Writing Group works quite successfully. When asked why, members offered the following reasons:

Clarity of Purpose. Members know that the group's focus is on communication. Participants join with the expectation that they must, at minimum, share their thinking through writing.

Risk, Commitment, and Investment. Commitment to the group seems to be directly related to the amount of risk that members are asked to take. Writing is, by nature, risky business; and sharing writing is even riskier. Both are required of members.

Community. Risk taking occurs in the Writing Group on an individual and on a community level. Commitment and investment (both related to risk taking) bond the group more tightly with each successive meeting. Members note that such bonding provides them with a special feeling of belonging.

Summary Reports. After each meeting, I synthesize the group's discussions into detailed notes that I mail to members about a week later. These reports are designed to move the group from one place in its thinking to the next, to synthesize seemingly disparate views, to allow group members to find their own voices in the proceedings of the latest meeting, to give members an additional sense of belonging, to provide continuity, and to allow me to keep the group subtly focused.

At the final session, I ask members to reflect in writing about their involvement in the group over the past year and to reflect about its progress. This writing is typed (without members' names) for distribution to members in late summer as a reminder of where the group has been and as a stimulus for members to think about where they might want to head in the coming year.

Leadership. The Writing Group agreed that its leader must have credibility as a writer (although the leader might not be an administrator) and that the leader must take the same risks that other members take. Thus, the Writing Group leader must be a participatory member. In addition to being a group participant, I also plan meetings, facilitate group discussions during meetings, lead training in writing and response, write and distribute meeting notes, encourage members to publish, edit and provide one-on-one response, plan and present workshops during the summer and the academic year, and write articles for the Principals' Center *Newsletter*.

Refreshments. Careful effort is given to providing members with more than just intellectual nourishment. Many members travel up to two hours to attend the meetings after a long workday. There is always a variety of cheese, crackers, and breads; candy, pretzels, and chips; soda, beer, and wine. Often conversations begun during a meeting are extended over coffee or a glass of wine. After the final meeting, the group has dinner together to celebrate.

While the structure of the Writing Group as a whole is easily described, the experience of each cohort is more variable. Although first-year members often intend to produce a publishable piece of writing, they typically spend most of the year discovering their own habits and processes as writers. Second-year members arrive more fluent and at ease in their writing than first-year members; they are also more eager to publish and more anxious about publishing. Veteran group members are the most likely to take a piece of writing to actual publication.

Each member of the Writing Group brings a unique set of personal expectations, which vary as greatly as the personalities that constitute the group. One member may need to write to reflect upon the pros and cons of a mid-career job change, while another may want to produce a piece of writing for professional advancement. Most members crave the collegiality that is cultivated among professional peers in a writing group. Some arrive without a clear agenda, hoping that one will develop with time and writing.

Practitioners come to the Writing Group for many reasons. Once they are part of the group, their experiences demonstrate writing's impact on writers, as well as its potential influence on schools.

An Excerpt and Reflections from the Journal
of One Writing Group Member
WILLIAM WIBEL

Bill Wibel is Principal at Lyle Middle School, Bourne, Massachusetts.

Phasing out! Is it a little like buttoning up? Is it something akin to going out of business? I wonder. Daily I enter the faculty room amidst the din and smoke to encounter a small look of despair. Maybe I should have seen it in the spring. The signs were too subtle. The classes were exciting, the activity-oriented instruction was superb. High levels of discussion and intimacies shared on intellectual levels between teacher and students abounded. No sign of demise.

June's children arrive in September in new faces and jeans; the challenge is ever so much the greater. I see the first signs of concern: the freshness gone, the empathy slipping (maybe that's what I missed last spring). I probe in quiet ways and am told he is overwhelmed. Teaching reading, having the same group daily is a burden. I wince; I know. I look the other way, engaging him on issues over which I can exercise authority and control. I offer out as an alternative. He smiles, not knowing how to deal with himself.

Arriving one early morning to the noise of hammers in the faculty room, I look quizzical. Amused at their humor and practical jokes, I proceed past. Returning later, I am struck by the most creative statement of burnout I have ever seen a faculty member offer: His mailbox is haphazardly nailed up with slats; "Phasing Out" etched in Magic Marker was the statement.

There was enough room to put things between the slats, but not enough room to take them out: creative, clever, but such a statement of truth.

"Phasing Out," a truly perfect statement from a wonderful teacher who is simply saying, "No more."

Having written this piece, I was able to talk further and more empathically with the teacher. Slowly the slats came down. Today the box stands bare of its early markings, and I am thankful. Had I not paused to write and then elicit feedback from Writing Group members, chances are I would not have responded productively. The school might have lost a precious resource.

Reflections in an Interview: Writing Beyond the Group

These comments were made by a school administrator who wishes to remain anonymous.

During the time I've been in the Writing Group, I've accomplished a number of things. I started to use my own notes from staff meetings to send messages to faculty and other administrators – in much the way the Writing Group Coordinator sends notes out to people in the group, summarizing the meeting themes and agendas. I stopped taking notes the way people usually take notes at meetings and I adopted a model that allows me to talk about what I think. It's not just a record of what happens. It takes the record a step further. Often people write back to me, and the notes become a way of continuing a conversation or shaping a subsequent meeting.

Recently we started a writing center at our school. The value I gained from writing in the Writing Group helped me to feel supportive of this initiative and made me want to be part of the process. The central idea of the writing center was like that of the Writing Group: a place to focus on writing and receive *peer support.* I contributed to the center by sharing some of the listening and feedback skills I learned in the Writing Group and by helping with training. Now students throughout the school come to the center with their work. Meanwhile, a colleague and I run a writing group for teachers as part of the staff development program. Periodically we take teachers or classes away from the school for a writing workshop – complete with tablecloths, flowers, and brand new notebooks. At the end of the day, everybody picks his or her best piece of writing. These are then put on a word processor and made into a book! We use the same process for students and for teachers, and they have loved it.

As I look back over the years I've been in the Writing Group, I recognize that my participation has influenced my development as both a writer and an adult. Reflection is a necessary ingredient in adult development, and I think the reflection inherent in writing has been an important stimulus for my growth. As a school administrator, I'm running around frenetically a good deal of the time. Even though I'm predisposed to being reflective and analytical, it's when I really sit down and think, and talk, and put pen to paper that I'm able to reflect productively. Writing is especially important to me because I save it and can therefore gather it together to see where it's growing and going. It's a way of collecting my thinking.

WRITING AT THE SUMMER INSTITUTE

Each year, the Principals' Center sponsors a summer institute, an intensive ten days of talking, reading, listening, and sharing for principals on school improvement. Writing is a central and powerful component of this experience.

Before the one hundred principals arrive, they receive a number of prereadings, including a statement about writing. Here we share with participants our beliefs in and commitment to writing as a vehicle for personal and professional development. We describe writing as a personal experience that can help individuals discover their thoughts, feelings, biases, and assumptions; react to people and issues; and reflect on theory and practice. Equally important, writing is an interpersonal experience, potentially initiating a shared conversation about practice.

On the first day of the institute, every participant and every faculty member receives a small notebook to be used as a journal. During our ten days together, we all use writing and the journals to capture the most important ideas of the institute. By the final day, as we are getting ready to say good-bye, guarding our journals represents a way of holding on to the experiences we have shared. One participant remarked that she would never part with her journal. I feel the same way about the journals on the bookshelf next to my desk, each representing one of the institutes I have attended. From time to time, I take them down, rereading and recapturing the spirit and substance of those times.

During the institute, participants have a variety of opportunities to write and to learn about writing: presentations about writing, short writing times at the end of sessions, extended times during each day, and group times where writing can be shared. At the end of the institute, participants volunteer one journal entry to become part of a collection of writings. Following are two examples.

A Letter from the Principal
LEONARD SIROTZKI

Leonard Sirotzki is Director of Staff Development, District U-46, Elgin, Illinois. Formerly he was Principal at Fairview Elementary School, Hoffman Estates, Illinois.

Dear Boys and Girls:

This summer I went to school at a place called Harvard. I know that's a funny name and not nearly as famous to you as McDonald's, but it's really a kind of neat place. I was there with about a hundred other principals from places all around America and the world. I know you are busy; you have places to go and things to do, but I want very much to tell you something I learned.

Sometimes we big people forget what it's like to be so young. Sometimes we forget how confusing things can be and how scary the whole world can seem. I want you to know that all of us principals are here to help you and to protect you from harm. Did you know that we were once children just like you? We were. We wiggled and giggled and played and sometimes cried. We know you come to school to learn. You want to read and write and work with numbers. You want to color and cut-and-paste, and recess is your very most favorite. And we know that you want to ask questions...millions and zillions of questions. We don't have answers to all your questions. Does that surprise you? It's true.

You know how badly you feel when you try really hard but still end up losing a soccer game? Well, sometimes that's the same way we principals feel. Sometimes we try our very best to do the right things for you but it just doesn't work out. Please don't give up on us; we'll keep on trying. What I learned in school this summer is that there are a whole bunch of principals who worry about you and care about you. We are all so full of hope that we can be better. If we can have hope, so can you. We need each other. I must go now, but there is one last thing I want you to know, and that is that we principals love you very, very much.

Your friend and principal

Being Good Enough
RICHARD C. VOSO

Richard C. Voso is Principal at Brevard Elementary School, Brevard, North Carolina.

Do I have enough strength to allow myself to be weak? That's a paradox I would not have admitted, or even dared to consider, just ten days ago.

I don't know the answer to the question I've posed. Yet, I see that an affirmative answer would inevitably lead to a new, total, and probably unsettling understanding of who it is I am today. I wonder if I can or want to come face to face with that truth.

So, what is it that I do know? I know I am not the same person I was ten days ago. I am different, very perplexed and somewhat frightened. I wonder if I am competent enough. I know that there are problems that I accepted as too complicated to be solved that may have simple but uncomfortable solutions which I have conveniently ignored. I know I have viewed complex situations as simplicities and missed real opportunities for positive change. I know that some of the calm waters are in reality stormy seas.

I have seen that excellence may not be effective, and that neither excellence nor effectiveness may be equitable, and good may not be good enough, but good enough may be okay. I know that intelligence is more than I thought, that congeniality is not collegiality, that praise may be harmful, and that coaching can be more powerful in the classroom than on the playing field.

I have come to see instructional skills as a complex and intricately woven tapestry of varied textures and patterns. I have accepted that adult developmental stages and phases may profoundly affect the learning of children.

And so I again return to the question: Do I have the strength to allow myself to be weak? Do I have the strength to admit and deal with my inadequacies and faults and thereby find a new, more powerful strength that enables growth and development?

I hope so, and if I do, I may find I'm not good, but good enough.

WRITING FROM SEPTEMBER TO JUNE

Two of the most striking results of the practice of writing are its continued use and its contagiousness. Not only do Writing Group members and Summer Institute participants continue to write once they have experienced the power and freedom of writing, but their enthusiasm often spreads to other adults and to children.

One story we like to tell around the Principals' Center is about a Writing Group member who became very interested in drama and wrote a play. He then boldly shared it with teachers and children at his school. Students liked it so much they staged a performance. A number of children became interested enough to try writing scripts of their own. Before long, some teachers joined in. The example set by one adult through writing and sharing led to a range of new learning opportunities as well as to the potential for expanded relationships among children and adults.

An elementary school principal who participated in the Summer Institute noticed she had a great deal of reluctance toward writing. "I always felt writing was a chore. I'd much rather talk than commit my thoughts to writing." Introduced to the practice of writing without editing and to journal writing, she gradually understood that her resistance was largely a fear of public scrutiny and negative judgment. Without this fear, she began to write, to enjoy writing, and to recognize that what she wrote was often quite good. "As long as nobody looked at it without permission, it felt good. I thought if this could work for an adult, it might also work for children."

Returning to her school in the fall, she began to carry a pad and to write things down as they occurred. Some of the writing she put in the school newsletter, resulting in interest from parents and the parents' and teachers' association. Planning with several teachers and backed by parents, she bought four hundred journals – one for every teacher and student. After wheeling the journals to each classroom on a pushcart, she passed them around and talked about the importance and fun of writing.

It certainly didn't go over right away. Just as I needed time, kids and teachers did too. Two years later, everyone writes for fifteen to twenty minutes every day. Whether they share is up to them. Teachers especially like the fact that we've created a positive learning tool without creating additional paperwork. Along with the fun and excitement that's been generated by the project, language scores have gone up. Even more important, since I don't believe tests reveal all that children can actually do, teachers feel that individuals are making gains in language as a result of daily journal writing.

This story might end here quite happily except for the fact that there have been several additional developments. As students have become more comfortable with writing, they have been willing to share their pieces with the principal and some have been published in the school newsletter, linking work that is going on at school with activities and interests at home. Future hopes and plans include the use of computers to write and an annual series of books with the children's thoughts and feelings.

In the following, another principal describes how writing has become an integral part of his professional life.

The Book
JOHN HALFACRE

John Halfacre is Principal at Springfield Elementary School, Charleston, South Carolina.

Some of the kids say it is my bible. Others call it a back brace. My secretary calls it "The Book." It is my security blanket and my lucky charm all rolled into one.

It is a blue vinyl binder with a replaceable five-by-seven-inch legal pad. The torn binding has been skillfully repaired with shipping tape. I carry it situated snugly inside the back of my pants with half of the pad showing above the belt line and the remainder neatly hidden. I know that it looks strange, but that's just the way it has to be. It's too large for my pocket. It's inconvenient carrying the pad in my hands, but I have to have it, and there's no other place. The kids have accepted my pad and its location. I'm not sure the teachers ever will.

I have a number of new pad holders that aren't cracked, but somehow I don't feel comfortable with them. The Book is a part of me. I feel lost without it. In fact, on the few occasions that I've misplaced it, I have experienced panic and a feeling of helplessness.

The Book reminds me of one of those multipurpose knives, the ones with the screwdriver, can opener, leather punch, and knife all rolled into one. It does a lot for me. The top page contains my "to do" schedule, a long list of tasks, some with lines drawn through them, some with asterisks, indicating high priority, as well as other familiar repeaters showing up day after day, serving as a friendly, ever present reminder of unpleasant situations needing my attention. Other pages contain notes to teachers and staff members – notes of praising, poking, reminding, thanking, asking, and begging. In addition, there are pages of doodles, agenda items for future meetings, and various names and numbers.

Helping me deal with my administrative tasks is one purpose of The Book. However, the feeling and relationship between The Book and me goes beyond time management, organizational efficiency, and communication procedures. For me, it has become a father confessor, confidant, good friend, and therapist. Leafing through these yellow pages, one becomes privy to my innermost feelings. The reader encounters an affective kaleidoscope of joy, excitement, anger, sadness, hope, and fear. There behind the smudges of a well-used felt-tip pen lies my personal vision for the school, those core beliefs about education that provide a framework for everything I want to do. There are the tear-stained words I wrote after a teacher said how much she hated me. There is the story of Jason, who after engaging in a fight with a classmate, explained to me how difficult it was to be a Christian when you're only eight years old. There is buried my unmailed letter of resignation, angrily written after my unsuccessful attempt to obtain air conditioning for thirty students in a 107-degree trailer.

It's all there in The Book, pressing against my back, symbolically pushing me forward when I hesitate, firmly supporting me as I stumble. The kids, with their honest curiosity, will continue to ask about it and then be on their way. The teachers will not ask; they'll just stare and wonder and think it strange. The Book will remain a part of me, helping me to grow as a person and, hopefully, as a principal.

WRITING FOR PUBLICATION

Although writing for publication can be intimidating, published writing brings a rare form of excitement and pride. Two related types of publications have surfaced through the Principals' Center at Harvard and the National Network of Principals' Centers (an informal group linking more than one hundred centers and leadership academies). A biannual *Newsletter* published by the Principals' Center exists as a forum for writing by practitioners about practice. School practitioners are encouraged to write by center staff, who often work closely with them on developing and articulating their feelings and ideas. Sometimes members of the Writing Group submit pieces to the *Newsletter*. Often we approach school leaders and suggest or encourage writing. Over the years, practitioners have written about an array of subjects, from middle school issues to teenage suicide to the effects of the most recent wave of school reform reports. Any school or organization can create a similar forum for writing.

Reflections is the name of a publication through the National Network of Principals' Centers that also encourages school practitioners to write about their practice. Two unique features of the publication are the pairing of writers and responders in the development and refinement of articles and a "floating" center of publication, moved each year from one center to the next.

These forms of writing serve as activities for sharing and as a means of amassing a literature on practice. Such a literature can potentially expand the knowledge base of leading and learning upon which others can build and elaborate. Groups of schools as well as local and national organizations can orchestrate similar networks for shared writing.

Individual and Group Supports

There are several keys to selecting individual and group supports that enhance adult development. Characteristics of the activity must capitalize on one or more of the conditions known to support and promote growth. Independent study, for example, exploits the adult learner's increasing capacity for independence. Mentor programs address both the young adult's need for guidance and the middle-aged adult's desire to nurture. Support groups, coaching, and professional-development organizations all take advantage of the adult's needs for peer interactions and inter-dependence. In educational terms, these developmental characteristics are variously labeled collaboration, cooperation, or collegial learning.

When I asked school practitioners to help me identify practices that support adult growth in their schools or districts, many were at a loss. Yet there are successful activities that incorporate important developmental elements. Recognition that these elements are also developmental supports may build confidence in these activities as well as increase enthusiasm and purpose. The practices identified in this chapter are examples of continuing and new individual and group professional development efforts.

INDEPENDENT LEARNING

Adult learners are becoming increasingly independent. They want to determine their own needs and objectives, and they require time to pursue individualized learning. Adults can work alone on projects of their own design and can be supported by others: staff developers, university faculty, advisors, learning partners, mentors. They can also be supported by specific structures. Some schools offer semester and/or year-long leaves or sabbaticals, during which educators can be paid part or all of their salary while working or traveling. Modifications of the traditional half-year or full-year sabbatical include month-long or even day-long leaves. Teachers and administrators can visit schools, attend professional meetings, or work on school-related projects.

Since personal and professional growth are intertwined, ideas for individualized development might be broadened to include time for hobbies or attention to family matters. When adults are preoccupied with concerns outside of school, overwhelmed with school work, or simply tired, such seemingly "unprofessional" activities can have a powerful impact on attitude and performance.

Individually tailored learning can be a regular and informal method of supporting adult development. I have found it useful, for instance, to ask adults to identify their learning goals and then to work with them to design appropriate learning opportunities. A staff member who wanted to improve his presentation skills was encouraged to make workshop introductions. Another, whose job responsibilities kept her confined to the office, wanted to work more closely with schools. Together we revised her job description to include regular school visits. Professional learning opportunities do not have to be formal occasions; nor do they have to focus on groups. Individualized plans for learning can foster ongoing professional and adult development.

PEER-ASSISTED LEADERSHIP

I think the greatest barrier to adult growth and learning is the inability to shift perspective. We just don't want to let go of our view or the way we do things so that we might see and act *in another way. Peer-Assisted Leadership is a specific mechanism to help do that.*[115]

Peer-Assisted Leadership is a training program developed through the work of the Far West Laboratory in California.[116] This program focuses on partnerships between principals; its structures and practices have relevance for teachers and administrators at all school levels.

What's special about this program, unlike support groups, is that it involves observation of practice in the work setting.

By shadowing (or observing), by providing reflective, nonjudgmental feedback, and by developing a personalized model of an individual's style of leadership, the program trains practitioners to be more observant and more self-conscious. Beginning as a companionship, much like coaching, peer relations can develop into a form of mentoring, "a teaching-learning exchange." The "grist" for the teaching and learning is not just what the principal (or teacher) is sharing from inside him – or herself, but the literal observation of that practitioner in the school setting.

Feedback is based on observation and is given without judgment in order to improve practice. This is a process sometimes available within schools among teachers or between teachers and supervisors or coaches. Principals, however, rarely have opportunities to develop this level of collegiality.

Just as clinical supervision and coaching require training – e.g., in observation, active listening, providing constructive feedback – Peer-Assisted Leadership is training-intensive. The extensive training required and the time it consumes sometimes dissuade practitioners from participating. Without it, the process could not work.

Even though the extensive training can be a major roadblock, it is precisely the level and depth of training required that make the program of value. If a person is genuinely going to benefit from this kind of experience, training is essential. There is no quick fix here, no quick clinic to give you the kind of reflection or introspection skills or the practice in feedback on *important* issues in a short amount of time. You might get a companionship going in a short amount of time; you can feel validated in a short amount of time, but it takes more to move to a plateau of learning in which you jointly examine what you're doing – not so much for validation, but for analysis and growth.

Validation and the development of trust are important first steps. Principals and teachers tend to be isolated; often they need someone to confirm that their jobs are complex, the level of ambiguity is high, time is fragmented, and there are inherent conflicts. Nor are principals and teachers accustomed to receiving good, frequent, regular, objective, precise, and concrete feedback about their practice. In this sense, peer observation and analysis is an unusual and high-risk activity.

There's a cultural conspiracy going on in which we all plot to keep life comfortable, nonthreatening, nonconfrontational, unquestioned. Praise quite often is given without a great deal of discrimination.

To the extent that Peer-Assisted Leadership creates a context for serious analysis, it pushes beyond the boundaries of characteristic professional relationships. Progressing through a cycle of trust building, to cooperative learning, toward autonomy, it offers practitioners the opportunity to become increasingly introspective, reflective, and self-monitoring. Over time, principals learn to observe themselves in action and adjust their own behaviors.

A promising practice for adult development, Peer-Assisted Leadership creates a context for increased self-awareness, learning, and change. The need for a partnership parallels the importance to growth of peer interactions. The ultimate goal of individual agency mirrors the developmental path toward independence and interdependence. Like adult growth, Peer-Assisted Leadership demands time. Two to three years is not an unusual expectation as a time frame for genuine change to develop.

Peer-Assisted Leadership demands more than a superficial relationship. Most important, you have to get past a superficial relationship with yourself.

MENTOR PROGRAMS

The term "mentor" derives from developmental theory. It describes the midlife adult in a supportive and trusting relationship with an early adult. More recently, the word has been generalized to signify an advisor or counselor, independent of place in the life cycle. While such relationships evolve and dissolve naturally during development, intentional mentor relationships can be established as a means of supporting and continuing adult learning. Experienced educators can be paired with novices to support the training of new teachers and administrators and to sustain the interests of veterans.

As in the development of peer-assisted partnerships, mentor relationships require extensive training. Beginning teachers and administrators need systematic, intensive supervision, and mentors need the skills required to demonstrate, observe, and coach. Particularly interesting and relevant components of the mentor approach are the underlying assumptions that adults have the capacity for continued growth and learning, that adults at more complex stages function differently and more effectively than those at less complex levels, and that adult development can be influenced by specific types of interventions.[117]

Careful study of mentor relationships reveals specific conditions conducive to success. Taking on significant and quality roles seems to make a positive learning difference. Mentors and their protégés also benefit from continuing reflection on practice over at least a one-year period – optimally, longer. Successful mentor relationships necessitate support and challenge.

Because training and coaching require different skills from teaching and administering, prospective mentors are selected and receive specialized training. More than a buddy or helpmate, the mentor gains and shares precise, concrete, and detailed knowledge of teaching, learning, and leading. In some cases, mentors are paid for their efforts. Remuneration as well as implicit acknowledgment for mentors make selection competitive and thereby problematic. Establishing a rotating pool of mentors can maximize inclusion. Nevertheless, the complex skills required of effective mentors do not lend themselves to easy acquisition. How to choose and train mentors remains a problem.

Although mentor programs require extended time commitments, practitioners reveal benefits to both mentor and protégé. New teachers and administrators learn to understand and analyze practice in ways that they are not taught in universities or colleges. Mentors not only develop supervisory skills, but enhance their own skills and development through the teaching and learning process.

COACHING

Like mentoring, coaching is a professional development design that builds on support and collaboration. The concept of coaching acknowledges the complexity of transferring learning to practice. As a result, the theory and knowledge base of new techniques are explored, techniques are modeled and practiced, and participants have the benefit of ongoing feedback. The essence of coaching includes watching and participating in as well as talking about practice.

Typically, coaching provides on-site support and technical assistance to teachers by other instructional experts. Through peer coaching, two classroom teachers attend the same training, collaborate on lesson development, observe one another, and offer constructive criticism.

Coaching can take various forms and have different objectives. It can pair teachers of similar skills with short-term goals of refining practice and developing collegiality and the long-term objective of establishing the skills and attitudes for self-monitoring and continuous teaching improvements. It can help teachers transfer training to classroom practice and can involve pairs of similarly skilled teachers or veterans and novices. Coaching can bring small groups of teachers together to work on particular teaching problems, and it can provide resource teachers – e.g., curriculum specialists or department chairs – to coplan, teach, and evaluate a lesson.[118]

Just as Peer-Assisted Leadership requires a firm belief in principals helping other principals, coaching depends upon the view that teachers and/ or administrators can help other teachers. Just as mentoring generally evolves as a relationship between a veteran and a novice, coaching often takes the form of a highly competent educator working with one who is less accomplished. In all cases, it is essential that the helper be proficient in the skill to be modeled.

As in all promising practices for adult and professional development, important components of coaching are time and support. It has been estimated that learning even a moderately difficult teaching strategy can take twenty to thirty hours of instruction in its theory, fifteen to twenty demonstrations using it with different subjects, and an additional ten to fifteen coaching sessions to attain higher-level skills.[119] Since teachers average only three or four days of staff development each year, the conditions needed for most time-intensive practices do not generally exist. It is here that support enters as an essential ingredient.

Support for staff development, in general, and for coaching, specifically, can take a number of forms. Often it means a principal committed to the practice and willing to provide resources and structures to make the practice work. Coaching requires training in a number of generic skills: interpersonal communication, observation, factual data collection, planning, and formative evaluation. Release time is needed for such training. While teachers are engaged in coaching, they need class coverage to allow for common observation and planning times. More basically, they need a school culture that encourages and rewards sharing.

The goal of coaching is improved instruction for students. In the process, coaching builds connections among teachers and administrators, helps develop positive self-concepts, improves the quality of the work environment, and enhances professionalism. Benefits thus accrue to both students and adults.

An important premise of coaching shared by other promising practices is the view of professional growth as ongoing learning. Conditions necessary for the professional growth of teachers parallel essential ingredients of adult development. Educators, like all adult learners, need the autonomy to direct and take responsibility for their own learning. They need to share and exchange with colleagues. And they need adequate time.

Coaching is an especially promising practice because it may require little more than coalescing the expertise that already exists in schools. To begin, teachers and administrators can identify specific instructional strengths and work to design in-service programs that model them. Teachers interested in developing these skills can practice them under simulated teaching conditions and then in the classroom. Separating the critical feedback that must accompany coaching from formal evaluation, teachers can then provide each other with help and support to acquire and refine new instructional practices. Not only is the acquisition of new skills a promise, but the building of new and strengthened relationships, as well as the enhancement of personal and professional self-worth, are likely results. Involving administrators and teachers can further expand the practice of coaching to benefit all the adults in schools.

ROLE TAKING

As distinct from role playing, role taking is the experience of assuming real tasks and responsibilities for a role somewhat more demanding and complex than the job a person has already performed. Kohlberg's work distinguished this activity as a catalyst for moral growth. In turn, advanced development has been discovered to enhance skills conducive to more effective teaching and leading.

Lack of a clearly defined and differentiated career path in education typically hampers efforts to provide teachers and administrators with legitimized role-taking experiences. Yet relative autonomy at the school level can open the way for creating multiple roles where educators will have opportunities to assume more complex tasks while remaining in the classroom or the building. On a system level, school people can consider interim positions that give teachers and administrators a chance to take on and benefit from more complex roles.

We know some conditions that stimulate development. Role taking, together with guided reflection, a balance of reflection and action, a combination of support and challenge and continuity, can stimulate growth.[120] In designing professional development experiences, we can use role taking as well as other activities that incorporate these conditions to intentionally build on our knowledge of adult development.

SUPPORT GROUPS

Many different kinds of groups can provide support for educators. Teachers can meet together within or across schools; administrators can meet together within or across districts. Groups can be all men, all women, or mixed. Descriptions of two groups provide specific examples.

An Individually Initiated Support Group for Teachers

> I've learned to know myself and other people. I've also learned more about the school.[121]

Interestingly, this support group grew out of a principal's interest in learning more about the needs of teachers for evaluation. A questionnaire circulated to the staff soliciting input for an evaluation process elicited the issue of how much teachers needed to be judged and how much they needed support. The teacher who told me about this promising practice shared:

> My personal reaction to an impending evaluation was a sense of threat, and that made me aware of the lack of support. I felt: "I need support *before* I'm evaluated – some means by which I have people whom I can trust to talk to about my teaching."

Feeling a need for support and having heard about a teachers' support group at a neighboring school, the teacher set out to learn more about the idea and how it was practiced. She liked the sound of what she heard.

> The idea immediately appealed to me, and when I learned how it worked, I decided I wanted it. The point was that I realized I needed support, but I didn't know how I was going to go about getting it. I didn't feel the administration had given it to me the way I wanted or needed it. I just wasn't content. I thought there must be some way of providing teachers with nonjudgmental feedback. A support group sounded good.

Raising the idea with other teachers brought expanded interest, and a group of about ten began to meet every other week for an hour and a half. Several issues immediately became apparent. Even before the group convened, teachers wondered about the response of the principal. Understanding his need to be involved in school-wide decisions and his tendency to want to grant permission, they sought out and obtained approval to meet at the school. Without such approval, the group certainly could not have met on school grounds. Whether teachers would have been comfortable or even willing to meet away from school against this principal's will is certainly a legitimate question.

When to meet was the next pressing issue. Although the teachers preferred to gather during the school day, they simply could not find a commonly available time. Meetings were therefore scheduled in the late afternoon. Time was an issue. While the benefits of support promised to be important, ongoing meetings were a commitment of time. Most teachers continually experienced some conflict. While they sometimes "dragged" themselves to group meetings after a long day, feelings of revitalization by the end of the meeting kept them committed. In fact, commitment to attend on a regular basis was an important criterion for joining.

Leadership was another question. Did the group need a designated leader or facilitator? In this case, members used consensus as a way of reaching decisions. Even though there has never been a formal leader, it is interesting that the group disbanded the year the initiating teacher went on leave. Reflecting on this point, the teacher agreed that she works well with groups and may be the "unofficial" group facilitator.

Would the group focus on personal as well as professional concerns? This question surfaced many times. And while the group decided to maintain a work-related focus, members often discovered that the two realms of their lives were not always easily separated. Such was the case one week when a teacher talked about not being able to pay her rent on the low salary she was making in teaching.

A school-based support group can create feelings of elitism or exclusion. Group members responded by encouraging others to meet and offering to help get them started. At one point, when space became available, a teacher disgruntled about the exclusiveness of the group was invited to join. Interestingly, he chose not to, suggesting that the very existence of the group, rather than his own participation, might have been a problem.

Within the group, teachers have felt supported and energized. At any given meeting, they might begin by a technique known to one member as a "go-round." Here, each group member has a chance to talk briefly about how he or she is doing. After everyone takes a turn, a topic is chosen for more in-depth discussion. In actuality, members are rarely disciplined enough to delay responding until everyone has a turn. As a result, the entire meeting can be consumed by what is meant to be an introduction.

After four years, the group has evolved to serve many purposes. One result of continued sharing is simply getting to know people better. The group brings together teachers from many different parts of the school who might normally have little cause for interaction. Discovering that other teachers have similar experiences and feelings also helps group members feel less isolated. Though the expression of a concern may not result in a solution, recognition of common experiences is comforting, a member said.

> Rarely is there any kind of resolution or advice, but there is sharing and a realization that ninety-nine percent of the time, whatever one person is going through, others are too. I figured that would be the case; I've found that it's true.

Sharing within the group also serves as a way of explaining and validating feelings.

> You're feeling depressed. You have no energy. You're sick of teaching. You share these feelings and often someone can point to an explanation. It's just before vacation; it's right after vacation; the kids are acting up. Whatever it is, it's almost always something others are also experiencing.

Beyond personal and professional sharing, the group serves as "a quality forum for discussing ideas." On one level, teachers talk about issues of teaching and learning, and group members say such discussion can make a positive difference to their teaching. On another level, group members discuss school-wide matters and have the potential to influence policies and decisions. Simply discussing an issue with the group prior to a school meeting gives members the advantage of having thought and talked about a matter, perhaps even developed a position. At times, this thinking and discussion benefit everyone, since most teachers have not had time for prior reflection. On other occasions, group members seem to form a coalition, having discussed an issue with the group and reached a common view. In this sense, a teachers' support group has the potential of being a political force in a school.

It is not surprising that a well-organized teachers' support group may threaten school administrators. Keeping principals informed so that teachers and administrators can work together on improving the school's culture is essential. Another possible limitation is the involvement of only a limited number of teachers in a single group. Encouraging all teachers to become involved and giving them the necessary supports – e.g., time, space, and group facilitation techniques – can broaden the benefits of support.

All teachers' support groups do not need a common focus. It is also important to recognize that groups can shift in purpose. Groups, like people, appear to develop. Initially, this group worked on issues specific to teaching. It was made up primarily of novice teachers, so issues directly relating to teaching were of primary importance. As the group and its members matured, discussions shifted to more general and less immediate issues, such as: What is good teaching? Group members were likewise better able to move beyond their own needs and focus on the needs of others. A type of reciprocal collegiality thus began to develop.

As the teacher I spoke with reflected on the importance of the support group as a promising practice for personal and professional development, she commented:

> Participation in the group has made me more a part of my community. I've gained a clear picture of how the school runs, and I think I can relate to the school better because I have an under-standing of it. As a teacher and as a person, I feel both more comfortable and more confident. Being part of the group allows me to keep tabs on myself, to be more self-conscious. It also makes me more aware of and sensitive to others. There are people out there. They're not a lot different from me. They're trying, too. They have bad days and good days. I feel respect for them and, in turn, I feel respected....
>
> I think a school would be a lot better place if everyone were involved in support groups. I think there would be a greater sense of respons- ibility for everything that happens. I think people would feel much clearer about what's going on around each issue, much clearer about what's going on with themselves in relation to the issues, and therefore they would be able to act upon the issues better and more responsibly. It's certainly been an education for me.

A Superintendents' Support Group

I include the story of a support group for superintendents to suggest the importance of support for administrators, to illustrate how a group of this kind can evolve, and to point out some of its special features. When the superintendent who told me this story took on his present position more than eight years ago, the support group was already in place.[122] Initiated by a psychiatrist with a belief in the need for ongoing discussion and support among educators, the group consisted of six superintendents meeting twice a month during the workday for two hours. Finding the group helpful and satisfying, this superintendent's predecessor suggested the new superintendent take his place.

For several years, the group stayed pretty much the same. As members left the superintendency for other positions and remained group members, the focus of the group broadened. One former superintendent is now a college president; another has become an insurance salesman. Not only is the superintendent who described the group to me the only currently practicing school administrator, but the psychiatrist-facilitator several years ago decided to become part of the group and stopped receiving payment (provided for by the school systems, where the need for such support was demonstrably valued). Several new members have since been recruited by group consensus when veterans have chosen to stop attending.

All-male at its inception, the group has continued to be for men, a choice that has been discussed and reconfirmed several times. Once a group of superintendents meeting from eight to ten in the morning, this now more diverse group of educators and businessmen meets over coffee at a member's house every other week from four to six in the afternoon. Meeting agendas vary depending upon what group members bring. Topics can range from highly personal issues about relationships between husbands and their wives or their children to work-related concerns. Like the teachers' group, this group is a resource for support and problem solving. Just as the teachers get to know one another, members of this group have become colleagues and friends. As male friendships tend to be limited, the bonds that have developed among these men have become especially important.

Given the range of age and experience in the group, the one remaining superintendent – as the youngest and least experienced group member – has received special benefits:

> For me, the group serves as a window on the future. What I get in the group is really slices of life from people in their forties, fifties, and sixties. It's a mentoring situation.

Being able to talk with men who are at varying stages in their careers also provides this superintendent with perspective on his own career. As he approaches midlife and becomes ready to be a mentor himself, the superintendent has expressed a desire to recruit younger group members.

Like the teachers' group, the superintendent has discovered the close relationship between personal and professional issues. Both invariably become the focus of group discussions. Personal well-being is fundamental to professional effectiveness. The superintendent explains:

> Ultimately, I see a blurring between the personal and the professional. If, for example, somebody is terribly unhappy about his marriage, I don't think he's going to be as productive at work – particularly in the education business, which is so highly personal. To the extent that people maintain healthy self-images and healthy relationships, I think they're going to be more effective at their work.

Although the superintendents' group started with a skilled facilitator, it is now leaderless. Members share responsibility for keeping discussions going and for getting their agendas met. Here and in the teachers' group, there has been a need for facilitative skills, however. The superintendent and the teacher agree that an outside facilitator is not essential, though a "critical mass of skill" is needed to keep the group moving and focused. In the superintendent's mind, school practitioners may have an advantage over other professionals because their jobs require interpersonal skills and offer experience in working with individuals and groups.

The teacher and the superintendent I talked with differ on how to start a support group and on the nature of its membership. While the teachers' group grew directly and informally out of one teacher's needs and interests and dealt almost immediately with personal and professional concerns, the superintendents' group began with a skilled facilitator and focused initially on the professional. Perhaps because of his experience, the superintendent recommends beginning with a trained group leader and dealing with professional issues until a firm level of trust has been established. This administrator's experience also leaves him open to considering both single and multi-career groups. On the one hand, professionals from the same career will share a lot in common. Alternatively, when groups bring together people from diverse careers, participants have opportunities to broaden their horizons.

Unlike the teacher, the superintendent is dubious about in-school support groups, worrying about their potential for creating "privileged relationships." Instead, he recommends membership from across schools and even across districts. One teacher's experience at one school demonstrates how a school-based group can work. One administrator's experience suggests a different model. Both groups can provide the peer support essential to adult development.

Organizational Supports

Beyond individual and group efforts, schools, districts, universities, staff development centers, state departments of education, and other organizations can promote growth. In this chapter, I describe a program for practitioners on leave from practice and in university residence. I discuss some components of the burgeoning principals'-center-and-leadership-academy movement. I conclude with a report on a teachers' network and a staff development center, each the product of a collaboration between a school and a college or university.

Like all promising practices for adult development, these supports are not effective by chance. They share in common such qualities as careful structures, designs for quality interpersonal relationships, and opportunities for intellectual and affective stimulation. Of particular importance is their acceptance and celebration of adults as learners. Planners of these organizations understand adults' needs, capacities, and interests in their own growth and in the development of others.

A VISITING PRACTITIONER PROGRAM

The experience has moved me to a new level in my development.[123]

Each year, a limited number of principals and other school leaders (e.g., teachers, superintendents) come to the Principals' Center at Harvard as Visiting Practitioners. On leave from their schools for a semester or a full year, they come to reflect and write about their years of practice and to be part of the center and the university. For the past several years, I have talked with practitioners just before the end of their stay. It is at their suggestion that I include this model of professional growth as a promising practice for adult development.

Thinking about his experience, one Visiting Practitioner reflected:

> What strikes me most about the year is the tremendous amount of responsibility I had for my own learning. That's just not the norm. In schools and universities, people are generally told what they have to learn, where to learn, and how to learn it. Even though I struggled during the first part of the year to find out what I needed and wanted to know, the freedom provided me with an opportunity to promote my own growth.

It's hard to describe the Visiting Practitioner year because it is so intentionally different for everyone. When school leaders come to learn about the program, we generally tell them the year is divided into three parts. Part one is having the opportunity to write, reflect, take courses, and engage in thinking and learning. After two days at the center, one practitioner exclaimed to a colleague on the phone: "This is the first chance I've had to think in twenty years!" While those who overheard the exuberant statement continued to chide him for the rest of the semester, there was some truth in his statement. The constant demands of working in schools leave little time for reflection.

Visiting Practitioners audit university courses, continue or initiate journals, and visit schools. One principal used some of his time to substitute teach. Not only did this activity allow him to visit many schools, but it reacquainted him with the work of classroom teachers.

Part two of the year is becoming actively involved in some aspect of the center. There is no money exchanged in the Visiting Practitioner program. Practitioners support their stay through district grants, sabbatical funds, and/or personal resources. Some take on part-time assignments during the year, such as teaching assistantships or the supervision of student interns. Working at the center is a way to become engaged in the professional development of colleagues and to learn how a center functions.

When practitioners arrive, they are given a copy of the previous year's final report and a list of center activities as potential areas for involvement. Typically, two practitioners plan and run a spring conference. Several serve on the center's *Newsletter* editorial board. Other activities have included assisting with teaching, developing programs, writing grants, and hosting visitors.

In the fall, practitioners take part in the orientation activities of the university and talk with people at the center before making commitments. One of their most formidable dilemmas is setting limits. By the end of their first two weeks, many are comparing the university and the center to a penny-candy store – there are many sweet options!

Part three of the Visiting Practitioner program is purely personal. When practitioners come to Massachusetts from out of the state or out of the country, we encourage them to explore New England and develop personal interests. Visiting Practitioners enjoy heading north in the fall to see the colors of autumn. One practitioner took time to learn to play tennis; another instructed himself in computer programming.

On balance, Visiting Practitioners come to the center for one or more of three reasons. Often they are weary of practice and in need of a break. Though I am always startled to hear them describe my frantically perceived work setting as relaxing, I can understand how it feels to be relieved of being center stage. A related reason for coming to the center is to shift from leader to learner and to steal time for reflection. Interestingly, the majority of practitioners who have come to the center have been at midlife and at the midpoint in their careers. Attracting applicants at a time of reassessment, the Visiting Practitioner program seems well matched to their naturally occurring developmental inclinations.

Two practitioners have been retired principals seeking a bridge between work and retirement. Two others have been anticipating retirement. One shared:

> I came because this was an exciting opportunity to learn, to be in a community of learners again. There were a lot of things I wanted to read and know as I prepared for the last part of my professional life.

A sixty-four-year-old independent-school head reported that the opportunity gave her time to be alone. Married for more than forty years, she explained: "It's been good for me to get away and to see that I can learn things on my own."

A third reason practitioners choose to spend time at the Principals' Center is to reassess their career options. Many come during periods of personal and professional transition. Sometimes they decide to return to their schools with renewed commitment; sometimes they resolve to seek alternative employment. A teacher came to the center to explore administration as a career option. She left recommitted to teaching. A principal sought refuge in a university to explore possible career opportunities in higher education. At the end of his semester, he realized he missed teachers and children and returned to his school with fresh ideas and renewed enthusiasm.

Why is this seemingly straightforward variation on the sabbatical a promising practice for adult development? I think there are several compelling reasons. If intellectual renewal is significant, being in a university can be particularly stimulating. If a practitioner is feeling isolated or worn down, the opportunity to connect with other practitioners, and to an organization whose focus is personal and professional renewal, is refreshing. Many Visiting Practitioners regain their sense of confidence while at the center and leave feeling reaffirmed. Their ideas have been recognized, they have encountered eager and responsive listeners, and they have been helped to remember that what they do is important. One principal said:

> A lot of what I know and believe has been confirmed, so that I really want to go back and do a great job in my principalship. I do believe principals make a difference.

Another shared: "I learned here that people value some of the things that I've done, and therefore *I* can value them again."

When Visiting Practitioners leave the center, they frequently say they have grown. They describe their growth as a shift in perspective:

> My sense of self and my thinking have shifted since I've been here because I've gotten some distance from my own school setting and have had a chance to look at issues from different perspectives. Being away has made me step back and look at my place in the school and at what I might want to do. I think of myself as a changed person as I go home.

Another practitioner talked about his development in similar terms:

> I know I've grown from the way I feel inside. I feel different as I look out at the world. Since I've been here, I've developed some different sensitivities. I have a different perspective on myself.
>
> Being here reopened my world. This was an opportunity to

recognize that there is a larger world of ideas, interactions, and intentions. The Principals' Center and the university were particularly fertile settings because there were people here willing to look at interesting ideas and committed to personal and professional growth.

Any organization has the potential to support a Visiting Practitioner program. Schools can collaborate with universities, state departments of education, or businesses to create time and support for adults. A number of variations on this model are also possible. School leaders might assume roles in nonschool settings. Teachers and administrators might exchange positions.

One of the most powerful and rewarding experiences reported by Visiting Practitioners is the opportunity and encouragement to write. A superintendent penned four hundred pages in one semester, responding to courses and readings. A principal faithfully kept a journal in which he drafted an article for publication, wrote poems and essays, and recorded his feelings. Another principal discovered writing as a vehicle for capturing his thinking.

In the past, writing something down would never have occurred to me. Now I'm in the habit of being able to capture a thought by writing it down. Writing is certainly something I plan to continue.

While being in a new setting is an important component of the Visiting Practitioner program, the particular nature of the experience and the culture of the hosting organization are equally essential. Most universities can provide opportunities for thought and reflection. The Principals' Center's general focus on professional development and its specific interest in adult development add vital dimensions. At the center, we talk and write about adult growth. We try to model continuous learning. We work to establish an environment that will support adult development.

We know that not all adults respond to the same conditions. Just as I am advocating listening to adults in schools and helping to fashion supportive work environments, I am suggesting a similar need for attentiveness to adults and their growing needs in any organization or program. The success of a Visiting Practitioner program rests on the successful translation of these ideas into everyday practice.

PRINCIPALS' CENTERS AND LEADERSHIP ACADEMIES

It is no surprise that principals' centers and other forms of leadership academies proliferated around the country in the 1980s.[124] The literature on effective schools and school reform reports reaffirmed the importance of strong leadership to school improvement.

In addition to the impetus of research, two basic realities created renewed interest in professional development for school administrators. Many principals were in their forties or fifties, when a shift in focus from concerns for career advancement to an interest in professional development is characteristic. Veteran principals often hunger for the stimulation and rejuvenation that principals' centers promise.

Focus on training and supporting school leaders was also timely because of the expected need for administrators. Since a large percentage of principals were expected to retire, training and selecting new principals as well as supporting practicing principals had both immediate and future relevance.

Perhaps the most salient feature of the more than one hundred centers, institutes, and academies established by the late 1980s was their diversity. Centers are large and small, simple and complex. They are variously associated with and funded by state departments of education, state and national associations, universities, school districts, businesses, and foundations. Many focus on professional renewal and development; others emphasize skill acquisition, assessment, or increased academic achievement for students. Centers operate year-round or in the summer. They offer workshops, conferences, institutes, courses, consultation, assessment, support groups, study groups, mini-grants, television series, and electronic mail hookups.

While individual organizations are idiosyncratic, centers and academies share a number of characteristics. Almost all centers serve a range of school leaders, including principals and assistant principals, superintendents and assistant superintendents, department heads, teachers, and sometimes school committee members and parents. All emphasize establishing connections among educators as a central component of their efforts. In the majority of centers, members are actively engaged in policy making, planning and offering activities, and evaluation. Whether they are affiliated with a state department of education, university, business, foundation, or school district, almost all of the centers support voluntary membership and participation.

Many centers and academies rely on the teachings of adult development and learning theories and on the principles of effective staff development. In keeping with these theories and principles, almost all of these organizations use a developmental rather than a remedial approach. Instead of trying to "fix" school people, they focus their attention on creating the conditions that will bring to life the inherent inclination that individuals share for learning and growth.

Not only is there no single center or academy model, but members of a national network of professionals engaged in promoting the development of school leaders celebrate their differences, proclaiming: "It's not the similarities that people in the network seem to focus on, but the differences that bond us."[125] If there is glue that unifies the centers, it is their shared beliefs, rather than their individual practices.

The following brief descriptions of several centers provide a sense of what a center can be and how it can work.

The North Carolina Leadership Institute for Principals

This institute is an office within the North Carolina State Department of Public Instruction. Conceived in 1979 and funded by the North Carolina legislature, the institute provides comprehensive statewide services for principals and assistant principals. Programs are determined on the basis of a yearly needs assessment, resulting in five to ten statewide and two regional training seminars. In addition to running seminars on such topics as legal issues, microcomputers, and management in education, the institute's staff produces two television series. The institute also arranges for principals to take part in short internships involving visits to other schools to observe principals with expertise in specific areas.

A special feature of the North Carolina Leadership Institute is its relationship to state business and industry. Businesses assist school administrators in strengthening their supervisory, administrative, communication, and interpersonal skills by offering the institute one or two slots in training programs developed for their employees.

Though participation in the North Carolina Leadership Institute is voluntary, ninety-five percent of the state's public school principals have taken part. Principals are actively involved in policy making and in planning, offering, and evaluating activities. Each year, two principals on leave from their school systems join the institute staff, taking on responsibilities for managing its day-to-day operations.

The Principals' Group in Washington, D.C.

In contrast to the North Carolina center, the Principals' Group in Washington, D.C., is a small, informal organization with no fixed site and no regular funding. Since 1983, twenty professionals have met every four to eight weeks to discuss topics of mutual interest, such as effective in-service training for teachers and school climate. Meetings take place at members' schools.

Besides talking among themselves about books, articles, and professional experiences, the group occasionally includes guest speakers. Speakers and topics are determined by participating members through informal discussion and consensus. Although a core group of school leaders has remained active since the beginning, others come and go.

In 1986, the Principals' Group received a small grant to be used for special programming. Group members worried that this formal support might be the group's undoing. Committed to the belief that school leaders need to learn from and with each other and that administrators need to work on their own growing, outside support posed a potential problem.

The Washington, D.C., Principals' Group is one of the few centers where public and private school administrators are actively working together. Principals from public and independent schools initiated the group and continue to participate.

The Principals' Center at Harvard University

The Center at the Harvard Graduate School of Education opened its doors in 1981, after a year of intensive planning by local principals and university faculty. Membership in the Principals' Center is open to principals and other practitioners who play a leading role in schools. After seven years of operation, there were some five hundred members, at least fifty percent of whom were principals. Members joined and participated voluntarily in the semiweekly workshops, seminars, and conferences.

Activities and policies are designed by a representative group of principals who serve on a program advisory board. Members have opportunities to shape these decisions through program evaluation and periodic needs assessments. The vast majority of Principals' Center members come from public schools and from the New England area; other members come from as far away as Oregon and Alaska, and from a number of foreign countries, including China, England, and Australia.

In addition to ongoing programs in such areas as leadership, policy, family and school, and curriculum and instruction, the center runs a ten-day summer institute on the principal and school improvement (see p. 251). The center is also an active participant in the National Network of Principals' Centers, an informal group of principals' centers and leadership academies nationwide.

Alaska Principals' Center

In rural Alaska, "bush principals," as they call themselves, have worked out yet another way of connecting. Alaska is a vast state, and principals live and work hundreds of miles apart. Some school districts in Alaska are as large as the state of Kansas. Principals may have to travel several hours by small airplane just to reach the central office!

Undaunted by these constraints, fifteen principals have established an informal consortium among themselves and with the University of Alaska. When they cannot meet face to face, they maintain communication by electronic mail. School administrators, it seems, can be extraordinarily inventive in developing and sustaining support for their ongoing professional training and development. More will be written about this unique collaboration as the principals involved meet together to determine their future plans.

Lessons Learned from the Movement

Professionals engaged in promoting the growth of school practitioners have recognized the importance of adult development and learning theories. School administrators, like other adults, learn best when they are voluntary and active participants in their own learning, when they have opportunities to take part in designing their learning agendas, when a variety of teaching and learning methods are used, when the people with whom they learn *do* what they profess, when they receive regular feedback and support, and when there is an atmosphere of trust and respect.

The principles of effective staff development and school improvement have also proved influential to the development of appropriate professional growth experiences for administrators. Though the literature on professional development for school leaders is only beginning to be written, many of the conditions conducive to the growth of teachers appear to be equally important for administrators' development. Some of the common points include: participant involvement in collaborative decision making regarding program, individualization of content, participant-identified needs, provision for both internal and external rewards, opportunities to see skills modeled, building on participant strengths, direct feedback, and ongoing support.

Equally important are points of contrast between teacher and administrator staff development. Whereas staff development for teachers has been shown to be most effective when delivered and followed up at the school site, principals seem to prefer a neutral and protected setting away from their schools. Whereas staff development for teachers has been shown to be most effective when its content is related and sustained over time, administrators seem to benefit from an eclectic approach to programming, characterized by short-term topical presentations. It may be that sustained interpersonal contact is as central to learning and staff development for administrators as scope and sequence of content.[126]

The principals'-center-leadership-academy movement has dramatized the importance of collegiality and sharing. Not only do contacts among educators alleviate feelings of isolation, they also create a context for sharing expertise and learning. In turn, the value of practitioners' knowledge has been reaffirmed.

The importance of reflecting on practice has been another valuable lesson, demonstrated in large part through writing (see Chapter 10). Writing helps practitioners think about, articulate, and refine practice and frequently leads to insights about school improvement. In contrast to the typical approach of identifying promising practices and molding or cajoling administrators to replicate them, reflections on practice have proved to be linked to greater awareness and greater understanding of practice. As a result, the center-academy movement has suggested an approach to encouraging and supporting change. This approach seems equally relevant to all practitioners:

| Reflect on Practice | → | Articulate Practice | → | Better Understand Practice | → | Improve Practice |

From the principals'-center-leadership-academy movement, in general, and from writing and other reflective activities, in particular, we seem to be learning that understanding practice is an essential precondition for improving practice.[127]

The Future of the Movement

It is difficult to tell where the principals' centers and leadership academies are heading. Given their diversity, they are likely to be heading in multiple directions. The proliferation of principals' centers and leadership academies suggests that the movement will continue to develop and expand. As the number of centers increases, there will be questions about how they relate to other established professional organizations, as well as how they will collaborate with one another.

Given the expanding need for school leaders, the focus of centers and academies will also likely expand to include training and assessment for the teachers and other educators who will be aspiring to school leadership positions, as well as providing professional support to veterans. Some centers already have formal or informal assessment mechanisms and certification programs. This expanding focus will require the centers to consider not only the conditions under which school leaders will actively engage in their own learning, but what is appropriate training for school leaders of the future.

Reports from educators indicate that principals' centers and leadership academies provide high-quality services, make a difference in the personal and professional lives of participants, and contribute positively to professional development activities within schools:

The Leadership Institute has consistently outstanding programs. I have never been disappointed at any activity I've attended.

Staff developers, always in the business of giving, inspiring, and nurturing, need some of the same. The principals' center "keeps me going during the inevitable periods of disenchantment, dismay, and isolation that often characterize work in the schools.

I find the principals' center valuable because it provides a wide variety of opportunities for many different staff. It stimulates discussion back in the system and ultimately serves as an outstanding form of professional development.

In one sense, these results should be enough to demonstrate that the movement is working. Adults in schools are valued professionals whose growth and development are important in their own right. In another sense, we always ask more from schools, and, most fundamentally, we demand excellence for children. A healthy work environment for the adults in schools is an important condition for a healthy and productive learning environment for students. Not only is this the premise upon which many centers and academies are based, it is the promise of the principals'-center-and-leadership-academy movement.

A TEACHERS' NETWORK AND A STAFF DEVELOPMENT CENTER

The Harvard Teachers' Network

The Teachers' Network at the Harvard Graduate School of Education began in 1985 to "generate and sustain processes that enhance teachers' professionalism, and thereby to better education."[128] Unlike the Principals' Center, the Teachers' Network is not a dues-paying membership organization. With the number of teachers far exceeding the number of administrators, this structure seemed unwieldy. Instead, the network is a loose association of area educators guided by an advisory committee. The committee is comprised of a diverse group of educators, Harvard students, and faculty members. Together they plan and provide for program implementation. Recommendations are then put into practice by a small staff, including a faculty sponsor, two graduate-student assistants, and a secretary.

Since its inception, the Teachers' Network has sponsored such initiatives as conferences, a study group to examine and write about the school reform reports of the 1980s, a periodic newsletter, and a variety of special-interest groups.[129] Beyond its specific activities, the network serves as a resource and meeting place for teachers concerned with the growth and development of the teaching profession.

I include the Teachers' Network as a promising practice for adult and professional development because it is informal, low-cost, wide-ranging, and effective. It illustrates the ways in which a university, and particularly a school of education, can be a supportive resource by providing a faculty advisor, student assistants (who are often teachers), space, and start-up financial assistance. Aided by an informal structure, teachers and other educators come together to maximize their knowledge and serve one another as resources.

Wisconsin's Regional Staff Development Center

Started in 1978 by the University of Wisconsin-Parkside, the Regional Staff Development Center serves the professional development needs of educators in twenty-three school districts and three colleges.[130] In many respects, the philosophy and programs of the center mirror those of the principals' centers and leadership academies. Bringing together faculty, administrators, board members, and union officials, the reach of the Regional Staff Development Center is broad. The center sponsors such wide-ranging activities as a beginning-teacher induction program, fourteen academic alliances, six mutual-interest networks, three study committees, an elementary-science training program, grant-writing teams, and a monthly newsletter distributed to 4,500 regional educators. It is this center's comprehensive approach to professional growth that merits its inclusion as a promising practice for adult development.

The structure of the Regional Staff Development Center encourages the participation of teachers at all levels. Similar to visiting practitioners, center associates are veteran classroom teachers on leave for a year from their districts to work at the center. A particularly interesting component of their work at the center is the opportunity it offers to take on new roles. Center associates assist in the development and implementation of programs, interact with personnel from diverse districts, and gain exposure to current research. In this sense, they have the benefit of role-taking experiences that potentially expand their development as adults and their effectiveness as educators.

Among the center's collaborative efforts are a series of alliances, or groups of school and university/college faculty, who regularly meet to share knowledge and experience in their disciplines. Other groups, called networks, are more general in focus. Networks already formed include a teacher support group, a middle-level educators' group, and a group on computers in education. Study committees are another structure for professional exchange and adult sharing. One elementary teacher exclaimed after a day-long experience:

> I came away with a feeling of pride. I was treated as an intelligent
> adult. It was wonderful to spend a day sharing ideas with adults.
> I went home refreshed and eager to go to school the next day.[131]

Staff at the Regional Center attribute its success to the collegiality and ownership experienced by members. Their acknowledgment of adult development needs is another critical factor.

Part Five

Looking Back and Looking Ahead

The Importance of an Adult Development Perspective

LOOKING BACK

Teaching is a difficult, demanding, and rewarding profession. Teachers get mixed messages about their value and rely primarily on their students for a sense of purpose. Schools generally do not attend adequately to the developmental needs of adults. Both their structures and norms circumscribe adult relationships.

I am convinced that most teachers and administrators have deeply felt positive experiences of their work. They also have an enormous wealth of wisdom about teaching and learning. Most of what is written about schools captures neither. This book is meant to celebrate both.

Theories of adult development are not well known or explicitly used in schools. Yet they offer an important tool for professional development and school leadership. Phase theory can provide a guide to the major life tasks and conflicts that preoccupy and motivate adults at specific times during the life cycle. Stage theory can identify the structures that adults build to understand themselves and the world. Questions of gender differences are heated and complex. It may be that certain occupations and work environments invite men and women with similar patterns of development. Working with children attracts many men and women with highly developed interpersonal skills and abundant levels of empathy and nurturance.

Listening closely to teachers and administrators using an adult development framework helps to clarify how adults are thinking and feeling and suggest developmentally appropriate responses. Both the principal and the school environment play central roles in supporting or inhibiting adult growth. The stories of individual teachers and administrators who have applied adult development theory to their lives and their work can be dramatic. Their sustained impact is predicated on a strong school culture as well as on positive parent, system, and community involvement.

Practices that support adult development in schools are only just beginning to surface. I have identified writing and individual, group, and organizational supports. Many of these practices require reflection, involve collaboration, and encourage a sense of ownership. Like most effective professional development strategies, they also require commitments of time, training, and resources. As the value of an adult development perspective is more widely recognized and embraced, additional practices will be shared and invented.

LOOKING AHEAD

Knowing More than We Do

There's an old Vermont farm story about a slick city salesman who comes to a farm to sell a newfangled idea to a hard-working farmer. Driving his tractor slowly across a field, the farmer listens politely to the sales pitch of the somewhat out-of-character man running along beside him – jacket, tie, and briefcase flying in different directions. "We know so much more than we did ten years ago," the breathless salesman insists. "Just think of all you could do with this new gadget," he implores. "Nope," replies the farmer with finality as he turns his tractor and heads off in the opposite direction. "I already *know* more than I *do!*"[132]

Much of what is important to know and do about supporting adults in schools is already known, if not practiced. We know, for instance, as a burly school superintendent from rural Alaska phrased it: "People are tender." No matter how hard each of us tries to appear in control and competent, everyone is vulnerable and no one is immune to being hurt. A related reality is the universal need for approval and recognition. Though these needs vary as we develop, no one ever outgrows his or her need to be needed and validated. Can you remember a time when you received too much positive feedback? I can't.

Much of what is important to know and do about supporting adults in schools comes directly from what we already know about children's development. We know, for instance, the importance of taking account of the whole child. Competent educators recognize the inextricable relationship between cognitive and social growth. In the same way, we must attend to the personal and professional lives of adults.

We've learned from Judy Cubbins, Janet Kramer, Don Bolter, and Nan Johnson that teachers can use their work as a source of stability when other aspects of their lives are in flux. On the other hand, adults whose personal lives are stable, or even static, may look to the profession for stimulation. By understanding the whole adult, principals and staff developers can make more-informed decisions about the kinds of supports and incentives needed and when they will be most effective. We generally assume professional development must be a constant. Yet there are times in an adult's life when a moratorium on professional growth is appropriate.

We know that children are continuing to learn and grow, and we *expect* that they will change. Establishing grade levels for children at different ages is an inexact expression of this knowledge. As children progress from grade to grade, our expectations and goals for them shift, their skills develop, and they take on new challenges. Like children, adults continue to change and grow. While teachers and administrators may not need totally new assignments every year, we can expect adults to want to modify their teaching and leading, adopt new curricula, change grades or schools, take sabbaticals, or otherwise alter their work to reflect their growth and development. One former principal I know asked teachers to bring to their end-of-the-year conference a plan or "dream" for the following September. If they could do anything at the school the next year, what might it be? Surprisingly, many dreams were modest enough to become realities. Most important, teachers were given permission and opportunities to develop.[133]

A staff developer I know has another good mechanism for surfacing adult development objectives. Playing on the term "Individualized Educational Plan" (IEP), created to identify the learning goals for children with special needs, this staff developer coined the term "Individualized Development Plan" (IDP) for adults who wish to design their own protocol for growing.[134] Such plans might include opportunities to attend professional meetings, visiting schools, or working on curricula. Teachers and administrators design IDPs together, creating the blueprint for an adult's year-long professional development activities and emphasizing the school's commitment to individually tailored staff development. Just as we expect children and adolescents to grow and change, we can anticipate, plan for, support, and stimulate adult development.

Through the work of Piaget and our own experience, we know that children understand themselves and their surroundings differently. One child insists the moon is following her. Another swears that the amount of juice in a large, tall glass diminishes when it is poured into a short, stout one, even though it returns to its original amount when the process is reversed. What is most interesting about talking with children about the world and themselves is *not* discovering if they know the "right" answers. It is not even discovering what answers the children *believe* to be right. More fundamentally, observing, asking questions, and attending to the responses uncover *why* children respond the way they do and what their answers reveal about *how* they are making sense of the world. In fact, it is often their "wrong" answers that most clearly provide access to the ways they are thinking and understanding.

Theories of adult growth also provide a basis for discovering how adults feel and understand. Like children, adults do not all see the world or themselves in the same way. Adult development theories underscore the importance of attending not only to *what* adults say, feel, and do; they invite us to look beneath these responses toward a more fundamental understanding of *how* they are making sense of themselves and others, and what these patterns of sense-making might mean for the ways we respond, the kinds of supports we make available, and even possibilities for expanding world views through the introduction of dilemmas.

Schools are complex social environments as well as places to gain skills and knowledge. Although teachers do most of the talking in schools and children are expected to do most of the listening, anyone who has ever stepped inside a school knows that activity and drama are unfolding in many places other than at the front of the classroom. A seven-year-old child can't seem to sit in one place for more than ten seconds. At the back of one room, attention is riveted on a note that is being passed among students. Between periods, the sounds of teenagers fill the halls that a moment before were empty and silent. Much of what is important to students in schools goes on outside the formal curriculum.

At thirteen, my daughter reminded me of this reality when she came home from junior high school to report that her day had been "rotten." As she rattled off the day's events, I remember hearing that she had a long history assignment, that she and her friend Jessie had had an argument, that the bus was finally on time, and that she had gotten a score of ninety-nine on her latest French exam. "Ninety-nine!" I exclaimed, momentarily forgetting the relative unimportance of academics to an early adolescent. "That sounds like a good day." "Haven't you been listening?" she replied, more than somewhat exasperated. "I said that Jessie and I had an argument." Social interactions, especially peer relationships, are at the heart of development for children and adolescents. Social interactions, particularly peer interactions, are central to the growth of adults. Most schools provide only limited opportunities for adults to come together. I remember talking with a group of adults about why they work. Being especially task oriented at the time, I was struck by one woman's unhesitating response: "I go to work to be with other adults." Now I understand more clearly what she meant and why it is so important.

An Expanded View of Professional Development and School Leadership
In addition to reminding us about what we already know, theories of adult development add important dimensions to our knowledge. The literature on school improvement persistently identifies school principals as central to the life of the school. Among their many required capabilities, principals are expected to be instructional leaders, building managers, culture builders, and visionaries. Principals must also be adult developers. Not only will this ability expand their professional development repertoire, but it will enhance their capacity to serve as strong and effective educational leaders.

This perspective on staff development and school leadership has implications for the selection, training, and ongoing professional development of school principals. Both the personality and the role of the principal are important. Peter Samson stands out for being a skillful person and a "rare" human being. Introspection, empathy, sensitivity, and reflectiveness are all central characteristics of an adult developer. The degree to which these and other essential skills can be learned is unclear. To the extent that the developmental orientation of a person in a helping relationship needs to be both distinct from and more advanced than the developmental level of the person he or she is trying to help, the principal's own development is of primary importance. Ongoing professional development opportunities for principals and other adult developers are therefore imperative.

Active listening is a key component of professional development and school leadership. Adults have varied needs about which they will be both aware and unaware. Adult developers in the school must listen closely to understand adult needs. It is striking how seldom adults in schools talk with and listen to one another about the things that matter to them, including the work of teaching and learning. A major professional development and school leadership goal must be to create a school culture that encourages such sharing.

Support is an essential precondition for growth. School principals and staff developers can use an adult development perspective to understand the nuances of support and to provide clues to the kinds of supports adults will need at different stages of development. When the supports offered are different from the supports needed, adults can feel threatened, undermined, attacked, or abandoned. One teacher finds praise insufficient, wanting challenge and debate; another finds questions unnerving and would prefer specific ideas that she can simply take and implement. When appropriate supports are lacking, adults seem to get stuck or even to regress; when appropriate supports are present, adults flourish.

Attending to the developmental needs of adults requires patience. Adult development is complex, slow, and untidy. When I returned to Archer Elementary after six years, I discovered that a great deal had remained unchanged and that very little of the change was dramatic. No effective professional development or school improvement approach is sustained by a "quick fix." Patience and persistence are demanded of staff developers and principals who are committed to supporting and promoting adult development.

An Expanded View of Schools

Like individuals, workplaces manifest developmental traits. Many organizations, and perhaps most schools, require and reward conformity rather than independence. It is not coincidental that adults who demand a great deal of autonomy can find schools confining and may choose to leave. For some, schools can place a ceiling on growth. When that happens, seeking an alternative work environment may be best. Since many workplaces and most schools do not attend adequately to the growing needs of adults, it is also imperative to work toward expanding the potential of schools to encompass the widest range of supports and incentives for adult growth. If we expect adults to grow, we must create contexts that support, encourage, and celebrate their development. What this means for individual schools will vary; what this means for all schools is structures and norms that encourage interdependence.

Where to Start, How to Continue

If you've gotten this far in the book (that is, if you're not a person who starts with the final chapter and reads backward), you have already begun to think about issues of adult development. Frequently schools build commitments to adult growth by learning about adult development theories through reading and/or by working with consultants. In every case I know, adults are immediately excited by having their needs addressed and legitimized and by beginning to learn and understand more about themselves. Most meetings among adults in schools focus on responding to the needs of others; addressing faculty needs can be a refreshing and energizing variation.

Faculties can work together to develop plans for making their schools more responsive to adult needs and aspirations. A small but meaningful change in one school was the initiation of fifteen minutes of daily and individually tailored "adult time." Teachers and administrators have also instituted faculty days; year, semester, and week-long sabbaticals; and coaching and mentoring relationships and support groups. On a larger scale, some schools have incorporated writing into the curriculum for everyone and have started leadership centers for teachers and/or administrators.

Readers can make direct use of the book by sharing the teacher portraits in meetings. The questions I raise in the introduction to Chapter 1 can be useful guides. You can begin to build a common understanding and vocabulary about adult development by introducing the stage and phase theories over time and thinking about their implications. The topic of gender differences is guaranteed to produce lively discussion, especially when adults begin their thinking with writing. Choosing one or more of the promising practices, making a commitment to learn more about it, and adopting an investigation and implementation plan for your school or district constitute another suggested step.

Along with other professional and school improvement tools, theories of adult development can expand the possibilities of staff development, leadership, and learning. Most fundamentally, discussion and debate about the realities and possibilities of human differences and human potential are central to the educational process. They promise to inform and enrich the way educators understand and respond to each other as well as to children.

Six Years Later...

Six years after completing the initial study, I went back to Archer for a day's visit. I was curious about how the school had changed. Had it grown larger as a result of school closings? Was it still a busy and productive learning environment for teachers and children? What had become of Judy Cubbins, Janet Kramer, Don Bolter, and Nan Johnson? I knew Peter Samson was still principal, because I had talked with him to arrange the visit. Was he still perceived as supportive, and was his presence still seen as central?

ARCHER ELEMENTARY: THE SECOND TIME AROUND
By the time I arrived on a Thursday morning, teachers and children were already engaged in the business of teaching and learning. Though some classroom doors stood ajar and others were closed, everyone was working within his or her classroom. In the halls, two custodians were repairing some broken chairs; aside from the sounds of their work, it was quiet in the building.

As I made my way to the front office (a sign read: "All Visitors Must Report to the Main Office"), I took pleasure in the colorfully displayed drawings and writings of children. On my right were life-size outlines of people filled in with the leaves of fall; in the front hallway was an exhibit on conservation. I remembered that the display of children's work had always been an important part of Archer's school environment.

I arrived at the office to find a packet of materials waiting for me. On top was a copy of the *Daily Bulletin*. In between an announcement of an upcoming field trip and the start of a "birthday club," I found a short paragraph alerting teachers to my visit. I had been scheduled to begin the day in Judy Cubbins' third grade and invited to "drop by other classrooms" at my discretion. So Judy Cubbins was still at Archer and still teaching third grade. Had she taught other grades in the intervening years? Was she still married? Did she have children?

I wandered slowly toward Room 14, wondering about the other teachers I had known. Was Nan Johnson still at Archer? She had talked about wanting to get more involved in system-wide curriculum development, but she had also said that she was often reluctant to tamper with things that were working. I remembered that she had been thinking about starting a family and was worrying about making a timely decision. I thought she might very well have one or two children by now. Although Nan was one of the most energetic persons I had ever met, I wondered if the strains of raising young children and working would leave even her weary. Had she taken time off? Did she feel the pulls between work and home? Was she planning to stay in education?

Janet Kramer, I guessed, would likely be gone. Though she was not a person who often took the initiative, perhaps her discomfort with her life had pushed her into a profession where she was more likely to meet men. If a relationship had come her way before that time, she could as easily have remained in teaching, though she might have taken time out from work to start a family.

Men who begin their careers as elementary school teachers often go on to teach junior or senior high school or leave the classroom for administration. Don Bolter had told me of his intention to remain a teacher. Where would he be, and what would he be doing? His commitment to teaching, his reluctance to change, and his devotion to family all made me believe he would still be in the classroom. Chances are, I would find him somewhere in the building. These and other thoughts swirled around in my mind as I opened the door to Room 14.

I spent the day observing in the school, talking with teachers, and meeting with the principal. I ate lunch in the teachers' room. I wandered through the cafeteria, around the library, and in the halls. I went into three classrooms: a third, a fourth, and a fifth grade. The most striking impression I and others had, as we reflected on the six intervening years, was how little had fundamentally changed. "We're all older," Peter Samson said. "There are some new programs," a teacher shared, "but the school is pretty much the same."

Though I had expected Archer's enrollment to be rising, as it had begun to do in neighboring towns, the number of students remained stable at about four hundred. Though some new teachers had come to the school, there was still a core of veterans. The principal had no immediate plans to leave; parents were said to be satisfied; there were few reported pressures from central office administration. Teaching and learning at Archer Elementary were going along smoothly and with little change.

In many ways, this was good news. Archer had been a positive environment for children and adults six years before, and it seemed to be continuing to meet the needs of most teachers, students, and parents. As Peter Samson searched his memory for changes in the school, he mentioned the shift in attitude and increased constructive involvement of parents: "Parents are less critical of the school than they used to be. They're very supportive, and they make an enormous contribution. It's as if we've finally proved ourselves to them."

Influenced by increasing public interest in the quality of schools and the more general criticism of education, I asked Peter how he would characterize Archer. Was it an ordinary school, a special place, or less than adequate in his opinion? Samson replied, without apology or hesitation:

In many ways, Archer's probably pretty ordinary. The school does have a special ability to respond to very needy children, and this ability has earned us some recognition. Parents, in general, and the parent organization, in particular, have a high regard for the quality of Archer's educational programs. In terms of test scores, the school's just about in the middle for the town. The level of teaching also varies. We have teachers whose teaching ranges in quality from just average to extraordinary.

Had Samson himself changed? I asked teachers and Samson this question. "I'd say he's more self-assured," one teacher commented. "He's still supportive, and he continues to create a positive school climate for everyone," another teacher shared. "Samson's probably the most intellectual principal in Scribner; he helps to keep us current professionally," a third said. As had been true from the start of my association at Archer, the role of the principal and the particular skills and personality characteristics of Peter Samson continued to surface when teachers spoke about the school. Even when they were not asked about the principal, Samson's name quickly surfaced in teachers' conversations.

"More self-assured?" repeated Samson when I shared one teacher's perception.

No, I don't think so. I know myself better, but I still have a lot of the same strengths and limitations. I listen, I'm supportive, I try to keep people thinking and growing, but I'm still afraid of some confrontations, and I'm still not a strong authoritarian. I can't answer all the needs of the children and adults who are here, but I do think I help make Archer an active and interesting learning and working environment. I've always been passionate about providing for kids' needs, and I also work hard to support and promote teachers' development.

The teachers I spoke with agreed. I talked with all four teachers whose stories I had chronicled. Judy Cubbins, Nan Johnson, and Janet Kramer were all still teaching at Archer. Don Bolter had recently left, having been transferred to the junior high school. As I listened to them talk about what had transpired in the past six years and where they thought they might be heading, I was intrigued by the congruence of the ways they approached the events in their lives and their more general developmental orientations.

JUDITH CUBBINS: BECOMING SELF-CONTAINED

Basically I'm a happy person, but I didn't realize how much happier I could be.

True to the way I had remembered it, Judith Cubbins' classroom was a masterpiece. (She was now Judith, not Judy, and I was to find out why.) Everywhere I turned, I saw something clever and colorful. Behind my seat there was a bright orange bulletin board. The names of books and the students who had chosen them were joined with a long rope. "Rope Yourself Some Good Reading," the accompanying sign read in letters carefully formed out of colored construction paper. In a lapse from note taking, my eyes strayed toward the window and the rainy morning. On the sill, three egg cartons captured my attention. Each contained rows of hollowed-out eggshell halves brightly decorated with faces, providing a home for grasses that were just beginning to germinate. Even the venetian blinds were drafted into service, holding the rules of punctuation on sheets clipped to the slats.

If anything had changed, it was the amount and sophistication of the materials her classroom displayed. It was filled with materials she had made and the results of projects she had initiated. Judith had always loved to create. "Putting together materials is part of the reason I love to teach....I love bulletin boards. That's me. And, in a way, teaching is an excuse for doing the things I like." This reason for teaching obviously still captured her interest. Judith had also described herself as a very organized and a very forceful person. The arrangement of chairs and desks in neat rows facing the front of the classroom, the teacher-directed activities I observed, and the impeccable neatness of the room all confirmed that these aspects of her style and personality had also stood the test of time. During the hour I observed in her classroom, Judith went over the answers to a grammar lesson, displaying the correct answers on an overhead screen; asked the children to write down a series of sentences that she dictated to them; and read part of a story while her students ate snacks during the start of recess.

In fact, others told me that Judith had grown more invested in teaching, more focused on her classroom, and more distant. Later she told me that she and her second husband had been divorced for several years, that she was feeling good about being single, and that she had been chosen Scribner's Teacher of the Year the previous spring.

As Judith spoke more about her divorce and its aftermath, she described the results of a continuing developmental transition. When I had first gotten to know her, she had come to a point in her development where she was just beginning to separate herself from others. In the shift from identifying herself with what she did and the people in her life, she had started to understand her own needs as separate from the needs of others. This allowed her, she said, to make space in her work and nonwork life without becoming so totally "immersed." Judith's second marriage temporarily focused her energies and attentions away from work. Now divorced and without children, she has accepted the challenges and liabilities of increased independence.

> Six years ago, I would have described myself as a person far more dependent on external reinforcement. I don't think I was able to give myself a pat on the back that I could believe or accept as permissible very often. Teaching gave me a great outlet for getting those pats so that I could feel my worth as a person.
>
> Six years ago, kids, parents, and teachers all told me I did my job well. That praise is still there, but it has changed in the way I

view it. Now I can say to myself: "You did a good job today."

Judith went on to describe her old sense of self:

> When I say "dependent," what I mean is, "Willing to sacrifice my
> own self to meet somebody else's needs – not paying attention to
> what my needs are." It's like holding onto someone out of the fear
> that there's not enough of you to let them hold onto. And that's a
> vicious cycle: The tighter you hold onto them, the less of you there is
> to hold. That's what I began to recognize. There was very little of me
> that I was holding onto.

As she described her emerging developmental orientation, Judith related
a growing ability to set limits on her development as a woman. Referring to
a book about women who are excessively loving, she said:

> When I read the book, I said to myself: "I wonder if you could class
> teachers, in general, and particularly those who are dedicated teach-
> ers, as women who love too much because they need to give in order
> to feel worth?" I see that as something society expects of women
> much more so than of men. Men are taught to set limits; women are
> taught not to set limits. And so my sense of being a woman has
> changed in that I have learned how to set limits without feeling guilt.

Judith's confidence and satisfaction with teaching have always
supported a movement toward independence. Even though she had relied
on other people's positive reactions, she had gradually accumulated enough
successful experiences to recognize her own professional worth. The initial
bond with her second husband also helped to maintain her developmental
balance. In the transition between the Conformist and Conscientious stages
or between Kegan's Interpersonal and Institutional positions, Judith's sense
of self-worth was defined by both external and internal forces. Six years,
continued success in teaching, and a painful divorce have now combined to
influence her ongoing development. More than ever before, Judith is able to
define herself by self-generated standards. She talks about the role of her
divorce, as well as the contributions of teaching, in these developments:

> Part of the shift was related to the pain of divorce. You can only deny
> so much pain. After we were separated, I was still hoping. I still really

believed in my heart that we could work it out and everything would be fine. I think I'd still be believing that today if I hadn't gradually recognized and overcome the great need to be needed and to have this person whose needs I could meet. Teaching continues to satisfy a piece of my old self. I still have a need to be needed and to be listened to, but I'm now more willing and able to meet my own needs and listen to myself.

Development is never simple or neat. Even as we gain new capacities, we remain tied to needs of the past. No one ever "outgrows" his or her need to be needed. Instead, the degree of our needs diminishes as our capacities to meet them ourselves increase. It is the increase of just such capacities that defines the new boundaries of Judith's development. While her sense of her self and the way she understands the world have shifted, many of her behaviors and her disposition remain. Judith is still forceful and directive, for instance. Although she says she has "extended" herself and her teaching, she continues to do things with her own class, in her own way, and in her own time. Several years ago, she initiated a teaching and learning program between students and residents of a nearby retirement home. She has limited the arrangement to her own class.

Although Judith says relationships are easier for her now that she has learned to set clear limits, she has become more selective about whom she befriends. Interestingly, she has drawn away from her colleagues over the past six years, feeling that the bitterness of some about remaining single has spilled over into their attitudes toward work. Many of her former friends have now left. With the exception of the principal – whom she still considers positively and who continues to provide her with the personal and professional support she needs to feel positive about her teaching, and autonomous in the classroom – she has few school-based friendships. Recognizing that her teaching style has always engendered some degree of jealousy and competitiveness, Judith's developmental orientation allows her to be less affected by the resulting isolation and negative feedback.

I am not as concerned with how people feel about my professionalism. I don't need approval from everybody to feel good or to be able to function. I mean, it's a fact of life that not everybody is going to approve of you – or even like you.

Within the school, both the teachers and the principal feel the results of Judith's professional success, as well as her personal distance. Tension and discomfort accompanied several teachers' reporting of Judith's Teacher-of-the-Year award. Others told me that she seemed to have become even more independent than she had been in the past and more reluctant to "let other people in." Judith understands and chooses this disposition. Some of what appears to be distancing, moreover, is the result of limited communication and lack of understanding. Teachers told me that Judith had abruptly changed her name from Judy to Judith, for instance, and they interpreted the change as a symbol of increased formality and aloofness. Has anyone talked to Judith about the choices and changes in her life? Has Judith volunteered an explanation? When I asked her about changing her name, she shared without hesitation:

It wasn't so much that I wanted to change my identity as that I wanted the identity that had always been mine. When I student-taught here, I was called Judy, a nickname. I was never called Judy before, except by my parents. But as a student teacher, I didn't say, "Hey, I'm Judith." So then I started teaching here and I was Judy – for all these years. Last summer, when I did part-time work, I introduced myself as Judith. It was the first opportunity in a working environment to say, "This is who I am."

Given the changes that Judith describes in her personal life and in her sense of self, it is not surprising that she has chosen to keep teaching. Teaching has been a continuing source of stability and achievement. That she has remained in the same school and with the same grade level for sixteen years may be more surprising. Judith explains:

I knew very early on that I wanted to teach, and I was fortunate enough when I was doing my student teaching to have choices about where I'd be and to pick the place that was right for me. I wasn't sure about the grade. At first, I fell in love with fifth grade, but the curriculum here in Scribner is what hooked me on third graders.

Judith's interests in curriculum and in teaching have thus been satisfied by her present position. At one time, she had thought about developing materials or teaching adults how to teach. In the last six years, she has satisfied her curriculum development urge by creating and publishing a number of learning materials. Her style and personality continue to be best suited to working with children. An increasing ability to see children and situations individually makes each student and every day different. As she completes her sixteenth year as a third-grade teacher at Archer, she has no plans for making a change.

Given Judith's developmental orientation and the circumstances of her life, it makes sense to me that her style with children and adults has remained orderly and directive. What has emerged is her ability to delineate a clear sense of herself and to draw boundaries between herself and others. I can also understand how difficult it is for colleagues to appreciate her limit setting and to accept her accomplishments. Whether she can or should interact more readily and willingly with other teachers in the building is an intriguing staff development question. For now, the classroom structure, the third grade, and her developmental orientation allow her to remain focused, in charge, protected, and self-contained.

JANET KRAMER: IN RELATIONSHIP

I'm happy! I can't believe it!

Not only was I surprised to learn that Janet had continued to work at Archer – without a break or a change – but I was puzzled to learn that she had persisted in teaching despite remaining unmarried. As I approached her classroom, I wondered what I would find. Would Janet look older and more weary? Would she be bitter and resigned?

Janet was working with several students as I entered her classroom. As she looked up, she smiled. She walked toward me and eagerly shook my hand. "Glad to see you," I said. "You look terrific!" Janet appeared comfortable and relaxed. She pulled over a chair from a nearby table and motioned for me to sit down. She and her twenty-one students were just finishing a geography lesson. Afterward, while the children worked independently, we caught up on the past six years.

Janet told me about herself and her life. She told me she was very happy with her teaching now, that she had taken some courses and looked into other fields, but hadn't found anything she liked as much. Over the past several years, Janet's parents had taken sick and ultimately died. This had been extremely hard on her. Continuing to teach, which she knew how to do so well, had freed her to attend to her out-of-school life.

"The best news is that I'm in a relationship!" Janet went on to tell me about a man she had met and about whom she was serious. She told me how important it was to have someone who cared about her in her life – especially since the death of her parents. "Otherwise, you're completely alone," she explained. "I'm so much happier now. I really hope this works out."

I asked Janet if having a family was still an important part of her dreams. "Perhaps," she answered tentatively. "For now, I'm concentrating on the relationship." Later, when I asked Peter about Janet's hopefulness and uncharacteristic optimism, he hypothesized that turning forty might also provide a partial explanation. "Maybe she hit forty and realized, 'This is my life. I might as well accept it.' In any case, she's had some hard times, and now things seem to be looking better." As Peter and I talked, we agreed on the importance of personal factors in professional development and the persistence of basic life tasks.

As Janet spoke about her new male companion, her feelings about being a woman and about her students and the principal, the important components of each relationship remained consistent. She was still very much bound to positive feedback from others for her sense of self-worth. About her new male friend, she explained:

> I'm just so happy to have found a man who's nice to me and who makes me feel good. I can't believe it. This has never happened before. It makes me feel complete.

Being cared about ~~by a man~~ has also influenced Janet's feelings about ~~being~~ a woman. Consistent with Kegan's Interpersonal developmental level, she relies upon positive input from her relationships to bring aspects of her self to life. Her sense of being a woman is further linked to her ability to express feelings.

> I feel like I *am* a woman now. I wasn't quite sure before. The man whom I used to spend time with never made me feel like anything but an object. This man cares about me; he's kind and nice to me.
>
> Feeling more like a woman means I don't have to feel guilty about my feelings. I can express my feelings. I used to think I wouldn't be respected for my feelings – as a person or as a woman. I'm getting to feel better about that now because I'm trying to express how I feel to this man – and he listens! The way I feel as a woman is bound up in my feelings and how I express them.

Referring back to the first time we had met, Janet links her negative attitudes about teaching both to an unsatisfying relationship with another man and to a particularly difficult class.

> I think I recall six years ago that I was feeling disillusioned, burned out, and tired of teaching, and that I had a very difficult class. Discipline was a big problem, and I just couldn't do anything to gain the kids' regard or respect. I started wondering whether I was doing the right thing. Since that time, the classes have been much better, and I've regained some sense of caring about the profession that I had when I first started out.

Now that Janet believes she has more positive feelings from her students, she feels more positive about teaching and about herself.

One of the things that stands out most starkly and painfully for her in the last six years was a breach in her relationship with the principal. Several years ago, the possibility of Janet being transferred from Archer had been hard on Janet and Peter's relationship. Needing to reduce staff size, Peter decided that Janet would be the most appropriate teacher to transfer. Janet believes she was chosen because she was "the least likely person to put up a fight." Peter remembers that his choice had been based on professional criteria. Though he told that to Janet at the time, he says she was very angry with him and told him she felt "betrayed." Aside from the professional implications, Janet felt Peter had violated their friendship. Peter told me, "She could not hear that the decision was a professional one and had nothing to do with our personal relationship."

As Janet recalls these hard times, she remembers it was the idea of having to disrupt her already established relationships and the feelings of being rejected by the principal that hurt most.

> I would say that it was probably the major trauma of my whole career: the thought of leaving a school where I had been for more than ten years and had established a good rapport with the kids and the parents. I felt like the principal didn't want me.

As it turned out, another teacher decided to retire, and the transfer was not needed. Both Peter and Janet remember that it took a long time for their relationship to mend. Peter waited and hoped that Janet would understand the educational logic of the decision. Janet needed time and evidence to regain a sense of trust. Until the relationship was repaired, a fundamental part of Janet's world view was at risk. Though the incident happened almost five years ago, it is still vivid in Janet's mind and heart.

Janet's sense of competence remains tied to how others perceive her. Not only does she feel reinforced when her students show her respect, positive regard, and disciplined behavior, but she feels most comfortable when expectations for her own performance are clear. When relationships are uncertain or unstable, Janet feels incomplete.

Janet's views of successful teaching are likewise linked to the characteristics of her developmental outlook. More than the accumulation of knowledge, Janet wants to help children gain self-confidence and feel good about themselves.

> I like to see the kids happy and feeling good about themselves and learning. My emphasis has always been more affective than cognitive.

Janet often experiences external requirements as impositions. This is how she describes the introduction of computers into the system, as well as the continuing demands of the town curriculum. Characteristically, she conforms to these outside influences rather than adjusting them to fit her own needs or standards. Describing the evolution of her teaching, she says:

> There have been changes in the curriculum that have led to changes in my teaching. I would say my teaching style changes in reaction to the kind of curriculum that's mandated.

Interestingly, Janet no longer feels she would think of the principal first when asked about the school. Instead, she believes it would be parental pressures and involvement. Though Peter's behavior has remained consistent and he continues to provide teachers with varied supports, Janet feels, "We have taken him for granted." Six years ago, Peter's style was in stark contrast to previous principals and provided exactly what teachers needed and wanted. Could it be that the principal's strengths are less valued now, or does he need to add other elements to his leadership repertoire?

Unlike others, Janet describes Samson as an instructional leader. As evidence, she points to the fact that he has taught a class for the last two years. Looking at the school more globally, she describes relationships among teachers as fragmented and the former team structure as almost defunct. She told me she hadn't seen Nan Johnson in four months. More important and satisfying to Janet than school-wide cohesiveness, however, are her immediate relationships to students and their parents and her interpersonal life outside of work.

Asked about the future, Janet explains that she wants the positive conditions that now characterize her life to stay in place. She wants to maintain the quality of her relationships and to minimize change. Far from feeling burned out, she is feeling energized and optimistic. She wants to be married and to make teaching at Archer her life's work.

> I'd really like to keep things the way they are. I'd like to solidify my relationship through marriage and make teaching my career. Although I know that changes do take place, I know what is expected of me at the moment. Basically, I see myself teaching forever and ever.

Enmeshed in positive relationships and clear about external demands, Janet's sense of self is completed and intact. Perhaps with these external supports in place, Janet will be freer to explore her teaching. Particularly if changes enhance her relationships to students, parents, and colleagues, she is likely to be comfortable about small shifts. The principal and others with whom Janet interacts will have useful and important criteria for determining how to work and live with Janet as they recognize the continuing importance of relationships to her sense of competence and self-worth.

DON BOLTER: MOVING ON OR SETTLING IN?

> I think there should be things that I'm told to do.

I had to drive across town to see Don Bolter. Shortly after I left, he had been transferred to the junior high school where he now teaches science. He had acquired an expertise at this level from years of summer school teaching experience. When I announced my presence at the front office, I heard Don's name being broadcast over the public address system. I remember thinking about the different atmosphere in what seemed to be a larger and more impersonal building. I also recall that things and people looked a lot bigger.

Don greeted me in the main hallway with a handshake and led me to a nearby conference room. As we sat down at the table, Don began to recount the circumstances of his transfer from Archer, certainly the event that stood out most in the six years since I had last seen him.

> It was a shock to everybody, especially me. Five years ago, there was one too many people for the number of positions at Archer; and at the time, everybody assumed someone would be transferred to a nearby elementary school where there were openings. Thinking of myself as a very important part of the staff, I felt secure. They certainly wouldn't dare transfer me!

As the time for the decision drew nearer, everyone was feeling increasingly nervous. Don, like others, was clear that he didn't want to endure the disruption of moving to another elementary school just to be doing the same thing. When Peter called him into his office and told him he would be assuming the junior high science position, Don remembers feeling both surprised and pleased. While he hadn't known the position was open, he knew it would be a positive move. He saw the choice by Samson as complimentary. Deep inside, he also knew he was getting tired of what he was doing and needed a change.

> I was comfortable at Archer, but I knew I needed to do something different. I had been in the same room teaching the same thing for five years. That was the longest amount of time I'd done any one thing, and I was ready for a change. I just didn't see any opportunities for change.

Asked if he would have pursued the junior high school position if he had been aware of it, Don said no. Though he was not sure at the time what change he sought, he thought he was probably looking for "something even bigger," something "even outside of education." It wasn't that he was dissatisfied, he explained with care; he was just "getting kind of itchy to do something different."

The circumstances of Don's move to the junior high school are particularly interesting in terms of his development. Several years earlier, Don had expressed interest in moving to the junior high but backed off when he realized he would have to take responsibility for bumping a non-tenured teacher. Now, though a teacher would still be moved out when he moved in, it wasn't me that was bumping someone out; it was the system doing it. I actually appreciated the fact that I was asked to move as opposed to me instigating it. I liked and appreciated the fact that I was not responsible for somebody else losing their position.

At the Conscientious or Institutional level, Don preferred being part of the organization as opposed to apart from it. He felt more comfortable going along with the way things were than bucking the tide. By being asked to move, Don could take advantage of an opportunity without having to take the initiative or to assume the responsibility. These same dynamics abetted Don's concerns about disrupting the lives of other teachers and what that might mean for his own acceptance.

Once I came here, I found I was accepted. I had some feelings about what the transition meant for other people. And when I was chosen, that at least let me off the hook in terms of my responsibility toward them.

Not only did these circumstances relieve Don of having to prove himself, but they allowed him to feel "selected." A person who is typically unsettled by change, Don felt more comfortable with the way things happened.

I really felt that the system had an obligation to me because they were the ones who were telling me to go as opposed to me having proved myself to them because I was asking to go. I enjoyed that position. I was able to...not exploit it, but use it to my advantage. I felt more comfortable coming that way. I was an invited guest rather than a party crasher.

Once at the junior high and in the science department, Don was motivated to take several graduate courses, something he had lost interest in after getting his master's degree fifteen years earlier. He discovered that course-work was not only fun but also stimulating. The whole experience of the move was rejuvenating.

Although Don says he's always had the feeling he wasn't going to teach forever, he does not have a clear idea about what he would do instead. At one point, he thought he might be interested in being an administrator, but he has since decided against that. Don's desire for a change thus seems more general than specific. Forty years old and the father of three children, he also realizes his options for shifting careers are narrowing.

When I asked Don about changes that had taken place in the last six years, he was hard pressed to enumerate them. Overall, he thinks his values and routines have remained the same. At the junior high, he has had opportunities to work with men and has found the variety interesting. As a science teacher rather than a teacher of nine- and ten-year-old children, he also feels he has become more identified with his discipline. Teaching one subject is also somewhat repetitious, and Don sometimes finds it hard to make teaching exciting. Once in the classroom, however, he regains his excitement.

> The thing that sustains me is the fact that I recognize that when I get into the classroom and start teaching, everything's good and I like it. I have to keep remembering that.

One difference Don definitely notices is the difference between Peter Samson and his present principal. Though he believes both principals are central to the life of the school, he continues to find the personal qualities of Samson unusual.

> At Archer, if you had a problem in the classroom, Peter would come in and help you out. He would do things with kids and work in the classroom. If you had lunch duty, he might come and take it for you, even if you never asked him to. He would just do the kinds of things that built relationships with the staff. He cared about us.
>
> That kind of thing doesn't happen here, partly because of the school's size and structure, partly because of the principal's style. Peter is rare.

Don intermittently talks about changing careers, but with more hope than focus. When he describes changes that might happen next year, they involve the specifics of his teaching assignment rather than exploration of a shift in career. Rather than taking an active role in shaping new options, Don characteristically waits until he has to respond. Foreseeing the possibility of both positive and negative changes, he concludes, "I'm not sure how I'm going to react." Since he doesn't see himself retiring from the position of teacher or becoming an administrator, I asked him if he anticipated a major career change. "Not necessarily," he responded. "I could just go on doing what I'm doing."

Given Don's desire to blend in with things around him, his need for security, and his ability to take direction, it is unlikely he will make a sudden move on his own. Responsibilities for his family also reinforce his conservative orientation. If an opportunity presents itself outside of education, Don could follow it. Lacking such an opportunity, he may well remain in the classroom. It is unclear whether he will move on or settle in.

NAN JOHNSON: A MATTER OF JUGGLING

Anytime I've made a change in my life, it's felt hard.

I recognized Nan Johnson as soon as I heard the familiar sound and pace of her voice, and as soon as I peered in and saw her busily engaged with one child and then another as she searched her desk for this or that in response to their questions. "Aren't you Nan Johnson?" I asked as I approached the doorway. Before I could finish reintroducing myself, there was a look of recognition, a broad smile, a big hug, and a steady stream of questions and conversation. I heard about and saw a picture of her children: Jennifer, age five, and Sam, age one. I learned about the different grades and grade combinations she had taught in the past six years and about her growing interest in curriculum and administration.

Both Nan and I remembered her deep ambivalence six years ago. Then, it was about whether to have children. Although her husband wanted to start a family, Nan was uncertain.

> I was in my early thirties at that point, and I think I felt the nurturing side of myself was being satisfied by teaching. Being involved with young children all day, I thought it would be too much coming home and starting all over again. Yet the biological clock was beginning to go tick, tick very loudly.

As Nan recalled these times, she described herself as "undecided" and "deeply ambivalent." "I remember agonizing over where my life was going." In fact, the solution presented itself to Nan when she discovered she was already several-months pregnant. Although she proceeded through six more months of her pregnancy in what she calls "prepartum depression," she characteristically allowed the events of life to pull her along.

Six years and two children later, Nan describes herself as "tired" and "sometimes trapped." In a traditional marriage, she finds herself doing most of the chores around the house and for the children. At the same time, financial demands keep her at work. Nan's tired and trapped feelings spill over into the way she talks about work. When she thinks about what stands out for her as a teacher in Scribner, she mentions the pressures of the curriculum and the demands of parents.

> Within the past six years, the elementary curriculum has become overwhelming. I'm trying to do a four-person job as a single person with very little support. The parents in this town really demand a lot. The expectations to do the three-ring circus all the time can get pretty tiring.

Interestingly, Nan's current description of herself and her feelings remind me of early conversations with Janet Kramer. Six years before, Janet had described herself as weary and confined. She, too, complained about the curriculum and about parents. While Janet looked to a relationship with a man to solve her dilemma, as was consistent with the terms of her development, Nan looks toward work and debates whether to seek a position outside the classroom. Nan actually uses the term "burnout" to describe her current state. "I feel sometimes that I'm on the edge of admitting that I have burned out and really want to move away from the classroom and do something different."

Much of Nan's current experience of herself and her world relates directly to conflicting pulls of work and family. The characteristic energies and ambitions Nan previously focused on work have now become divided, leaving Nan with less time and energy for work. The part of Nan that needs to feel productive is coming up short. Her failure to maintain her high internal standards leaves her feeling dissatisfied and frustrated.

> I don't feel as successful now as I once did. I can't pay as much attention because of some of the other pulls on my life. It's not just that there's so much in the curriculum; it's also that I have less time.
>
> I feel guilty when I have to dash things together. And I'm even more frustrated now because I know what I'd like to be doing with the kids and I have the skills to do it. I just don't have the time to get organized and do it the right way.

Though Nan feels frustrated and disappointed with herself, others continue to see her as active and energetic. Peter Samson and Janet Kramer both confirmed the persistence of Nan's high energy level. About conflicts between work and family, Peter said, "If anything, I think her family might want her to pull back from work. Nan is still a dynamo in the classroom and in the system." Janet's description of Nan coming into school on a weekend with one child in tow and the other strapped to her back reinforced Peter's perception of Nan's dedication to teaching.

From the inside, things look and feel quite different. Although Nan is energetic, she is stretching herself to the limits.

> Things feel on the edge now. Just getting here in the morning is really difficult – getting everyone off and running. I really feel like I'm carrying two full-time jobs. Thankfully, I have a lot of energy and I don't require a lot of sleep. The middle of the night is about the only time there is any time for me. I felt guilty about the crazy hours I keep until I talked with other mothers and found out that's how a lot of working mothers live.

While Nan's drive may keep her going, her pride keeps her isolated. Never having many close friends on staff, she now feels "pretty alone."

> There are a lot of unmarried and childless women in the school. At forty, I'm still one of the youngest staff members, and I'm sure for some there are issues about what they might have missed.

The potential for teachers at the school to support or alleviate some of Nan's conflicts through shared experiences or friendships is thus almost nonexistent. Only Peter Samson remains a "very close friend." Nan's tendency to see him in this way and to minimize his role as instructional leader is likely to be related, in part, to her intense need for friendship.

Several years ago, Nan started working with adolescents at a nearby community center and found she loved the age group and the informality of the teaching and learning experience. More recently, she has become trained in counseling and finds her increased participation at the center a good way to meet people and form new relationships. While all this has given her "a lot of good feelings," she simultaneously feels pressures to leave teaching and enter social work – pressures she is not yet prepared to accept. "There are days when people say I should go into social work, but I'm not sure I'm ready for it."

Nan's positive experiences with the community center and her fantasies about changing careers make the confinements of teaching even more evident.

> I sometimes envy the community center director and her different helping role with people, her freedom to set up her own schedule in the day. I think part of feeling trapped in teaching is the rigidity of the school schedule and the never-ending quality of teaching. I guess it all relates to the "have to's." I'm not feeling free, either financially or in terms of my work choices.

Making choices has never been one of Nan's strong points. This quality must make the repetitious and conflicting pulls of work and family even more difficult. Lacking sufficient support from school and home, Nan has continued to manifest a familiar developmental orientation: moving between an addiction to the "shoulds" of life (seen at the Conformist level) and the unrelenting need for accomplishment (characteristic of the Conscientious stage). Perhaps the particular constraints of school and home have even depleted her characteristic drive, exaggerated her tendency toward indecision, and left her feeling tethered to her present life circumstances. Painting a picture of her relationship to work, Nan describes the school as an "ocean liner" and herself as "a tugboat," tied to and being carried forward and backward by the flow of the ship.

Six years ago, Nan was sitting on the fence, trying to decide whether to have children, on the one hand, and thinking about moving out of the classroom, on the other. Just as the issue of motherhood was "solved" for her when she discovered she was pregnant, taking an administrative position or even leaving the profession may be determined more by what others do than by her own actions. Increasingly subject to external circumstances, Nan has stayed both in the classroom and on the fence.

> From the outside, it looks like I'm a good teacher. From the inside, it feels crazy. It's really a matter of juggling.

Unless Nan's independent self gains more strength and support, in another six years she will likely be wherever life takes her.

AT DAY'S END
Overall, I was intrigued by how much of importance was shared with me during my visits to Archer Elementary and to Scribner Junior High School.

In particular, I was struck by the subtle discrepancies between what people told me about themselves and how they were perceived by others. Judith Cubbins, for instance, appears aloof and distant to her colleagues, while she is really making some significant developmental strides. Nan Johnson seems to be coping well with the demands of work and home, while she is actually overwhelmed and exhausted. Considering how readily these adults explained their thoughts and feelings, I wondered why they had not done so with colleagues. Have they not been asked? Have they shied away from volunteering? What can be done to create an atmosphere in schools that allows and encourages people to exchange the personal and professional nuances of their lives?

Next, I was reminded of the complexities of development, its gradual pace, and the degree to which the school environment can support, ignore, or inhibit growth. All the adults I spoke with surfaced memories as if they were yesterday's occurrences. Neither the context nor the dynamics of their life stories had shifted greatly over a six-year period. Are we to conclude, then, that growth is not continuous or that change is so slow and subtle it is hardly worth noting? The major conclusions to be drawn, I think, are that adults manifest different life stages and phases and that it is helpful to recognize the particular nature of their development in order to understand their immediate needs and to provide appropriate supports for stability and incentives for movement.

The interaction between personal and professional growth is the second important observation. In every case, personal or professional forces influenced these adults' development. Judith Cubbins' continuing growth derives from a combination of the changing events in her personal life, on the one hand, and the stability of her professional accomplishments, on the other. Judith, Janet, and Nan all used their teaching as an anchor while they were adrift in their personal lives – through divorce, child rearing, the death of parents, and the formation of new relationships. Don has relied on the strength of his family ties to modulate his investment in career change or advancement. He has used his responsibilities toward family to maintain his continued involvement.

In most instances, the school seems to be less an incentive to growth than a neutral or even negative environment. Both Nan and Don seem stuck, for instance. The demands of motherhood have taken their toll on Nan's available energies for teaching and career advancement. Trying as she is to perform the roles of teacher and mother has left her conflicted and exhausted. Could the principal or the system have taken a more active role in recognizing her dilemma, in providing time off or suggesting interim, part-time options? Simultaneously, could Nan have been supported in her desire for career advancement without feeling she might lose the chance to return to teaching or the credibility to assume a curriculum specialist's position?

Don went to the junior high as he was told to do. In fact, he liked the feeling of being selected. Recognizing he was ready for a change, he viewed the move as timely. Still feeling restless and thinking about a major career shift, Don seems very alone. Who is available to talk with Don about his teaching and his career? Are there supports within the school for helping him safely explore alternatives inside education as well as in other professions? Rather than reinforce Don's tendency to respond to decisions and events after they happen to him, could the principal, his department chair, or colleagues help him in being more proactive?

Janet's teaching appears to have remained strong and consistent over the years. Even though the death of her parents and an unproductive relationship with a man disrupted her personal life, she believes she didn't bring these problems or her feelings of disillusionment into the classroom. Whether this is true, only she and perhaps Peter Samson know. Just as Janet's vibrance and energy are so evident now that the relationships in her life are working, I find it hard to believe her former frustrations were completely hidden. What support could the school have provided when Janet was experiencing hard times? Given that she complained of professional burnout, did the school have a particular obligation to respond? Now that Janet's world view and her life circumstances are in alignment, how might the school capitalize on her positive energies and outlook?

Judith's world view is clearly shifting from the Conformist/Conscientious constellation to the Conscientious stage. Here she is able to set clearer boundaries around herself, generate standards for her own success, and escape the full weight of external judgments. She has taken a number of positive initiatives in her teaching. Her classroom is a wonderful teaching and learning environment. She has made it possible for students to learn about and form relationships with older people. Judith's developmental shift was largely facilitated by crisis in her personal life. While she finds outlets for its productive expression at work, she keeps herself separate from others and rarely shares ideas and resources. How can Judith be encouraged to share her developmental wealth? Can she interact more freely with other teachers and the principal around professional issues without infringing on the independence she cherishes in her self-contained classroom? If team teaching would be too much of an infringement, could Judith run workshops in the school or in the system? Could visitors come and observe her teaching, take notes, and even borrow some of the materials she has created to enrich their own classrooms? For now, the structure of the school and the limits of Judith's new developmental orientation are serving to keep others out when everyone (adults and children) might benefit from increased flexibility and sharing.

Peter Samson continues to manifest a consistent developmental orientation. He has a relatively clear sense of self and an increasingly clear understanding of his strengths and weaknesses. While he is not seen by most as an instructional leader, he is characterized as a "rare human being." Perhaps his greatest strength is his sensitivity to individual needs and his tendency to allow teachers the freedom to work as they determine. But this can be a weakness, too: When he sees problems, he can be reluctant to confront them; when he recognizes strengths, he may not exploit them. Samson had the sensitivity and foresight to transfer Don Bolter. Might the move have been more productive if he had talked about the opening with Don beforehand so the two could have shared the decision and the responsibility for moving? Would more active experiences of decision making and change ultimately be in Don's best professional and developmental interest? Could it be that Don would now be seeking help and advice if he had tasted the benefits of joint decision making and self-initiative? Doesn't Judith Cubbins have strengths that could be exploited for the benefit of others in the school, the system, and the community? Can Janet Kramer's present optimism be translated into educational innovations?

At day's end, I am struck by how little adults in schools talk with one another about the things that matter to them and about the work of teaching and learning. It may be true that adults in schools are more likely to talk to an outsider than with colleagues or the principal. Shouldn't a major goal of the principal be to create a school environment that encourages such sharing? Shouldn't it also be the responsibility of the principal and the teachers in the school to continuously raise basic questions about the teaching and learning of both children and adults? Such questions can form the basis for instructional and staff development options.

Finally, I am persistently convinced of the need for support as a precondition of growth. Each person defines support so that it is consistent with the particular nature of his or her development. For Janet Kramer, support is clearly positive reinforcement; for Nan Johnson, support may currently be recognizing the pulls on her energies, helping to alleviate or reduce some of her current tasks, and sorting out with her the conflicts surrounding her interest in moving out of the classroom. However support is defined, it must be present as a basis for thought and action. When it is not present, adults seem to get stuck or to regress as they struggle to satisfy their most basic needs. With it, they appear to gain the perspective and strength that allow them to capitalize upon their potential and even move forward.

Seen from a developmental perspective, my closing interchanges with several of the teachers and the principal seem particularly appropriate. "Come back whenever you want," Peter invited. "You're always welcome to visit if you need to know more." Peter's openness to reflection and scrutiny and his interest in supporting the work of others are characteristic.

"Thanks for letting me observe," I called to Judith Cubbins as I saw her making her way toward the parking lot. "You're welcome," she said. "I love an audience!," said Judith, keeping a distance. Confident of her abilities as a teacher, she welcomed observers and took for granted a positive response.

"Come and visit me at the Principals' Center," I suggested to Janet after lunch. "No, I'd never be comfortable there. You come back here to visit." It made sense that Janet would feel uncomfortable in a new setting. This would be especially true of a university and an organization for principals, both signifying a somewhat intimidating status. Janet wanted to maintain connection; she also wanted the surrounding context to be familiar and safe.

Finally, Nan Johnson hurriedly handed me a slip of paper with her name and address. She asked to be on the Principals' Center mailing list and agreed to participate as the "teacher expert" in an upcoming program on curriculum development. Though she wondered out loud where she would ever find the time, she wanted very much to keep up. Linking up with a professional organization and sharing her expertise with others were well matched to her energy, ambition, and level of experience. That she took this initiative at such a busy time in her life was both hopeful and problematic.

Certainly, many things had changed for the adults who worked at Archer Elementary since I had first met them six years earlier. The school had new teachers and students, classroom and even school assignments had shifted, and individuals were older and facing new life choices. There was still much to be learned and understood by taking a developmental perspective. I was glad to have returned.

Epilogue: Fifteen Years Later

In the summer of 1989 I left Harvard to become head of an elementary school. For me it was a natural transition. After years of research and teaching *about* schools, it was time to be *in* a school, immersed in the lives of the children and adults about whom I had been learning from a distance.

I remember colleagues in both schools and universities praising me for my courage. I remember thinking that courage was a strange word to describe what felt to me like a logical next step. Some described the change as a "leap of faith;" others used phrases like "career shift" and almost everyone was puzzled by my desire to leave a prestigious university for a small elementary school in a Boston suburb.

These reactions *did* make me somewhat apprehensive. Phone calls and letters from faculty, staff and parents – even before I started my journey from theory to practice – added to my nervousness. As I became and have continued to become a part of the day-to-day life of a school, I have been almost literally swept off my feet by the whirlwind of exhilaration and responsibility that characterizes a school leader's work.

Every now and again, I run into the teachers and principal I worked with at Archer. After bumping into Nan Johnson at a local supermarket, I joined her and principal Peter Samson for coffee and dessert. One day, I was astonished to pick up the phone and hear the familiar voice of Janet Kramer. Might my current school be a good match for *her* son? Could she come and visit?

What I most want to share with you years after I first walked into Archer Elementary and now some years since becoming head of a school is the persistent relevance and importance of the premises that shaped my original interest. I also want to share several ideas and strategies that I have derived from practice.

It is vital to see schools as places where both children and adults work and learn. Schools must be responsive to the development of *all* their constituents. Attending to the developmental needs of the adults who work in schools is a worthy goal in its own right. Even more compelling is the connection between the vitality of the adults in schools and the learning of students.

Understanding and working on my *own* development has been very important and extremely helpful to me in my role as principal. I had learned from my original study that the developmental stage of the school leader is critical. Peter Samson was successful in supporting and promoting the growth of faculty and staff, in part, because he had already completed many of the tasks they were facing. Articulating my commitment to learning and demonstrating that commitment have proved essential. Children often surprise adults with their uncanny ability to grasp new ideas. At the end of my first year as principal, three fifth graders presented me with a wooden plaque for my office door. On the plaque they had painstakingly carved the words: "Head Learner."

Understanding and supporting the growth of *others* has been another crucial part of my role. I never doubted the importance of this role. I have learned, however, that supporting and promoting adult growth is a complicated and difficult undertaking. Fifteen years after walking into Archer Elementary filled with ideas, ideals, and convictions, I am much more humble about what it means and even whether it is always possible to promote growth for every adult in the school. I am convinced, however, that personal and professional issues are present and often pressing for teachers and administrators (whether they are recognized or not), that support is essential, and that there are constant needs for individual support as well as for the creation of a "culture of support" within the school.

Everyone in the school community needs to feel supported. While the specific ways in which we need support may vary related to our development, support must flow in *all* directions – not only from the head to teachers; from teachers to parents; and from parents, teachers, and the head to children. But reciprocally from teachers, children, and parents to the principal; from parents and children to teachers, etc. When individuals feel their efforts are recognized and valued, they work and play hard and with a sense of purpose.

Hard and purposeful work and play create, in turn, a "culture of support" that pervades the entire school community. A culture of growth and support is sustained by a commitment of resources, such as materials, money and time. Establishing these conditions for children and teachers is one of the principal's greatest and most important opportunities and challenges. Being head learner and head leader, moreover, are both full-time preoccupations. Add all the other responsibilities of the principal's role and the result can be daunting.

Being a leader and learner in a school and working to support and develop other leaders and learners is very special work. It's fun; it's hard; it's frustrating; it's rewarding; it's vital. Whenever it seems relevant, I remind myself, colleagues, parents, and children that there is no more important work than teaching and learning.

Within the school I have experienced three especially powerful ways through which a culture of support can develop. These are: the ongoing help of a consulting psychologist; an allocation of time that allows for regular learning and collaboration among and between students and teachers; and opportunities for faculty and staff to assume authentic leadership roles.

For one-half day each week, faculty and staff have access to a clinical psychologist. Her role is to consult with teachers about children, families, and colleagues in the school as well as to listen to and provide perspective on personal and professional matters. I am especially proud of myself for recognizing my own need for such support. While the weekly time I spend with the consultant certainly demonstrates how much I value her services, it has become a major source of support and growth for me in its own right.

Time is a precious commodity in schools and there is never enough. A teacher reminded me of this reality not long ago in response to yet another great idea I thought I had that, coincidentally, required a lot of work. "Teaching is work," he said. "In fact," he continued, "good teaching creates work. It demands planning, developing, evaluating, reporting...." I got the point. All the best intentions to enhance teaching and learning are hollow without time for planning, implementation and assessment.

Given that time is limited and primarily for classroom teaching, how is it possible for adults to assume leadership roles in the school? It's a good question with no simple answer. I think a partial response entails striving for balance or, at least, the integration of leading and learning. I do know that teachers who assume leadership roles in the school model leading and learning for children and colleagues. They inevitably learn and grow. And though the work is demanding and time-consuming, the experience often leaves teacher/leaders with even more energy for their day-to-day work.

During the past fifteen years, research on women's and girls' development has deepened, enriched and complicated our understanding of growth. While there remain more differences within groups than between them, knowledge of the ways in which girls and women develop and the implications for teaching and learning are growing. I draw your attention to the updated suggested reading list which includes a number of important publications on this topic.

Exploring what my journey from theory to practice has meant to my understanding of schools and adults is another book. You may find two general points of discovery interesting. First is an even more vivid recognition that my own development plays a pivotal role in my ability to support and promote adult growth in the school. Second is my discovery that supporting and promoting adult growth in schools adds a measure of instability to the school leader's life and to the life of the organization.

When I reached mid-life, for example, I noticed my primary issues and preoccupations shifting in ways that dramatically affect my perceptions and actions. At a time in my life when climbing up the ladder is less appealing than stretching out alongside it, I feel more comfortable about both short- and long-term issues and more available to let people and things develop in their own ways and in their own time. At a developmental period when a black and white view of the world is replaced by an appreciation of the multiple shades of gray, I am less patient with the idealism of the young teacher. I used to delight in the young teacher's optimism and passion. Now I can bristle at the accompanying rigidity and unrelenting persistence that are also developmentally appropriate.

I have discovered that creating a school culture which values growth and change has both its excitement and its drawbacks. The adults I have found to be most attuned to their development often are the ones who make personal and professional changes. The nature of these changes characteristically involves a high degree of initiative and a willingness to take risks. A very capable beginning teacher I mentored during my first years as principal decided to pursue a doctorate. "You're the reason I'm leaving," she explained. "You taught me to value my growth and to search for ways to enhance my professional development." I lost an early childhood educator with great promise. So much for encouraging development, I thought! I am certain, however, that she will go on to learn and share her knowledge and experience with a wide audience.

Over time, I have noticed a pattern of growth and risk-taking that I have often promoted: a vivacious and well-liked teacher taking a year's leave to be home with his infant daughter; an extraordinary third grade teacher leaving the profession after many year to try a new career. When our school librarian decided to retire, I encouraged other teachers to think about applying for her position. Not only did several teachers take me up on this suggestion, but before the domino effect subsided, three teachers had taken on new responsibilities in the school.

With limited opportunities for career development within school, and especially within a small school, I am delighted to encourage teachers to grow in these ways. I am also increasingly cognizant of and directly responsible for dealing with the questions and concerns about organizational stability that may result. I am also left with the important and energy-depleting task of hiring new adults and helping them integrate into the school culture. "Promoting adult development," I thought to myself one rare, quiet moment, "certainly makes things exciting." After responding to the next five difficult situations that arose in rapid succession, I completed my thinking: "But it can also generate a lot more work!"

As I reflect on the up- and down-sides of supporting adult growth in schools, the benefits far outweigh the costs. Working with a group of professionals who are excited about what they do is exhilarating. A most important benefit is the positive impact on children. I see evidence of the tangible results every day: when the energies of an animated teacher are reflected in the curiosity and excitement of his students; when a teacher who is moving to a new grade can't stop reading, thinking, and talking about early childhood development and her excitement and exhilaration manifest themselves in creative new activities for children in both grades. The feeling in her classroom is electric.

When teachers are engaged and growing, so are their students. During this process everyone in the school community – children, teachers, staff, and parents – benefits.

Notes

CHAPTER 1

1. Seymour B. Sarason, *Work, Aging and Social Change* (New York: The Free Press, 1977), 2.

CHAPTER 2

2. Ray Raphael, *The Teacher's Voice: A Sense of Who We Are* (Portsmouth, NH: Heinemann Educational Books, 1985), 97.

3. Dan C. Lortie, *Schoolteacher* (Chicago: University of Chicago Press, 1975), 82-108.

4. R. Kottkamp, E. Provenzo, and M. Cohen, "Stability and Change in a Profession: Two Decades of Attitudes, 1964-1984," *Phi Delta Kappan* 67 (April 1986): 564-65.

5. Lortie, *Schoolteacher*, 99.

6. Willard Waller, *The Sociology of Teaching* (New York: John Wiley, 1932), 60.

7. Seymour B. Sarason, *The Culture of the School and the Problem of Change* (Boston: Allyn and Bacon, 1971), 168.

8. Sara Freedman, Jane Jackson, and Katherine Boles, *The Effect of Teaching on Teachers* (Grand Forks, N.D.: Center for Teaching and Learning, 1986), 2.

9. Myron Brenton, *What's Happened to Teacher?* (New York: Coward-McCann, 1970), 42-43.

10. J.W. Little, "Norms of Collegiality and Experimentation in the Workplace," *American Educational Research Journal* 19, no. 3 (Fall 1982): 320-40.

11. Linda Darling-Hammond, *Beyond the Commission Reports: The Coming Crisis in Teaching*, The Rand Publication Series (Santa Monica, Calif.: Rand Corporation, 1984), 1-19.

12. Kottkamp, Provenzo, and Cohen, "Stability and Change in a Profession," 559-76.

13. Ibid., 561.

14. Ibid., 164-65.

15. John I. Goodlad, *A Place Called School: Prospects for the Future* (New

York: McGraw-Hill, 1984), 14.

16. R. S. Barth, "The Principal and the Profession of Teaching," *Elementary School Journal* 86, no. 4 (March 1986): 10.

17. A Nation at Risk: The Imperative for Educational Reform: A Report to the Nation and the Secretary of Education, U.S. Department of Education, by the National Commission on Excellence in Education (Washington, DC: The Commission; Superintendent of Documents, U.S. GPO, distributor, 1983), 65.

18. K. P. Cross, "The Rising Tide of School Reform Reports," *Phi Delta Kappan* 66 (Nov. 1984): 167.

19. Goodlad, *A Place Called School*, 264.

CHAPTER 3

20. Erik H. Erikson, *Identity, Youth and Crisis* (New York: W.W. Norton, 1968), 97.

21. Little, "Norms of Collegiality," 325-40.

22. Erik H. Erikson, *Childhood and Society* (New York: W. W. Norton, 1950), 231.

23. Raphael, *The Teacher's Voice*, 97.

24. Gertrude McPherson, *Small Town Teacher* (Cambridge, Mass.: Harvard University Press, 1972), 201-2.

25. Daniel Levinson et al., *The Seasons of a Man's Life* (New York: Knopf, 1978), 7.

26. Daniel Levinson, "A Conception of Adult Development," *American Psychologist* 41, no. 1 (Jan. 1986): 7.

27. Levinson, et al., *The Seasons of a Man's Life*, 53.

28. R. Kegan, "The Evolving Self: A Process Conception of Ego Psychology," *Counseling Psychologist* 8 (Oct. 1978): 27.

29. Roger L. Gould, *Transformations: Growth and Change in Adult Life* (New York: Simon and Schuster, 1978), 25.

30. Ibid., 77-151.

31. Ibid., 153-215.

32. Ibid., 217-307.

33. Chris Argyris, *Reasoning, Learning, and Action: Individual and Organizational* (San Francisco: Jossey-Bass, 1982), 85.

34. Little, "Norms of Collegiality," 325-40; Jon Saphier and Matthew King, "Good Seeds Grow in Strong Cultures," *Educational Leadership* 42 (March 1985): 67-74.

CHAPTER 4

35. Lawrence Kohlberg, "Moral Stages and Moralization: The Cognitive Developmental Approach," in *Moral Development and Behavior: Theory, Research, and Social Issues*, ed. Thomas Lickona (New York: Holt, Rinehart and Winston, 1976), 2:31-53.

36. Levinson et al., *The Seasons of a Man's Life*, 320.

37. Jane Loevinger, "The Meaning and Measurement of Ego Development," *The American Psychologist* 21 (March 1966): 220.

38. S. Glassberg and N. Sprinthall, "Student Teaching: A Developmental Approach," *Journal of Teacher Education* 31 (1980): 31-38.

39. Lawrence Kohlberg, *The Psychology of Moral Development* (San Francisco: Harper and Row, 1984), 468.

40. Lawrence Kohlberg and Rochelle Mayer, "Development as the Aim of Education," *Harvard Educational Review* 42 (Nov. 1972): 449-96.

41. Jane Loevinger, *Ego Development: Conceptions and Theories* (San Francisco: Jossey-Bass, 1976), 27.

42. Monroe C. Gutman Library, "Kohlberg Faculty Files," Gutman Library, Cambridge, Mass.

43. R. Selman and M. Glidden, "Negotiation Strategies for Youth," *School Safety* 3 (Fall 1987): 18-21.

44. Lawrence Kohlberg, "Just Community Approach to Moral Education," in *Moral Education: Theory and Application*, ed. Fritz Oser and Marvin Berkowitz (Hillside, NJ: Ehrlbaum Associates, 1982), 27-87.

45. Loevinger, *Ego Development*, 54-67.

46. Jane Loevinger and Ruth Wessler, *Measuring Ego Development* (San Francisco: Jossey-Bass, 1970), I:7.

47. Loevinger, *Ego Development*, 26.

48. Loevinger, Department of Psychology, Washington University, St. Louis, Mo., personal communication, Nov. 1987.

49. Loevinger and Wessler, *Measuring Ego Development*, 3-7.

50. W. Perry, "Cognitive and Ethical Growth: The Making of Meaning," in *The Modern American College*, ed. Arthur Chickering (San Francisco: Jossey-Bass, 1981), 76-116.

51. Sarason, *The Culture of the School*, 121.

52. R. Kegan, *The Evolving Self: Problems and Process in Human Development* (Cambridge, MA: Harvard University Press, 1982), 246.

53. Ibid., 105.

54. Ibid., 249.

55. Waller, *The Sociology of Teaching*, 1.

56. Ibid., 243.
57. Lucianne B. Carmichael, former elementary principal, New Orleans, LA, journal entry, 1982.
58. S. L. Levine, "A Developmental Perspective on School Leadership," *Principal Magazine* 63 (Nov. 1983): 23-28.

CHAPTER 5

59. Norman A. Sprinthall and Richard C. Sprinthall, *Educational Psychology: A Developmental Approach* (New York: Random House, 1987), 176-77.
60. Jean Baker Miller, *Toward a New Psychology of Women* (Boston: Beacon Press, 1974), 3-12; Carol Gilligan, *In a Different Voice: Psychological Theory and Women's Development* (Cambridge, MA: Harvard University Press, 1982), 9.
61. L. C. Woo, "Women Administrators: Profiles of Success," *Phi Delta Kappan* 67 (Dec. 1985): 287.
62. Ibid.
63. C. Shakeshaft, "A Female Organizational Culture," *Educational Horizons* 62 (Spring 1986): 117-22.
64. Sara Lawrence Lightfoot, *The Good High School: Portraits of Character and Culture* (New York: Basic Books, 1983).
65. S.K. Bilken and M.B. Brannigan, eds., *Women and Educational Leadership* (Lexington, MA: D.C. Heath, 1980): 2.
66. Lightfoot, *The Good High School*, 333.
67. Ibid., 329.
68. E.E. Maccoby and C.N. Jacklin, eds., *The Psychology of Sex Differences* (Stanford, CA: Stanford University Press, 1974) 10:349-55.
69. Ibid., 373-74.
70. Ibid., 373.
71. Ibid.
72. Erikson, *Identity, Youth and Crisis*, 261-94.
73. Ibid., 265.
74. Robert W. White, *Lives in Progress: A Study of the Natural Growth of Personality* (New York: Holt, Rinehart and Winston, 1952), 199.
75. Ibid., 283.
76. Gould, *Transformations*, 128-29.
77. Woo, "Women Administrators," 286.
78. Gould, *Transformations*, 103.
79. Miller, *Toward a New Psychology of Women*, 40.

80. Jean Baker Miller, *The Development of Women's Sense of Self*, Stone Center Work in Progress Series, no. 12 (Wellesley, MA, 1984), 9-10.

81. Judith Jordan, *Empathy and Self Boundaries*, Stone Center Work in Progress Series, no. 16 (Wellesley, MA, 1984), 2; Janet Surrey, *Self-in-Relation: A Theory of Women's Development*, Stone Center Work in Progress Series, no.13 (Wellesley, MA, 1985), 1-15.

82. Gilligan, *In a Different Voice*, pp. 1-23.

83. Ibid.

84. Mary F. Belenky et al., *Women's Ways of Knowing: The Development of Self, Voice, and Mind* (New York: Basic Books, 1986).

85. W. Stuart, "A Psychosocial Study of the Formation of the Early Adult Life Structure in Women" (Doctoral thesis, Columbia University, 1977).

86. Ibid.

87. Gail Sheehy, *Passages: Predictable Crises of Adult Life* (New York: E.P. Dutton, 1974), 293-94.

88. Ric Masten, *Deserted Rooster* (Carmel, CA: Sunflower Ink, 1982), 19.

89. N. Chodorow, "Family Structure and Feminine Personality," in *Women, Culture, and Society*, Michelle Rosaldo and Louise Lamphere, eds. (Stanford, CA: Stanford University Press, 1974), 43-66.

90. Jordan, *Empathy and Self Boundaries*, 8.

91. P. Welsh, *Tales Out of School* (New York: Penguin Books, 1984), 21-22.

CHAPTER 6

92. Levinson et al., *The Seasons of a Man's Life*, 235.

93. Ibid., 233.

94. Ibid., 331.

95. Ibid., 332.

96. Ruby Whalley, high school assistant principal-on-leave, Eagle Point, OR; currently high school principal, Waldport, OR; personal communication, 1986.

CHAPTER 7

97. Loevinger, *Ego Development*, 19.

98. McPherson, *Small Town Teacher*, 201.

99. Jessica Daniel, Associate in Psychology in the Department of Psychiatry, Children's Hospital, Boston, 1987.

CHAPTER 8

100. *Education Week,* May 14, 1986, 5

101. Levinson et al., *The Seasons of a Man's Life,* 46-47.

102. A. L. Manasse, "Vision and Leadership: Paying Attention to Intention" (Washington, DC: The Cortland Group, 1986), 5.

103. Waller, *The Sociology of Teaching,* 442.

104. Levine, "Relationships Between the School as an Organizational Context and the Potentials for Adult Development" (Doctoral thesis, Harvard Graduate School of Education, 1980), 270.

105. Manasse, "Vision and Leadership," 27; Thomas J. Sergiovanni, *The Principalship: A Reflective Practice Perspective* (Boston: Allyn and Bacon, 1987).

106. Lightfoot, *The Good High School,* 329.

107. Arthur Blumberg and William Greenfield, *The Effective Principal: Perspectives on School Leadership* (Boston: Allyn and Bacon, 1980), 7.

108. Loevinger and Wessler, *Measuring Ego Development,* 7.

109. C. H. Persell and P. Cookson, "The Effective Principal in Action" (National Institute of Education grant, Washington, DC, 1982); Joan Lipsitz, *Successful Schools for Young Adolescents* (New Brunswick, NJ: Transaction, 1984), 173-78; A. L. Manasse, "Improving Conditions for Principal Effectiveness: Policy Implications of Research on Effective Principals" (Washington, DC: Stanford Engineering and Management Systems, June 1983); Sergiovanni, *The Principalship,* 3-18, 337-48.

110. Lightfoot, *The Good High School.*

CHAPTER 9

111. Levinson, et al., *The Seasons of a Man's Life,* 177.

CHAPTER 10

112. S. I. Levine and V. A. Jacobs, "Writing as a Tool for Staff Development," *Journal of Staff Development* 7 (Spring 1986): 44-51.

113. The Principals' Center is a membership organization dedicated to the professional development of school leaders.

114. Activities are based largely upon those used at the Bard Institute for Writing and Thinking (Annandale-on-Hudson, NY) and on Peter Elbow's *Writing with Power* (New York: Oxford University Press, 1981).

CHAPTER 11

115. Charles Christensen, teacher trainer, former middle school principal, Harvard, Cambridge, 1987.

116. For more information, contact Peer-Assisted Leadership Program, Far West Laboratory, 1855 Folsom St., San Francisco, CA 94103.

117. L. Thies-Sprinthall, "Promoting the Developmental Growth of Supervising Teachers: Theory, Research Programs, and Implications," *Journal of Teacher Education* 35 (May-June, 1984): 53-60; L. Thies-Sprinthall, "A Collaborative Approach for Mentor Training: A Working Model," *Potpourri* (North Carolina State University Newsletter, Nov.-Dec. 1986): 15-16.

118. R. Garmstron, "How Administrators Support Peer Coaching," *Educational Leadership* 44 (Jan. 1987): 18-26.

119. Ibid., 19; L. Shalaway, "Peer Coaching . . . Does It Work?" cited in Garmstron, "How Administrators Support Peer Coaching," 19.

120. Thies-Sprinthall, "Promoting the Developmental Growth of Supervising Teachers," 53-60; Sprinthall and Thies-Sprinthall, "Teachers as Adult Learners," in *Staff Development*, ed. C. Griffin (Chicago: University of Chicago Press, 1983), 24-31.

121. This description of a teacher-initiated support group was told to me in an interview with an elementary/middle-school teacher who wishes to remain anonymous.

122. This group was described to me by a superintendent who will remain anonymous.

CHAPTER 12

123. Quotes within this section come from Visiting Practitioners at the Principals' Center between 1985 and 1987.

124. This section is based on Levine, "The Principals' Center Movement: When School Leaders Become Adult Learners," *Journal of Staff Development* 7, no. 2 (Fall 1986): 28-41.

125. R. van der Bogert, "Tillers of the Soil," *Reflections* 1 (1986): 11

126. Sarah Levine, Roland Barth, and Kenneth Haskins, "The Harvard Principals' Center: School Leaders as Adult Learners," in *Approaches to Administrative Training in Education*, ed. Joseph Murphy and Philip Hallinger (Albany: State University of New York Press, 1987), 160.

127. Ibid.

128. The Harvard Teachers' Network, "First Annual Report," August 1986, Cambridge, MA.

129. Study groups include "Teachers as Learners," "Grants for Teachers," and "Methods for Teacher Empowerment." The Educators' Forum, a group predating the Network, is also part of its offerings. The Forum encourages teacher-initiated research.

130. S. Gould and E. Letven, "A Center for Interactive Professional Development," *Educational Leadership* 45 (Nov. 1987): 49-52.

131. Ibid., 51.

CHAPTER 13

132. I first heard a version of this story from Roland S. Barth, Senior Lecturer on Education, Harvard Graduate School of Education, Cambridge, MA.

133. Barth, *Run School Run* (Cambridge, MA: Harvard University Press, 1980), 27.

134. J.-A. Krupp, "Understanding and Motivating Personnel in the Second Half of Life," *Journal of Education* 169 (Nov. 1987): 29.

Suggested Readings

ADULT DEVELOPMENT

Covey, S.R. (1989). *The 7 Habits of Highly Effective People: Powerful Lessons in Personal Change.* New York: Fireside.

Cross, P.K. (1981). *Adults as Learners.* San Francisco: Jossey-Bass.

Daloz, L.A. (1986). *Effective Teaching and Mentoring: Realizing the Transformational Power of Adult Learning Experiences.* San Francisco: Jossey-Bass.

Erikson, E.H. (1968). *Identity, Youth and Crisis.* New York: W.W. Norton.

Gould, R.L. (1978). *Transformations: Growth and Change in Adult Life.* New York: Simon and Schuster.

Kegan, R. (1994). *In Over Our Heads: The Mental Demands of Modern Life.* Cambridge, MA: Harvard University Press.

Kegan, R. (1982). *The Evolving Self: Problems and Processes in Human Development.* Cambridge, MA: Harvard University Press.

Kegan, R., and Lahey, L.L. (1984). "Adult Leadership and Adult Development: A Constructivist View." In B. Kellerman (ed.), *Leadership: Multidisciplinary Perspectives* (pp. 199-230). Englewood Cliffs, NJ: Prentice-Hall.

Kohlberg, L. (1984). *The Psychology of Moral Development.* San Francisco: Harper and Row.

Levine, S. L. (1987). "Understanding Life Cycle Issues: A Resource for School Leaders." *Journal of Education, 169 (1),* 7-19.

Levinson, D., Darro, C.N., Kline, E.B., Levinson, M.H., and McKee, B. (1978). *The Seasons of a Man's Life.* New York: Ballantine Books.

Loevinger, J. (1976). *Ego Development: Conceptions and Theories.* San Francisco: Jossey-Bass.

Miller, J.B. (1974). *Toward a New Psychology of Women.* Boston: Beacon Press.

Oja, S.N. (1991). "Adult Development: Insights on Staff Development." In A. Lieberman and L. Miller (Eds.), *Staff Development for Education in the 90s: New Demands, New Realities, New Perspectives* (pp. 37-60). New York: Teachers College Press.

Osherson, S. (1986). *Finding Our Fathers: How a Man's Life Is Shaped by His Relationship with His Father.* New York: Ballantine Books.

Sheehy, G. (1974). *Passages: Predictable Crises of Adult Life.* New York: E.P. Dutton.

Tannen, D. (1990). *You Just Don't Understand: Women and Men in Conversation.* New York: Ballantine Books.

GIRLS' AND WOMEN'S DEVELOPMENT

American Association of University Women. (1991). *Shortchanging Girls, Shortchanging America.* Washington, DC: AAUW.

Apter, T. (1990). *Altered Loves: Mothers and Daughters During Adolescence.* New York: St. Martin's Press.

Belenky, M.F., Clinchy, B.M., Goldberger, N.R., and Tarule, J.M. (1986). *Women's Ways of Knowing: The Development of Self, Voice, and Mind.* New York: Basic Books, 1986.

Brown, L.M., and Gilligan, C. (1992). *Meeting at the Crossroads: Women's Psychology and Girls' Development.* Cambridge, MA: Harvard University Press.

Boyd, B. McCrary. (1992). *The Revolution of Little Girls.* New York: Vintage Contemporaries.

Debold, E., Wilson, M., and Malave, I. (1993). *Mother Daughter Revolution.* Reading, MA: Addison-Wesley.

Fine, M. (1988). "Sexuality, Schooling and Adolescent Females: The Missing Discourse of Desire." *Harvard Educational Review, 58,* 29-53.

Gilligan, C. (1982). *In a Different Voice: Psychological Theory and Women's Development.* Cambridge, MA: Harvard University Press.

Gilligan, C. (1990a). "Joining The Resistance: Psychology, Politics, Girls and Women. *Michigan Quarterly Review, 29 (4),* 501-536.

Gilligan, C. (1979). "Woman's Place in a Man's Life Cycle." *Harvard Educational Review, 49,* 431-446.

Gilligan, C., and Attanucci, J. (1988). "Two Moral Orientations: Gender Differences and Similarities." *Merrill-Palmer Quarterly, 343,* 223-237.

Gilligan, C., Lyons, N. P., Hanmer, T. J. (eds.) (1989). *Making Connections: The Relational Worlds of Adolescent Girls at Emma Willard School.* Troy, New York: Emma Willard School.

Gilligan, C., Rogers, A.G., and Tolman, D.L. (eds.) (1991). *Women, Girls and Psychotherapy: Reframing Resistance.* New York: The Haworth Press, Inc.

Gilligan, C., Ward, J., and Taylor, J. (eds.) (1988). *Mapping the Moral Domain: A Contribution of Women's Thinking to Psychology and Education.* Cambridge, MA: Harvard University Press.

Hancock, E. (1989). *The Girl Within: A Groundbreaking New Approach to Female Identity.* New York: Fawcett Columbine.

Heilbrun, C. (1989). *Writing a Woman's Life.* New York: Ballantine.

Jordan, J., Miller, J.B., Stiver, I., and Surrey, J. (1991). *Women's Growth in Connection: Writings from the Stone Center.* New York: Guilford Press.

Josselson, R. (1992). *The Space Between Us: Exploring the Dimensions of Human Relationships.* San Francisco: Jossey-Bass.

Noddings, N. (1984). *Caring.* Berkeley, CA: University of California Press.

Sadker, M., and Sadker, D. (1994). *Failing at Fairness: How America's Schools Cheat Girls.* New York: Charles Scribner's Sons.

Sadker, M., and Sadker, D. (1986). "Sexism in the Classroom: From Grade School to Graduate School." *Phi Delta Kappan, 43 (7).*

SCHOOLS

Barth, R.S. (1980). *Run School Run.* Cambridge, MA: Harvard University Press.

Barth, R.S. (1990). *Improving Schools From Within: Teachers, Parents, and Principals Can Make a Difference.* San Francisco: Jossey-Bass.

Bilken, S.K., and Brannigan, M.B. (1980). *Women and Educational Leadership.* Lexington, MA: D.C. Heath.

Blumberg, A., and Greenfield, W. (1980). *The Effective Principal: Perspectives on School Leadership.* Boston: Allyn and Bacon.

Fullan, M., and Hargraves, A. (1992). "Teacher Development and Educational Change." In A. Hargraves and M. Fullan (eds.), *Understanding Teacher Development* (pp. 1-9). New York: Teachers College Press.

Glickman, C.G. (1990). *Supervision of Instruction: A Developmental Approach* (2nd ed.). Boston: Allyn and Bacon.

Goodlad, J.I. (1984). *A Place Called School: Prospects for the Future.* New York: McGraw-Hill.

Hickcox, E.S., and Musella, D.F. (1992). "Teacher Performance and Staff Development." In M. Fullan and A. Hargraves (eds.), *Teacher Development and Educational Change* (pp. 1-9). Washington, DC: Falmer Press.

Lickona, T. (1991). *Educating for Character: How Our Schools Can Teach Respect and Responsibility.* New York: Bantam Books.

Lieberman, A., and Miller, L. (1978). *Staff Development: New Demands, New Realities, New Perspectives.* New York: Teachers College Press.

Lieberman, A., and Miller, L. (1992). *Teachers - Their World and Their Work: Implications for School Improvement.* New York: Teachers College.

Lightfoot, S.L. (1983). *The Good High School: Portraits of Character and Culture.* New York: Basic Books.

Lortie, D.C. (1975). *Schoolteacher.* Chicago: University of Chicago Press.

Loucks-Horsley, S. (1982). *Continuing to Learn: A Guidebook for Teacher Development*. Andover, MA: The Regional Laboratory for Educational Improvement of the Northeast and Islands; and Oxford, OH: The National Staff Development Council.

Murphy, J., and Hallinger, P. (eds.) (1987). *Approaches to Administrative Training*. Albany: State University of New York Press.

Oja, S.N., and Smulyan, L. (1989). *Collaborative Action Research: A Developmental Approach*. New York: The Falmer Press.

Perkins, D. (1992). *Smart Schools: From Training Memories to Educating Minds*. New York: The Free Press.

Sarason, S.B. (1971). *The Culture of School and the Problem of Change*. Boston: Allyn and Bacon.

Sarason, S.B. (1993). *The Predictable Failure of Educational Reform*. San Francisco: Jossey Bass.

Sergiovanni, T.J. (1987). *The Principalship: A Reflective Practice Perspective*. Boston: Allyn and Bacon.

Shakeshaft, C. (1987). *Women in Educational Administration*. Newbery Park, CA: Sage Publications.

Sizer, T.R. (1992). *Horace's School: Redesigning the American High School*. New York: Houghton Mifflin Company

LEADERSHIP

Astin, H.S., and Leland, C. (1991). *Women of Influence, Women of Vision: A Cross-Generational Study of Leaders and Social Change*. San Francisco: Jossey-Bass.

Bolman, L.B., and Deal, T.E. (1991). *Reframing Organizations: Artistry, Choice, and Leadership*. San Francisco: Jossey-Bass.

Cantor, D.W., Bernay, T., and Stoess, J. (1992). *Women in Power: The Secrets of Leadership*. Boston: Houghton Mifflin Co.

Gardner, J.W. (1990). *On Leadership*. New York: The Free Press.

Greenleaf, R.K. (1991). *Servant Leadership: A Journey into the Nature of Legitimate Power and Greatness*. New York: Paulist Press.

Hershey, P. (1984). *The Situational Leader*. New York: Warner Books.

Kouzes, J.M., and Posner, B.Z. (1987). *The Leadership Challenge*. San Francisco: Jossey-Bass.

Senge, P.M. (1990). *The Fifth Discipline: The Art and Practice of the Learning Organization*. New York: Doubleday.

Sergiovanni, T.J. (1992). *Moral Leadership: Getting to the Heart of School Improvement*. San Francisco: Jossey-Bass.

Index

About the Author

For over twenty-five years, Sarah Levine has been a teacher of children and teachers. A developmental psychologist, she has a special interest in schools as contexts for the growth of children and adults. Currently, she is Head of School at the Belmont Day School, an independent, coeducational elementary school just outside of Boston. Between 1983 and 1989, Dr. Levine served as Associate Director of the Principals' Center at Harvard University. At Harvard, she was Lecturer on Education and Director of the Principals' Institute, for practicing principals, and the Principals' Certification Pattern, for aspiring school principals. Dr. Levine has been a teacher, teacher educator, curriculum developer and evaluator, researcher and clinician. Her interests include her family, exercise, movies, and her golden retriever, Max.